From the library of:

Shipwrecks on the Virginia Coast

and the Men of the United States Life-Saving Service

Shipwrecks
on the Virginia Coast

and the

Men of the United States Life-Saving Service

BY RICHARD A. POULIOT

AND

JULIE J. POULIOT

Centreville — *Maryland*

Tidewater Publishers

Library of Congress Cataloging in Publication Data

Pouliot, Richard A., 1945-
  Shipwrecks on the Virginia coast and the men of the
United States Life-Saving Service.

    Bibliography: p.
    Includes index.
    1. Shipwrecks—Virginia.   2. United States.
Life-Saving Service.   I. Pouliot, Julie J., 1948-
II. Title.
G525.P59   1986   363.1′23′09755   85-41004
ISBN 0-87033-352-6

Manufactured in the United States of America

First edition, 1986; second printing, 1994

To our children, Richard and Robin, without whom
we would not have had the inspiration to complete this work;
to our parents, without whom we would not have had
the education necessary; and to each other,
without whom there would have been no book at all.

Contents

List of Illustrations

Preface

This book came to be written because there simply was no comprehensive work covering shipwrecks along the Atlantic shores of Virginia between the years 1874-1915. I believe that these disasters and the individuals that worked at the life-saving stations are as much a part of our maritime history as the well-known saga of the clipper ship era, for example, and should be chronicled and their history preserved. In pursuit of this subject, that has been very close to my heart and to which Julie, my wife and eventual coauthor, also became dedicated, I have invested five years of my life.

Shipwrecks have long held a fascination for me. While I served for more than eight years as a United States Navy Diver stationed with Underwater Demolition Team 22 and SEAL Team 2, I was given the opportunity to dive in the Caribbean, the Atlantic, and in the Mediterranean Sea where numerous shipwrecks have lain undisturbed for decades. After I settled in Virginia Beach and completed my undergraduate work at Old Dominion University, I began my graduate studies and was introduced to the methods of research necessary for the investigation I had undertaken. At this point my wife Julie accepted the challenge either to join me or to take second place in the priority of my concerns in life. She can type—I can't. But, she also assumed many authorial roles. She accepted the task of editing, filing, collating, illustrating, and keeping this work in some semblance of order. She is truly its coauthor.

There is currently an increased interest in the subject of maritime history and in shipwrecks in particular. We hope that this book will contribute in some degree to the documentation of shipwrecks as well as to the activities of those brave men of the past who were members of the United States Life-Saving Service and who did so much to reduce the volume of tragedies at sea.

Acknowledgments

We are grateful for the assistance of the staff of the National Archives in Washington, D.C., in particular Ms. Terry Matchett. They helped us find the material on the Life-Saving Service so vital to this work. Thanks also to the Mariners' Museum in Newport News, Virginia, whose staff and extensive research library were kindly placed at our disposal. We must also thank Reid Perry and Jack Brown at The Memory Bank in Virginia Beach for their assistance with our Apple computer, without which we would still be using index cards and shoe boxes! The history department of Old Dominion University and Dr. Peter C. Stewart, in particular, also deserve our gratitude, for it was Dr. Stewart who taught Richard the necessary research techniques and told him that this research could lead to the publication of a book.

We wish to extend our gratitude to Richard's employer of twelve years, Dixie Manufacturing Company in Norfolk, and in particular to W. MacKenzie Jenkins, Jr., John S. Mitchell, and William E. Watson, who provided time, support, and encouragement to complete the book. Julie and I would also like to thank all our many friends for their understanding and patience during our five years of closed-door research and writing, and for helping to keep our two youngsters occupied while Mom and Dad were "working on the book, again."

Special appreciation is extended to T. William Robson of Boice-Robson Studios in Virginia Beach for his time and talent in reproducing some of the aged photographs in this book. He has always responded to our requests for photographs with professional speed and friendly advice.

Our greatest thanks, however, must go to the Virginia Beach Maritime Historical Museum in Virginia Beach, Virginia. The Museum's Executive Director, Admiral Richard E. Rumble, Research and Education Director Atsuko Biernot, and Community Relations Director Martha Price unhesitatingly provided encouragement, advice, information, and support. Julie and I have been made part of the Museum's family, and for this we are truly grateful.

Shipwrecks on the Virginia Coast

and the Men of the United States Life-Saving Service

Chapter 1

The Development of the United States Life-Saving Service

During the nineteenth century the stretches of the Atlantic coast of the United States where shipwrecks most frequently occurred were desolate, sparsely populated, and far from urban centers. The United States, unlike other nations at that time, developed a federally-supported life-saving service. As early as 1847 Congress appropriated five thousand dollars toward furnishing lighthouses on the Atlantic coast with facilities for aiding shipwrecked mariners. Before this time there were no life-saving organizations except through voluntary action taken by the inhabitants of an area. For example, the Massachusetts Humane Society was first established to aid shipwreck victims, and was entirely voluntary. As coastal and overseas shipping increased during the middle and later decades of the nineteenth century, Congress made periodic appropriations, and life-saving stations gradually multiplied along the Atlantic coasts of Massachusetts, Virginia, North Carolina, New York, and New Jersey. In the absence of any general regulations or guidelines, each station acted independently. The first stations along the shores of New York and New Jersey were built to protect America's shipping hub, New York City.

Before 1871 the life-saving establishment along the coast of the United States was at an all-time low. It was during this period that some unsavory individuals who lived along the shore would show false lights on the beach to draw ships into shoaling waters and disaster in order to plunder them. These "shore pirates" were known simply as "wreckers." Any effort to build an organized, government-controlled life-saving service was minimal and was kept to the small number of lighthouse

3

Dangers of a shipwreck. A nineteenth-century wood engraving.

keepers who tried to save the few lives they could with their meager supplies and equipment. All efforts died with the outbreak of the Civil War.

During the years of the Civil War, there was more interest in "blockading" and in running those blockades than in saving lives, as is true in most wars. After the war the existing, old, and poorly equipped stations, mostly in the northeast between New Jersey and Boston, were still manned only by local volunteers. However, with the nation rebuilding and shipping expanding after the war, there was a parallel increase in the number of fatal shipping disasters along the coast. Public sentiment was aroused and Congress warmed to its humanitarian duties.

In 1871 Sumner I. Kimball (1834-1923) was appointed by President Grant to head the Revenue Marine Bureau of the Treasury Department. It was under his leadership that the life-saving program came into its own. Born in Lebanon, Maine, and educated at Bowdoin College, Kimball was admitted to the bar in 1858 and elected to the Maine legislature in 1859. In 1861 he moved to Washington, D.C., to begin his government career as a clerk in the office of the second auditor of the treasury. Once there, he quickly rose to the grade of chief clerk.

From 1871 to 1878, Kimball fostered the work of the Revenue Cutter Service, which was within his Revenue Marine Bureau, leading to a gradual increase in the life-saving stations along the coast of the United States. Kimball was neither a maritime nor a life-saving expert particularly, but he was an extremely good organizer. He excelled at whatever jobs were given him, and as a result, in 1878 President Hayes appointed him General Superintendent of the newly-formed United States Life-Saving Service (USLSS). The Senate confirmed his appointment unanimously, without the usual reference to a committee, which was quite a distinction at that time.

At the helm of the infant USLSS, Kimball immediately took stock of its existing condition—the poor and virtually useless equipment, the badly neglected stations, and the unfit employees. Kimball began his reorganization by preparing a uniform code of regulations: the duties of each man employed were detailed; the stations were refurbished; and the equipment repaired or replaced. Most of the "unworthy" employees were dismissed and replaced with professional watermen—no longer were jobs in the USLSS handed out as political favors. Without waiting for congressional action, Kimball attempted to enforce his simple principle that the "appointment of district superintendents, inspectors, and keepers and crews of life-saving stations" should be "made solely with reference to their fitness and without reference to their political or party affiliations."[1]

By 1889 the USLSS consisted of a General Superintendent, receiving a yearly salary of $4,999; an Assistant General Superintendent, with a yearly salary of $2,500; a corps of clerks; a civil engineer; a topographer; a hydrographer; and a draftsman. The third-ranked official in the USLSS was Inspector. He was an officer detailed from the Revenue Cutter Service upon the request of the General Superintendent, and was headquartered in New York City. His duties included the periodical inspections of the stations and of the goods purchased to supply the stations. Under the Inspector was an assistant, also an officer from the Revenue Cutter Service. Whenever a loss of life occurred in a shipwreck, the Assistant Inspector was dispatched to investigate all circumstances surrounding the incident in order to ascertain the cause of the disaster and to determine whether there was any neglect on the part of the lifesavers.

The results of Kimball's reorganization were astounding. During the first year of operation under his new system, every person imperiled by shipwreck on the coasts of New York and New Jersey was saved. By the winter of 1872-73 the United States Life-Saving Service had expanded to eighty-two stations in three districts: Cape Cod, Rhode Island and Long Island, and New Jersey.

On these dangerous portions of the Atlantic coast in the winter of 1873-74, some forty-eight vessels were driven ashore. The vessels had a total value of over $2,300,000 but the aggregate loss was less than $460,000. Although there were 1,166 lives imperiled, only two lives were lost. And, both of these deaths were caused by the mast falling when a vessel ran aground. (Although incomplete—for example, they do not tell us how many vessels were lost—the early USLSS statistics were a great improvement over the figures available earlier. Before the establishment of the USLSS, such statistics were gathered with much difficulty from very diverse sources from wreck commissioners, officers of the customs, lighthouse keepers, underwriters, and any other available source.) In addition to the life-saving stations, the total number of navigational aids in use under the auspices of the United States government was 546 lighthouses, 23 lightships, 42 fog signals, 382 beacons, and 2,865 buoys.

The success of the Life-Saving Service in the winter of 1872-73 induced Congress to extend the system. In March 1873, one hundred thousand dollars was appropriated to build new stations between Maine and North Carolina. These new coastal stations included five in Maine, one in New Hampshire, five in Massachusetts, one in Rhode Island, three in Virginia, and seven in North Carolina. By the winter of 1873-74 these stations were completed, manned, and ready for service. In June 1874 Congress again appropriated funds for an additional eight stations to be constructed on the coasts of Maryland and Virginia. With these new stations came the addition of three new districts: District One now encompassed the coasts of Maine and New Hampshire; District Five covered the coasts of Maryland and Virginia (to Cape Charles); and District Six included Virginia (from Cape Henry) and North Carolina (to Cape Hatteras). The stations in District Five along the Eastern Shore of Virginia were: Assateague Beach, Cedar Inlet, Hog Island, Cobb Island, and Smith Island. The life-saving stations in District Six, in what is now Virginia Beach, were Cape Henry, Dam Neck Mills, and False Cape.

Through what seemed magnanimous legislation, the work of the USLSS was crowned with brilliant success, and the creation of new stations increased steadily until 1877. But the very success of the Life-Saving Service contributed to a slowdown in the building of new stations. Considerably below the estimates submitted by the management of the service, the appropriation of 1877-78 prevented new stations from opening for the winter season before 1 December 1877.

A disaster in the Sixth District on the coast of North Carolina only six days prior to the opening of the stations focused attention on the remaining gaps along the coast. On 25 November 1877 the steamship *Huron* stranded near the Nags Head Life-Saving Station and ninety-eight persons perished, most of whom doubtless could have been saved had the stations been in operation. The *Huron* disaster was so tragic and enormous in its proportions that the entire nation was "roused into interrogation." As if the *Huron* disaster alone was not enough to make the case for more stations to begin the winter season earlier, another steamship, the *Metropolis,* stranded on the beach near Currituck, North Carolina, and eighty-five more lives were lost.

As early as 1876 a commission, appointed by Kimball to ascertain where new stations were needed most, reported that

> the portion of the coast embraced between Capes Henry and Hatteras does not appear to be sufficiently provided with stations. The distance between the stations now located thereon averages ten miles, which is too great to admit of the complete surveillance by the patrol.[2]

The twin disasters on North Carolina's "Graveyard of the Atlantic" helped to reeducate the nation's lawmakers. An Act of Congress dated 18 June 1878 authorized the establishment of additional life-saving stations on America's sea and lake coasts. The appropriation called for fifteen stations to be built on the shores of Virginia and North Carolina, ten of them at intermediate intervals between the existing stations. The Sixth District then encompassed the coast between Cape Henry, Virginia, and Cape Fear, North Carolina.

Life-Saving Stations in Virginia, 1878

Fifth District

Popes Island
Assateague Beach
Cedar Island
Hog Island
Cobb Island
Smith Island

Sixth District

Cape Henry
Seatack (Va. Beach)
Dam Neck Mills
Little Island
False Cape

In addition to the new stations, the Sixth District also had telephones for use during the winter season (1 December through 30 April). The United States Signal Service had telegraph lines running along the coast between Capes Henry and Hatteras in the immediate vicinity of the life-saving stations in the Sixth District. This existing line was used to run the telephone lines, and thus the Sixth District became equipped with one of the most up-to-date forms of communication. This, however, was a mixed blessing in that the telegraph lines were operative in fair weather, but, more often than not, out of commission during violent northeasters, gales, and hurricanes when needed most.

On Sunday 24 May 1874, *The Norfolk Virginian* announced on its front page that the contracts for the construction of life-saving stations between Capes Henry and Hatteras had been awarded to the A. A. McCullough firm of Norfolk. The stations were to be "20 [by] 43 feet in size, two stories high, and built of the very best lumber obtainable, all of which is to be dressed in oil to preserve it."[3] The majority of the stations were sturdily-built, two-story frame structures with a lookout platform on top. The stations were placed above the high water mark, safe from high storm tides. The first floor was divided into four rooms: a mess room for the crew, a storeroom, the station keeper's room, and the boat room. Wide double doors, leading to a sloping platform outside, were located in the boat room to aid the crew in taking heavy equipment out for a rescue or drill. The second floor had two rooms: a bunk room for the crew and a spare room which was used for storage as well as a shelter for those rescued from the sea. By the late 1800s the roofs of all the stations were painted dark red to make them more visible from the sea. It was also

Popes Island Life-Saving Station. Courtesy: U. S. Coast Guard.

mandatory that a sixty-foot signal pole be erected to be used with flags to warn and send messages to passing vessels.

Each station was equipped with two surfboats (a surfboat was a wooden boat with a sharp bow and oars to row it through the surf) and a surfboat carriage (also made of wood, on the style of a carriage base, equipped with strong wooden wheels covered with iron) to enable the

Little Island Life-Saving Station. Courtesy: U. S. Coast Guard.

Interior of a boat room. From the authors' postcard collection.

crew to transport the boats along the shore. In addition to the surfboats, the stations were supplied a firing device with which the rescue could be attempted by the use of hauling lines. Originally there were three such devices: the Lyle and Hunt guns and the Cunningham rocket apparatus. All three employed a fired projectile to which a line was attached. After intensive comparison, the Lyle gun was chosen to be standard equipment for this use. Once a successful shot had been fired from the Lyle gun, communication could be established between the wreck and the shore, a vital link in the rescue operation.

After the initial shot was fired and a line secured to the vessel in distress, those on board, who were able, would haul up a heavier line, as well as hawsers, to set up devices which would carry everyone to safety. During the latter half of the nineteenth century there were three devices for rescue employing hauling lines: the boatswain's chair, the breeches buoy, and the life car. The boatswain's chair (still in use today) is a simple swing attached to a hawser. The person being rescued sits in the chair and is pulled landward by the lines. This method works well as long as weather conditions are mild, the surf calm, and the person strong and able-bodied. The second and most popular device, the breeches buoy, was a common circular life preserver or life ring made from cork and covered with heavy canvas. Attached to the life ring was a short pair of heavy canvas breeches into which the rescued person would sit chest deep with his legs hanging through. The breeches buoy was hauled to the beach in the same manner as the boatswain's chair. The third and least popular device was the life car which held up to four people and

The Lyle gun. A nineteenth-century wood engraving.

The breeches buoy. A nineteenth-century wood engraving.

was a small, covered, metal boat with openings for ventilation. Like the other two devices, it hung down from the hawser and, with rings on either end, could be pulled to and from the wrecked vessel.

Each district within the United States Life-Saving Service was under the immediate charge of a superintendent who served as a disbursement officer, a general business manager, and as a supervisor of all operations

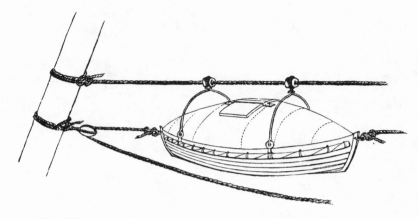

The life-saving car. A nineteenth-century wood engraving.

Winding line on a faking board. Courtesy: The National Archives.

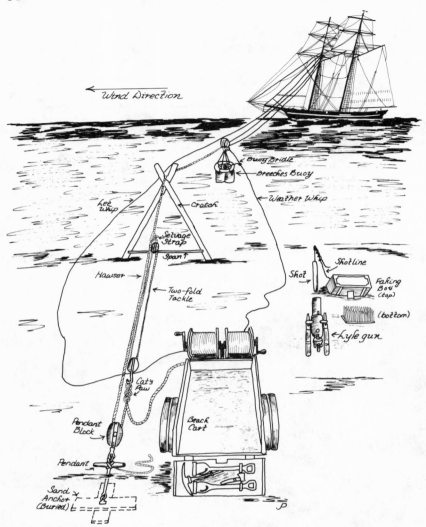

Breeches buoy rescue apparatus. Drawing by J. Pouliot.

and personnel in the individual stations. In addition, he made requisitions to the General Superintendent for supplies. It was his duty to visit each station at least once a quarter and assess the condition of the station and the crew. The District Superintendent was also ex officio Inspector of Customs, it being his responsibility to look after the government's interests when dutiable property was wrecked within his district. By the late 1880s his compensation ranged from one thousand to eighteen hundred dollars annually, depending upon the size of his district.

Each station keeper had direct control over all affairs of his station. He was, therefore, selected with the utmost care by the District Superintendent. In the vicinity of nearly all the stations built during this period on the Atlantic coast were fishermen and salvagers who had lived and worked their entire lives on the water and who had become experts in handling boats in the surf in all weather conditions. From this group of professionals came both the keepers and the surfmen needed to man the life-saving stations. The keeper was someone who, by common consent, was recognized not only as an excellent practitioner but also as a leader among his fellows. The keeper had to be a man of exceptional character, for so much depended upon his actions and reactions in times of crisis. The keepers were held to a "strict accountability for the proper care, preservations, and good order of the apparatus, boats, buildings, and their appurtenances, and for the economical use of all supplies of every kind placed in their charge."[4]

In addition to being able-bodied, physically sound, and a master of boats in the surf, the keeper had to be competent enough to transact the station's business. There were monthly reports to be written, and the keeper had to act as agent for the Collector of Customs. Filling the vacancies that occurred when a keeper died or left the service was not as difficult as finding those first keepers. Successive keepers were selected from among the most competent of the station surfmen. In 1878 the keeper was paid on the average of fifty dollars per month.

The total number of men composing the station crew was first determined by the number of oars required to pull the largest boat belonging to the station. There were some five-oared boats in the Atlantic coastal stations, but at nearly every station there was at least one boat which required six oars. Six men, therefore, made up the regular crew of the life-saving stations. The keeper selected the crews from qualified men residing in the vicinity of the respective stations. This privilege was granted the keeper in view of the necessity for mutual confidence between a leader and his men in a very hazardous situation involving not only their own lives, but the lives of others. With six men needed to fill the crew in a sparsely populated area, the keeper was sometimes handicapped by the regulation which forbade him to employ his father, brother, or son except where adherence to this rule would have been extremely detrimental to the service. This regulation was

Crew launching a lifeboat. A nineteenth-century wood engraving.

enforced because to do otherwise could possibly have impaired the keeper's judgement in a life-or-death situation.

At the beginning of the winter season the surfmen assembled at their respective stations. The winter season for the fifth and sixth districts was from 1 December to 30 April. Each crew member was paid forty dollars per month, and all men were required to reside at the station during the winter season. The keeper, also a resident, organized his crew by arranging and numbering the members in order of competency, from Surfman Number One through Surfman Number Six, from the most senior to the youngest and, most likely, the least experienced. This was the life-saving station's chain of command, and if the keeper were ever absent, Surfman Number One would immediately assume command. These proficiency numbers were changed when vacancies were filled or when the performance of an individual surfman warranted it.

With the ranking of his men established, the keeper assigned quarters to each man and prepared the station list for the day watch, night patrol, boat, and apparatus drill, as well as scheduled the daily maintenance both on the building and the equipment. Patrol limits were established by the district superintendent for both directions, north and south of each station. The day watch was kept from sunrise to sunset by a surfman, assigned daily, who served his duty stationed in the lookout tower. During stormy weather the beach was patrolled twenty-

Surfman on beach patrol. A nineteenth-century wood engraving.

four hours a day. The station lookout kept a log of all vessels he sighted passing the station.

The beach patrol was distinctively American in origin. It was wholly devised by the United States Life-Saving Service in the early 1870s. In the Fifth and Sixth Districts the beach patrol was divided into four watches: sunset to eight o'clock; eight o'clock to midnight;

midnight to four o'clock; and four o'clock to sunrise. Two surfmen were assigned for each watch. At the start of the patrol the two surfmen set out in opposite directions along the beach, keeping a sharp lookout for any sign of trouble: a light in the surf zone or wreckage drifting ashore. With the exception of the Cape Henry Life-Saving Station where the surfmen on north patrol proceeded only halfway to the Lynnhaven Inlet, and any station located on an island, the patrolling surfman met his counterpart traveling in the opposite direction from the adjacent station. For example, the south patrol from Cape Henry Station would walk the beach until he met the north patrol from Seatack Station. They would then exchange metallic "checks," each marked with the station's and surfman's number. When this system of checks was first introduced the surfmen generally regarded it unfavorably. But by the early 1880s they saw the system not as degrading but as a safeguard for them; it relieved them of any suspicion of not having performed their duty. As with most professionals, these surfmen were very jealous of their reputations.

Each patrolling surfman was equipped with a lantern and several red Coston lights. When the discovery of a vessel in distress was made, the surfman ignited his Coston light, or flare, which resembled a large Roman candle. On a clear night, the red flame of this light could be seen for up to twenty miles. During this period in maritime history, there were few captains afloat who were so sure of their "reckoning" that they did not look very cautiously when a red Coston light was burning on the shore. The Coston light served a double purpose: it warned mariners of danger, and assured them that help was at hand if they were in distress. Any time that the patrolling surfman spotted a vessel too near the shore, or, as often happened near Cape Henry, headed straight towards the beach, he burned a Coston light and the captain of the vessel would take the necessary action to correct his course.

Once the surfmen were settled in the stations, a regular daily routine was established. On Monday would be a drill and practice with the beach apparatus and an examination of the boats and all gear. Tuesday was reserved for boat practice. On Wednesday the surfmen rehearsed the International Signal Code. Thursday they would hold a practice with the beach apparatus again, and on Friday they went over "the method adopted for restoring the apparently drowned," as resuscitation was then described. The surfmen cleaned the station on Saturday. Whenever there was a lapse in the regular performance of any of these

Warning a vessel of danger. A nineteenth-century wood engraving.

duties, the omission was logged in the station journal, and the routine in question was performed as soon as possible.

For the required practice with the beach apparatus there was a drill ground located near each station. A replica of a ship's mast, called a wreck pole, was planted to represent the mast of a vessel in distress. The men operated fifty to seventy-five yards away from this wreck pole in an area representing the shoreline. On Monday and Thursday, the station crew was mustered in the boat room. When his number was called, each man would recite, in the proper sequence, every act he would perform in the exercise as prescribed in the manual of the Life-Saving Service. Upon the keeper's command they would fall into their numerical places at the

Loading the Gun.

Firing the Life-line.

71-8

A life-saving station crew drilling. From the authors' postcard collection.

drag ropes of the apparatus cart, and pull it to the drill area. Then they would perform a mimic rescue by using the wreck pole and taking a survivor off it and back to "shore" safely in the breeches buoy.

Tuesday's boat practice and Wednesday's signalling were less time-consuming than the apparatus drill. Boat practice consisted of launching and landing through the surf, with at least half an hour's exercise in pulling the oars under the keeper's direction. The drill in flag signalling was conducted by interrogating each surfman as to the meaning of various flags learned from the International Code of Signals. The flags and code book were used when direct communication between the lifesavers and a vessel offshore was impossible. Frequently, when weather permitted, practice was held between the stations and revenue vessels.

The district superintendent accompanied by his immediate supervisor, the inspector, who had general supervision of two or more districts, made annual inspections of each station in great detail. The USLSS regulations stated that

> all the apparatus, boats, boat carriages, cars, hawsers, and gear, with the public property of every description, will be closely inspected and compared with the inventory, to see that every article is on hand or properly accounted for.[5]

These two officers inspected the appearance of the crew. More importantly they reviewed the proficiencies of the keeper and his surfmen in the various drills. The station crews were graded on a scale of one to ten, and transcripts of this rating were sent to General Superintendent Sumner I. Kimball. The crew had to perform their mimic rescue within five minutes; if this goal was not achieved, the crew had thirty days in which to improve their drill. They were cautioned that if upon the next visit of the inspector, a marked improvement was not shown, more decisive action would be taken. In most of the districts a highly spirited rivalry existed among the stations for excellence in the mimic rescue drill. The fastest time may never be known, but by 1890, Kimball was quoted as saying that the drill had been executed without error by several crews in two minutes and thirty seconds. Of course, nothing of such certainty could be expected in actual rescues when violent weather and pounding surf, strong shore currents, and the lack of skillful cooperation on the part of the sailors impeded the surfmen's efforts.

Chapter 2

Early Casualties

JANUARY 1875 – FEBRUARY 1881

From the organization of the United States Life-Saving Service on the coast of Virginia in 1874 until its merger with the Revenue Cutter Service in January 1915 to form the United States Coast Guard, there were more than six hundred incidents in which the USLSS was involved. In all but three of the documented disasters, the life-savers did all that was humanly possible to save the lives of those endangered by the sea. More than 6,812 lives were imperiled in the stranding of vessels on the shores of Virginia. A total of 102 lives were lost and 220 of the vessels became rotting hulks along the coastline.

Incidents According to Vessel Type, 1875-1915[1]

Vessel Type	Number
Schooner	325
Steamship	91
Bark	35
Sailing ship	14
Sloop	77
Brig	8
Barge	6
Barkentine	4
Motor launch	3
Sailboat	1
Destroyer	1
Small boat	1
Fishing boat	1
Unknown	2

22

Incidents According to Months, 1875-1915[2]

Month	Incidents	Month	Incidents
January	74	July	13
February	56	August	18
March	64	September	28
April	52	October	67
May	25	November	55
June	8	December	109

Among the primary reasons for shipwrecks along the coast of Virginia were the quickly changing and violent weather conditions which often caused experienced captains to lose their bearings and run their vessels onto the beach or the sandbars that were located close to the shoreline. The first vessel to come ashore after the United States Life-Saving Service built stations along the coast of Virginia Beach was the 2,238-ton steamship *San Marcos*. The steamship was lost in a dense fog when she grounded on 3 January 1875, four miles south of the False Cape Life-Saving Station. Bound from Galveston, Texas, to Liverpool, England, the *San Marcos* was due at Norfolk to be supplied with coal for her ocean crossing. The ship's cargo consisted of two hundred bales of cotton and two hundred boxes of canned beef. For five anxious days the life-savers watched as the *San Marcos* scraped upon the sands; because of the incredibly rough seas and dense fog the would-be rescuers could not launch the surfboat to reach the stranded steamship. On 8 January the sea subsided enough so that three tugboats, the *Resolute*, the *George W. Childs*, and the *Relief*, were able to pull the *San Marcos* from the shoal which had held her fast. There were no lives lost, and the *San Marcos* continued on her voyage after being towed to Norfolk for repairs.

Controversy surrounded the wreck of the *Fannie K. Shaw* in 1876. This 295-ton schooner drove ashore during a heavy northeast storm. *The Public Ledger* of 15 December 1876 told a much different story from the facts which appeared in the *Annual Report* of the USLSS. Captain John H. Belano of the *Shaw* wrote an open letter to the newspaper in which he accused the life-savers of the Cape Henry Station of being cowards and called for an investigation into the matter by the Superintendent of the Sixth District.

Captain Belano stated that all life-savers except for the keeper and one surfman refused to come to the aid of his vessel after a distress signal was made from the *Shaw*. He claimed that all on board, including his wife, would have perished from the freezing temperature and gale force winds had he and his first mate not brought them ashore in the schooner's own boat. Captain Belano then went to the life-saving station and secured the aid of the Keeper and one surfman to rescue the remainder of the *Shaw*'s crew.

A careful search of both the newspapers and the USLSS *Annual Report* for that year indicates that there was no basis for the accusations made by Captain Belano. In fact, no further mention of the wreck of the *Fannie K. Shaw* was found, and it can only be assumed that the matter was settled to the captain's satisfaction. The *Fannie K. Shaw* was the only vessel to wreck on the shores of Virginia Beach during 1876, which could have been the reason for Belano's story being printed in *The Public Ledger* at all.

The early success of the Life-Saving Service caused a further split between those who supported the Service and those who did not. There was a public outcry for more stations, and for each of the existing stations to have a longer season, while at the same time there were those who thought the Service should cut back and engage volunteers to supplement its activities. Two shipwrecks, occurring within hours of each other, served to polarize public opinion in favor of the Life-Saving Service.

On 25 November 1877 a fierce northeasterly gale was blowing off Virginia's Eastern Shore. The 181-ton schooner *Frank Jameson* was being driven towards the shore by the storm. The schooner was on a coastwise voyage from Rockland, Maine, to Richmond, Virginia, carrying her precious cargo of ice. The storm battered the schooner, and she lost her steering gear, became unmanageable, and drove ashore at midnight directly opposite the Smith Island Life-Saving Station. By daybreak the *Jameson* had completely broken up, and her crew, with one exception, had been washed from her decks and drowned.

The lone survivor was washed ashore and doubtless would have died had it not been for the attention he received from the surfmen. The entire crew of the *Jameson* could probably have been saved had the Smith Island Station been open, or had the life-savers been summoned earlier. As it was the lighthouse keeper at Smith Island was aware of the vessel's position, but incorrectly assumed that she was riding out the storm at anchor. More than six hours passed before anyone notified the

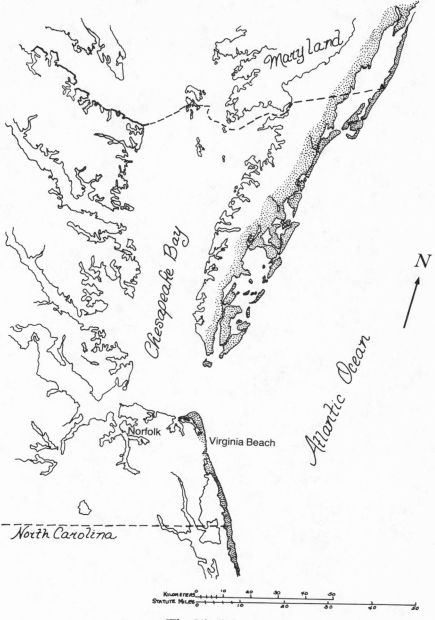

Maryland

Chesapeake Bay

Atlantic Ocean

N

Norfolk
Virginia Beach

North Carolina

KILOMETERS 0 10 20 30 40 50
STATUTE MILES 0 10 20 30 40 50

The Virginia Coast

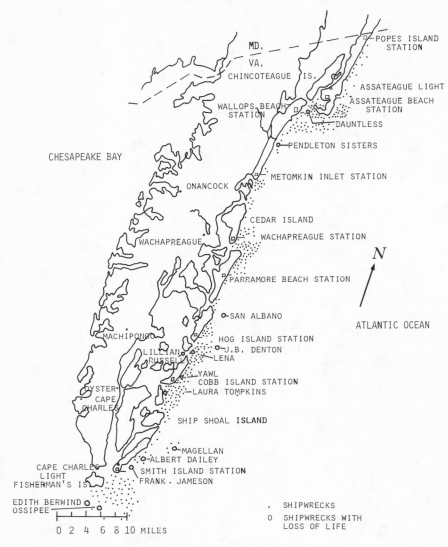

MD.
VA.
CHINCOTEAGUE IS.

POPES ISLAND
STATION

ASSATEAGUE LIGHT

WALLOPS BEACH
STATION

ASSATEAGUE BEACH
STATION

DAUNTLESS

PENDLETON SISTERS

CHESAPEAKE BAY

METOMKIN INLET STATION

ONANCOCK

CEDAR ISLAND

WACHAPREAGUE STATION

WACHAPREAGUE

PARRAMORE BEACH STATION

N

SAN ALBANO

ATLANTIC OCEAN

MACHIPONGO

HOG ISLAND STATION

LILLIAN
RUSSELL

J.B. DENTON
LENA

YAWL

OYSTER
CAPE
CHARLES

COBB ISLAND STATION

LAURA TOMPKINS

SHIP SHOAL ISLAND

MAGELLAN

ALBERT DAILEY

CAPE CHARLES
LIGHT
FISHERMAN'S IS.

SMITH ISLAND STATION

FRANK. JAMESON

EDITH BERWIND
OSSIPEE

0 2 4 6 8 10 MILES

.   SHIPWRECKS
O   SHIPWRECKS WITH
     LOSS OF LIFE

Shipwrecks on Virginia Beach, 1874–1915

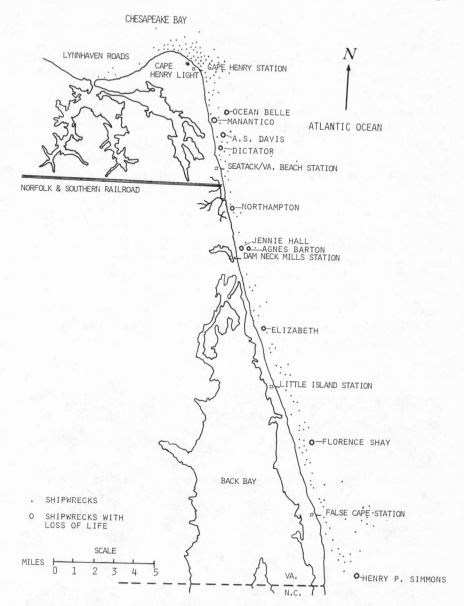

CHESAPEAKE BAY

LYNNHAVEN ROADS

CAPE
HENRY LIGHT

CAPE HENRY STATION

N

ATLANTIC OCEAN

O—OCEAN BELLE
O—MANANTICO

O—A.S. DAVIS
O—DICTATOR

SEATACK/VA. BEACH STATION

NORFOLK & SOUTHERN RAILROAD

O—NORTHAMPTON

O—JENNIE HALL
O—AGNES BARTON
DAM NECK MILLS STATION

O—ELIZABETH

LITTLE ISLAND STATION

O—FLORENCE SHAY

BACK BAY

FALSE CAPE STATION

· SHIPWRECKS

O SHIPWRECKS WITH
   LOSS OF LIFE

SCALE

MILES

0 1 2 3 4 5

VA.
N.C.

O—HENRY P. SIMMONS

Shipwrecks on Eastern Shore Virginia, 1874–1915.
(Maps by Julie Pouliot)

off-duty surfmen, who then hurried to the scene only to find the broken
schooner, her crew drowned, and only one survivor.

The wreck of the brig *Ossipee* occurred twelve hours prior to that
of the *Frank Jameson;* she was blown ashore with her sails in shreds
shortly after noon on 25 November. The northeasterly gale had pushed
the *Ossipee* far to the south of her course, on her way from Denia, Spain,
to New York City hauling a cargo of almonds and raisins valued at over
thirty thousand dollars. The brig hit the sands seven and one-half miles
south of the Assateague Beach Station and immediately began to break
apart. A few members of the crew were successful in releasing the brig's
boat and reaching the beach safely, but in returning for the remainder of
the crew, their inexperience in handling the boat in such rough surf
caused the deaths of two men. The keeper of the Assateague Beach
station stated that in his judgement all nine of the *Ossipee*'s crew could
have been saved had his station been open. At that time the life-saving
station's winter season was from 1 December to 30 April.

One of the most violent hurricanes on record occurred on 22-23 October
1878. The storm raged along the Atlantic coast from North Carolina
through the large urban areas of Virginia, Maryland, Delaware, New

Surfmen pulling the apparatus cart on a flooded beach.
A nineteenth-century wood engraving.

Jersey, Pennsylvania, New York, and the New England states. The coastal barrier islands were either flooded or pounded by surf that was being pushed by more than eighty-miles-per-hour winds. In fact, a wind speed of eighty-four miles per hour was recorded at the National Weather Service station at Cape Henry, Virginia, on 23 October 1878. The extraordinary fury of this storm was such that some thirty churches and hundreds of other buildings were damaged in Philadelphia, and a schooner in the Chesapeake Bay was carried up into the woods, quite far from her anchorage. Many of Virginia's life-saving stations were damaged; not one of the stations on the Eastern Shore escaped some damage—one of which was lifted from its foundation and carried nearly one half mile where it was left standing upright.

In many locations, new inlets cut through the beaches, breaking up the normal path of the surfmen's beach patrol. Five surfmen from the Seatack Station agreed that although they had lived their entire lives on the coast, they had never seen such a combination of sea conditions, wind, and rain that raged that night. In the height of all this fury, the *A. S. Davis* drove ashore.

The ship had sailed from Callao, Peru, three months earlier, on 23 July 1878, for Hampton Roads and Norfolk with a cargo of guano consigned to Hobson Hurtado and Company. A large ship of 1,399 tons, the *A. S. Davis* was manned by a crew of twenty men. Of that number only William H. Minton survived to tell of the sudden stranding and complete shattering of his ship.

The Norfolk Virginian, on 29 October 1878, reported Minton's account of the wreck as it had appeared in the report filed by Lieutenant Charles F. Shoemaker of the Revenue Marine Bureau to the Superintendent of the Life-Saving Service. At 6:00 P.M. on 22 October the *A. S. Davis* was sailing in a moderate gale and Captain James W. Ford gave orders to shorten the sails. After her ten-thousand-mile journey, the ship was within hours of port. The large three-masted ship sailed swiftly towards Cape Henry and by midnight

> Her lower topsail, which was new, was blown out of the bolt-ropes and the mizzen lower topsail was taken in. Finally, with only her fore topsail and fore topmast stay sail set, she was racing through the darkness with headlong velocity, amidst the roar of the hurricane, when suddenly, with a shivering shock, she plunged aground.[3]

At once the captain and crew headed for the rigging, for the sea was washing completely over the entire length of the ship. Because she was driving so hard before the storm, the *A. S. Davis* hit the beach bow first at a ninety degree angle. The surf rose up from behind and crashed upon the stern of the ship, literally shaking the three-year-old ship to pieces. Lieutenant Shoemaker stated, "I visited the scene of the wreck about sunrise on the morning of the 23rd, and could not conceive it possible that a ship could be so completely broken up."[4]

Surfmen James Balass and John T. Atwood were on south and north patrol respectively from the Seatack Station during the wrecking of the *A. S. Davis*. Atwood had to take cover when the hurricane reached its peak during the early hours of 23 October. He was north of the wreck scene, and shortly before daybreak, having completed his patrol, started to make his way back towards the station. The wind shifted as the center of the storm passed, and again he walked directly into the wind on his return. Halfway back to the station Atwood noticed pieces of all sizes from a wreck, and the number increased until the beach was "fairly covered with broken planks and timbers in every variety of mutilation and fracture."[5]

Once Atwood saw the first piece of the wreck, he searched for signs that someone might have come ashore. His well-trained eyes spotted bare footprints in the sand and he followed them for about one hundred yards into the dunes. There he discovered the sailor, Minton, who said he had fallen from the rigging onto the cabin and from there was swept off into the surf where he managed to grab and hold on to a piece of the ship's rail. Minton must have lost consciousness because his next recollection was of lying on the shore with only his shirt on. He knew that to survive he would have to find shelter.

> I managed to get up and walk off to the beach hills a distance of about twenty to thirty feet, where I dug a hole in the sand and covered myself up with the exception of my head, in order to obtain warmth. Remained in this position until daylight, when shortly after emerging from my place of refuge, was discovered by Mr. John T. Atwood.[6]

With Atwood taking charge of the situation, the only survivor of the wreck was saved from death by exposure. The nineteen men to perish in the wreck of the *A. S. Davis* were Captain James W. Ford, First Mate C. P. Quinn, Second Mate Berry, Seamen Thomas Deving, Thomas Thompson, John O'Connor, Matthew Simpson, Harry Gover, and five seamen whose names were unknown; the ship's carpenter, cook, and steward (names unknown); and the ship's boys, George Reynard, Robert Jons, and a third boy whose name was also unknown. Of these nineteen men, there were only seventeen bodies found within forty hours after the wreck, their clothes in shreds and their remains grotesquely mangled by the wreckage.[7] The captain and ten of his crew were buried in a mass grave one and one-half miles south of the Cape Henry Life-Saving Station; the others were buried just to the north of the wreck site. It was the tragic end of a once majestic merchantman and the beginning of a long history of gallant service for the men of the United States Life-Saving Service on the coast of Virginia.

Sometimes it took more than the life-savers could give to save a ship from disaster. Fate played a part in the wrecking of both the *Peerless* and the *Flora Curtis* in December 1878. The *Peerless* was on her way from her home port of Baltimore and stranded in a smooth sea while attempting to sail through the Virginia Capes out to sea. She slid to a stop about five miles west southwest of Smith Island Life-Saving Station at 2:00 A.M. on 1 December. The life-savers boarded the *Peerless* at 8:00 A.M., but when the schooner's captain refused to leave his vessel, the life-savers returned to their station. The wind steadily increased throughout the morning and reached gale force by noon. Again the life-savers pulled their surfboat abreast of the schooner, but three attempts to maneuver the surfboat alongside failed. Shortly after the life-saver's third attempt, the *Peerless'* masts crashed to her deck, and her hull ripped apart with a wrenching thunder. Her crew still clung to whatever piece of rigging they could, the seas breaking in mountainous swells above them. With great risk to their own lives, the life-savers plucked the sailors from their holds in the rigging, steering the surfboat as close to the wreck as they dared, and finally landed the crew safely on the beach. The surfmen and sailors watched from the beach as the *Peerless* broke apart, a total wreck.

In contrast, the *Flora Curtis* stranded during the height of a strong southeast gale on 2 December, three-fourths of a mile offshore and three miles south of the Assateague Beach Life-Saving Station. The station crew set out to aid the stricken schooner in the surfboat; after a fierce struggle with the heavy surf, the rescuers succeeded in reaching her, and found her lying broadside to the beach with heavy seas breaking over her. The surfmen boarded the schooner and ran out her kedge anchor (a small portable anchor). By dropping the schooner's anchors and using her winches, they succeeded in pulling the schooner off the shoal, thus preventing her from becoming a total wreck.

The storm was relentless. The wind rose to a howling gale, and the seas were so heavy that the life-savers, after leaving the *Flora Curtis* to ride out the storm safely at anchor, were unable to land the surfboat near their station. They had to row the surfboat and put in at an inlet two miles south of their station where they waited until the storm abated somewhat, and then rowed safely back to their station.

Not all of the vessels sighted by the life-savers required their assistance. Some schooners were even luckier than the *Flora Curtis* in their battles with the sea. On 8 February 1879 the keeper of the Cedar Inlet Life-Saving Station reported that an unknown schooner was prevented from running ashore by a surfman's red Coston light—the vessel's captain had seen the bright flare and had successfully tacked offshore to the safety of deeper waters. The life-saving station logs are filled with accounts of vessels saved from danger by the diligent and watchful efforts of the surfmen.

The first loss of life within the scope of the USLSS on the Eastern Shore of Virginia occurred on 13 October 1879 near Cedar Island Life-Saving Station. At 7:00 A.M. the weather was clear and bright with a moderate wind, but rough surf. A yawl was putting out to sea through an inlet which had formed during a recent storm about one-half mile north of the station. Because of the turbulent sea conditions, the Cedar Island keeper kept his eye on the little yawl; he anticipated trouble and ordered his crew to stand ready with the surfboat. As the yawl reached a sandbar about three hundred yards from the beach, a huge wave broke upon and partially filled her. A second breaker knocked one of the oars from its oarlock, forcing it from the hands of one of the crew. A third breaker came over the bow; the boat was swept fore and aft by the water which completely engulfed it. With a great deal of difficulty, the yawl's crew steered her toward the shore.

The keeper ordered the surfboat launched for the rescue. While his orders were being carried out, he watched as the yawl capsized throwing the crew overboard. He was aghast as he saw the steersman going overboard with the steering oar still clenched in his hands, and men disappearing as soon as they struck the water. The life-savers pulled vigorously for the capsized yawl and the men whose lives were in danger.

As they passed the yawl and other floating wreckage, there was no sign of the crew until Thomas Nock was spotted clinging to the floating foresail. Although the surf was beating Nock into unconsiousness as the life-savers retrieved him, he was able to tell them that it was useless to search for the two other men—he had seen both go down very soon after the yawl capsized. Nock had held on to one man until he himself was nearly drowned. The life-savers returned to shore with their passenger and gave him brandy and dry clothing in the safety and warmth of the station. The body of one of the men, James Davis, was found washed ashore the next day; while the other, Thomas Sturgis, was never found.

At 8:00 A.M. on 31 March 1879, the keeper of the Cape Henry Life-Saving Station saw a schooner driving hard before a strong northeast gale. He correctly judged that the vessel would certainly come ashore. In her mad dash to escape to the relative safety of the Chesapeake Bay, the schooner's jib blew away, her fore boom broke, and she became unmanageable. The surfmen followed the schooner along the shore, dragging the beach apparatus cart two and one-half miles across the flooded beach. The keeper of the Seatack Station, having had the situation explained to him via telephone, hurriedly saddled a horse and immediately set out.

The *James M. Vance*, on her way from Philadelphia to Norfolk, had stranded in the northeaster and was quickly breaking apart, the giant swells crashing over her decks. The life-savers had little trouble, however, in rigging the breeches buoy and in rescuing all six of the crew. The crew was then cared for at the Cape Henry Station until they were provided with transportation to Norfolk.

On 22 October 1880, the sunrise brought with it enough light for the surfman on south patrol from the Hog Island Station to see a vessel pounding on the shoals three miles south of the station. He burned his Coston light to alert those on board that they had been seen and then hastened to the station to notify its keeper. The vessel was the Italian bark *Giambatista Primo*, its home port in Genoa, on her way from England to Baltimore in ballast. The Hog Island Station crew hauled the surfboat to the beach and readied it for launch. When the crew determined that the surf was much too rough to allow for a safe launching from the beach they hauled the surfboat a mile and a half to an inlet where they launched the boat. Because of the flood tide, high seas, and gale force winds, it was impossible to row the twenty-six-foot surfboat any farther than the mouth of the inlet. The boat drifted, despite all efforts, onto the beach at Prout's Island, on the south side of Rowe's Inlet.

Unless help was forthcoming, the Hog Island Station Keeper believed that the *Giambatista Primo*'s crew of thirteen would be lost if the storm continued. He took three of his best surfmen with him and walked six miles along the beach south to Cobb Island Life-Saving Station where he requested and obtained additional surfmen to aid in the rescue attempt. The keeper and crew of the Cobb Island Station launched their surfboat and, with the Hog Island surfmen, pulled north inside the beach of Cobb Island toward the inlet. Their intentions upon reaching Rowe's Inlet were to double bank the oars using the two station crews. Reaching the inlet, they found the *Primo*'s crew had abandoned her in their long boat and had pulled to the schooner *W. G. Tufts*, which was riding out the storm safely at anchor about a mile away. The bark's long boat, damaged in several places, had filled with water, and the crew had made themselves ready to swim to the schooner. They reached the schooner safely where the life-savers found them. The battered survivors were taken to the Cobb Island Station where they were given dry clothing, and housed at the station for two days before they left for Norfolk on board a wrecking schooner.

As was usual after the destruction of a vessel, pieces of the *Primo* washed up on the shores for days following the wrecking. Local residents were responsible for putting to good use any timber, lumber, barrels, cargo, or anything that was not salvaged by the owners of the vessel. In this instance the life-savers found clothing and other personal articles belonging to the crew of the *Primo* which they dried, packaged, and forwarded to the Italian consul in Norfolk. The bark, however, was a total loss.

After these losses, two years passed wherein only eight vessels were assisted by the Life-Saving Service in Virginia Beach. However, on the night of 10 February 1881 a surfman on south patrol from the Cape Henry Station, walking the beach in an extremely dense fog, discovered wreckage scattered along the beach, a clue that there was a stranded vessel. "Looking intently seaward for some time, [the surfman] managed to catch an occasional glimpse of a light, which most of the time was entirely obscured by the heavy fog."[8]

When the surfman was assured he saw the light of a vessel, he ignited a red Coston light and went back to his station. The life-savers took the surfboat out and had no difficulty in hauling the boat cart to a point on the shore believed to be abreast of the vessel since it was low tide. Again, it was quite difficult for the surfmen to find the vessel's light in the dense fog; but once located, they launched the surfboat and discovered the British bark *Joanna H. Cann,* a large vessel of 1,169 tons, stranded only 250 yards from shore. The surfmen quickly rowed the surfboat alongside the bark, and the Cape Henry keeper boarded her, offering assistance. At first Captain Tooker declined any help; he thought that the bark was on "middle ground between Capes Henry and Charles, and would get clear at high water."[9] Once the captain realized his mistake in location, he gladly accepted the keeper's offer. When the Cape Henry crew returned to shore, they found the Seatack Station keeper and crew ready to help.

With weather conditions threatening, the Seatack crew decided to rig the breeches buoy to bring ashore the survivors of the *Cann.* When the crew was safely ashore, the life-savers turned their attention to the stranded *Cann.* They obtained a tugboat from Norfolk, but she failed to haul the bark from her position on the outer sandbar. The *Cann* had lost her keel when she was driven aground and so the officials decided the only option was to strip and salvage her.

In the performance of their duties at the wreck of the *Joanna H. Cann,* the two life-saving crews made twenty-two trips to the vessel with the surfboat, unloading sails and any rigging they could along with what personal effects of the crew they could gather. Of the total value of the *Cann* at sixty-five thousand dollars, only $600 was saved. But, of course, no value could be placed on the lives of the crew—all of whom, rescued by the surfmen, were to sail again along the coast of Virginia.

Chapter 3

The Sea Takes Its Toll

APRIL 1881-JANUARY 1883

The Eastern Shore of Virginia, especially the barrier islands, was not heavily populated during the late nineteenth century. Most of the villages that centered around the fishing industry, which supplied the small populations with their livelihood, were secluded and desolate, with only a minimum of conveniences. The watermen who lived in these villages were a robust, self-sufficient lot, taking care of their own. The men of the Life-Saving Service on the Eastern Shore had been selected from these hardy individuals and it is understandable that they would still rely on their neighbors to help them take care of shipwrecked mariners that happened to stumble on to their shores.

In contrast to the relatively unchanging Eastern Shore, Virginia Beach, then known as a part of Princess Anne County, was developing into a minor but impressive hunter's paradise and vacation spot. Its shores followed the routes of commerce and travel among the cities of Baltimore, Washington, Annapolis, and other growing metropolitan areas. Steamships and packets brought travelers down the calmer and more sheltered bay waters to Norfolk and Hampton Roads for weekend holidays and week-long vacations. Schooners and sailing ships could be seen from the shores of Virginia Beach as they plied the Atlantic waters. These vessels were the coastwise carriers and deep water traders on routes from Europe and South America as well as those from the closer ports of San Francisco, New York, and Charleston. Unfortunately many of these vessels would become wrecks along Virginia's beaches both on the Eastern Shore's inlets and near the more populous areas of the western shore.

One of these wrecks was the Norwegian bark *Dictator* of Tved-strand, Norway, which stranded shortly after 1:00 A.M. on 21 April 1881. (This 578-ton bark should not be confused with the Norwegian bark of the same name which stranded with a tragic loss of life on 27 March 1891.) The *Dictator* of Tvedstrand was sailing in ballast from Boston, England, to Baltimore, Maryland, with a crew of thirteen men when she came ashore three and one half miles south of the Little Island Life-Saving Station. The surfman on south patrol was near the end of his beat when he saw the bark dangerously close to shore. He tried to warn those aboard the *Dictator*, but his Coston light failed to ignite, and the bark struck bottom shortly afterward. By 2:00 A.M. the surfman had sounded the alarm at his station, and the surfboat was launched immediately, but it took the better part of an hour for the crew to row the distance to the *Dictator*. Once alongside the bark, the keeper boarded her with considerable difficulty, and "made her captain understand that he and his men were there to render whatever service was needed, gratuitously. There was, however, no immediate danger to life."[1]

With their surfboat tied alongside the bark and ready for any emergency, the Little Island crew remained on board the *Dictator* until daylight. At dawn the surfmen rowed ashore and met the crew of the False Cape Life-Saving Station who had arrived with their beach apparatus cart. The breeches buoy was rigged, and the two crews alternated watches. Messages were sent by telephone to the Cape Henry Station where they were relayed to Norfolk by telegraph. By 1:00 P.M., just twelve hours after her stranding, the Barker Wrecking Company's steam tug *Resolute* left Norfolk to go to the assistance of the *Dictator*. At the request of Captain Christensen, the life-saving crews remained by the bark until she was hauled free by the *Resolute* and towed for the sum of three thousand dollars into Norfolk harbor.

On 23 November 1881, the schooner *James W. Brown*, a small vessel of 161 tons, on her way from Baltimore to Jacksonville, Florida, with a general cargo, stranded near the entrance to the Lynnhaven Inlet. (Lynnhaven Inlet was seven miles from the Cape Henry Life-Saving Station and far beyond the beach patrol's limit.) The weather was thick and foggy when the schooner's master, Captain Elwell, became lost and thought he had passed safely out of Lynnhaven Bay. Actually, he had headed south and was stranded, still in the bay. At 11:30 A.M. on 24

November the Cape Henry Station received word of the incident and, without delay, manned the surfboat and pulled for the wreck.

Captain Elwell was able to reach the shore in one of the *Brown*'s small boats and went to the Lynnhaven Inlet signal office to report the disaster. At midday on 24 November a gale force wind developed, and the Cape Henry surfmen had to beach their surfboat and have the boat pulled by a team of horses to a point opposite the wreck. It wasn't until 4:00 P.M. that the surfboat was again launched into Lynnhaven Bay, and the remaining four crew members from the *James W. Brown* taken safely ashore. The schooner became a total wreck and only a small portion of her cargo was saved, but the surfmen had saved the lives of the *Brown*'s crew.

On 21 February 1882 two lives were lost on the Eastern Shore when the sloop *Dauntless* stranded. The sloop's home port was Chincoteague, and she was on a short coastal voyage from New Inlet, Virginia, back to Chincoteague with a cargo of seed oysters when disaster struck. There was a fresh southerly gale prevailing most of the day which caused rough seas, but as the day wore on, the crew of the *Dauntless* was forced to double reef the mainsail to make her more manageable in the wind.

In the investigation of the wreck which followed, the sole survivor, John W. Howard, told Assistant Inspector Lt. T. Walker of the Revenue Marine Bureau that he had advised the vessel's master, Captain Sewell Collins, to put into Metomkin Inlet before sundown; Howard feared his captain would try to enter Chincoteague Inlet after dark—something even the most experienced captain rarely attempted, and then only when weather conditions were favorable. It was because of Captain Collins's error in judgement that the *Dauntless* was wrecked and the lives were lost.[2] The story of what happened follows.

When the *Dauntless* was just off Wallop's Island shortly after sunset, she lost her deck load of oysters as heavy seas washed over her decks. Her sails were ripped to tatters, but the captain pushed her onward. As she neared the outer buoy off Chincoteague Inlet, the direction of the wind shifted, coming out of the west pushed by a dark and threatening thunderstorm. Captain Collins knew that the only way into the inlet was a dead beat to windward. It was in the *Dauntless*' favor that the tide was not extremely high, or she would have swamped long before she did.

Howard said that the sloop had the usual running lights which were in working condition, but that no lamp except one small oil lamp in the cabin was lit. The sloop made two or three tacks in the channel as her skipper used all his skills to try and enter the inlet. Captain Collins soon realized his mistake and called for Howard to relieve him at the wheel while he ran forward to let go the anchors. When the anchors grabbed and held, the sloop came to rest in the breakers on Fox Shoal, a spit of sand extending south from the end of Chincoteague Island. The *Dauntless* quickly filled with water and sank.

With the sea crashing mercilessly over her decks, the *Dauntless* pounded heavily on the shoal. Captain Collins and Howard climbed to the starboard rigging while James Taylor, a nineteen-year-old seaman, clung to the port side rigging. Howard recalled that his captain had quite a reputation for daring and reckless deeds. But even this adventuresome captain realized he had gone too far this time. He seemed, finally, to be overcome by a realization of his mistake and the danger in which he had put himself and his crew. Collins soon gave up, fell from the rigging, and was washed away. Shortly after the death of his captain, young Taylor was torn from the rigging; he grabbed a line and crawled back above the deck of the sloop. Bitter cold numbed Taylor's hands and he too slipped back into the frigid water to his death.

Howard was perched on the lower masthead, his arms clutching the topmast, but the sloop was pounding in the surf so violently that he was almost thrown from the rigging. As the tide continued to ebb, Howard's position became more secure. Throughout the night he kept himself awake and fought the cold by beating his body with his hands.

The *Dauntless* was discovered by the Assateague Beach Life-Saving Station lookout shortly after sunrise on 22 February. The surfboat was launched without delay, and the crew rowed furiously to the sloop. When they arrived, the *Dauntless* was full of water, and her stern had been ripped apart. The surfmen could find no one on board the wreck and rowed back to the beach. There they discovered footprints leading in the direction of Chincoteague Village.

What happened was that at sunrise Howard had descended from his position in the rigging and with the water only knee deep, waded quickly the short distance to shore. Once on the beach he walked to the nearest inhabited building where he was given food and dry clothing. Then he went into the village and sent telegrams, notifying James Taylor's parents and Captain Collins's family of the deaths.

Meanwhile, the surfmen had followed the footprints until they found that Howard had reached shelter. The life-savers never made contact with any crew member of the *Dauntless*, living or dead. Had the life-savers been aware of the wreck earlier, would they have been able to save the lives of the Captain and young Taylor? We can only wonder.

At 4:00 A.M. on 24 February 1882, the schooner *Pearl Nelson* stranded nearly in front of the False Cape Life-Saving Station. The schooner was discovered by one of the patrolmen on his return to the station to wake up his relief. The *Pearl Nelson* was on a coastwise voyage from Wilmington, North Carolina, to Plymouth, Massachusetts, with a cargo of twelve hundred barrels of tar when she encountered a strong northeasterly wind along with heavy seas which caused her to strand one hundred and fifty yards offshore.

The False Cape crew dragged the surfboat on its cart to the shore and launched it into the heavy breakers. Once alongside the schooner, "the sea was so rough that, notwithstanding the exertions of the men to keep their boat clear of the schooner, it was dashed violently against the anchor and badly stove."[3] The surfboat was so badly damaged that it had to be hoisted aboard the schooner for repairs in order to be seaworthy enough to return to shore.

After the damaged boards in the surfboat had been caulked, the vessel's crew refused, understandably, to be taken ashore in the surfboat.

Surfmen dragging the surfboat on its cart to the scene of a wreck.
A nineteenth-century wood engraving.

The life-savers returned to their station and hauled the beach apparatus cart to the scene and quickly set up the breeches buoy. The crew of the *Nelson* still refused to be taken off until noon when five men were safely hauled ashore. The captain of the *Pearl Nelson* remained on board until sunset when he made a signal that he, too, wished to be rescued. The captain and crew of the schooner were then made comfortable for the night at the False Cape Station. The next day the *Pearl Nelson* was successfully hauled off the sand by a wrecking tug and towed to Norfolk to be checked for whatever repairs were needed. The life-savers, too, were hard at work making permanent repairs to their surfboat.

The last vessel to come ashore on Virginia Beach during 1882 was the three-masted schooner *Boston*. On 30 December 1882, the schooner encountered a severe northeast storm on her way up the coast from New Bern, North Carolina. The *Boston* was loaded with a cargo of lumber and shingles bound for her home port of Philadelphia when she began to leak so rapidly that Captain William Jones, her master, started to steer her straight for the beach to save the lives of himself and his crew.

The south patrol from the False Cape Life-Saving Station soon discovered the schooner heading for land and burned a red Coston light to warn her off. Within fifteen minutes, however, the *Boston* struck the outer sandbar two hundred yards from shore. The surfman on patrol started at once for his station to give the alarm. The False Cape crew, arriving at the wreck at 10:00 A.M., fired only a single shot from the Lyle gun and successfully placed a line on board the schooner. The very high tides and strong shore current pushed the *Boston* south; the life-savers followed with their gear along the beach. This caused a great delay in the rescue operations, but in time the breeches buoy was rigged and by noon on 31 December all crewmen aboard the *Boston* were safely landed.

On 1 January 1883 the northeaster abated somewhat and the False Cape life-savers rowed to the schooner in the surfboat, recovering as much of the crew's possessions as could be found. Those shipwrecked were well cared for at the station for five days until transportation could be arranged for them to be taken to Norfolk, then on to Philadelphia. The schooner was declared a total loss, with nothing saved other than some of her sails, rigging, and a small portion of her cargo.

After a rescue operation, those on board the vessel were taken to the Life-Saving stations where they were provided with food, dry clothing, and a warm place to rest. If they suffered injuries, they were cared for by the life-savers. Frequently, nearby physicians were summoned to handle more serious injuries. It was not, however, until the 1882-83 winter season that the station crews were given specific help in the care of those shipwrecked. During this period the Women's National Relief Association (WNRA) was organized, the core being made up of the wives of prominent men in Washington and New York. The WNRA president was Mrs. James A. Garfield, the wife of the President of the United States, who was not simply content to give her name to the movement, but was one of the most active women in the organization.

The basic function of the WNRA was to give whatever assistance it could to the Life-Saving stations. Their charitable function was to put beds, blankets, warm clothing, and other items of necessity in each of the life-saving stations for the aid and comfort of those who were rescued from marine disasters. The federal government provided a well-stocked medicine chest, but in most cases, the victims needed rest and dry clothing more than medical assistance. Until aided by the WNRA the surfmen often gave up their own beds in the station and provided their own clothing.

The life-saving stations were also provided with a small library of books and, in the not-so-remote areas, newspapers to relieve the tedium of the enforced detention, lasting days and even weeks in some instances after a shipwreck. These libraries were donated by the Seaman's Friend Society. In addition several newspaper publishers sent their papers to many of the stations as a courtesy.

The next shipwreck which involved loss of life along the coast of Virginia was that of the 238-ton schooner *Albert Dailey,* and took place on Smith Island on 7 January 1883. The schooner was a "coaster" (a schooner that plied the waters close to the coastline) whose home port was in Augusta, Maine. She was on her way from Baltimore to Bridgeport, Connecticut, with a load of coal. She ran aground because of an extremely dense fog and strong current about two hundred and fifty yards from shore, some three miles northeast of the Smith Island Life-Saving Station. She had been grounded for five hours when, to the patrolling surfman on the shore, she suddenly appeared like a phantom out of the fog. The surfman burned his Coston light but received no response from the vessel. Waiting for a time, he burned another light to which the *Albert Dailey* finally responded. Immediately the surfman set out for his station to sound the alarm.

As the Smith Island Station crew hauled the surfboat north along the darkened beach, the fog closed in more heavily. The crew dragged their boat to a point they thought was opposite the schooner and launched it into a relatively calm sea, but the night was so dark and thick with fog that Keeper Hitchins could see nothing beyond the area lit by the surfboat's lantern. Still, the surfmen rowed, groping in the darkness, searching for the vessel. Shortly before dawn the schooner once more loomed out of the fog within fifty feet of the surfboat.

The *Albert Dailey*'s captain requested that Keeper Hitchins and his men stay on board the schooner, which they did, until 1:00 A.M. when the surf began to rise. Then the surfmen took the schooner's crew along with their personal effects and the ship's papers, safely to shore and escorted them to the Smith Island Station.

The next day Captain Goldthwaite of the *Dailey* and his crew were taken back to their schooner in the surfboat. The tasks which faced the surfmen and sailors were to try to get the schooner off the shoal and to save as much of the cargo as possible. When the surfmen were unable to move the schooner off the sands, they made an agreement with Nathan Cobb of the Cobb Wrecking Company to try to refloat the vessel. Keeper Hitchins then took Captain Goldthwaite and started back to the shore in the surfboat; Cobb remained on board with three of his men and the crew of the *Dailey*.

A blinding snowstorm developed and the wind increased and shifted to the northeast, and once again the surfmen pulled their surfboat to the *Dailey*, but no one on board wished to be taken off. With the Cobb Wrecking Company's boat alongside the schooner, those on board felt they had a means of escape if their situation became dangerous; they could signal the life-savers with a flag until dark, and the schooner's fog horn would serve to alert the life-savers on shore at night.

In the late afternoon the weather worsened, and, according to regulations, Keeper Hitchins had the surfmen patrol the beach; they were instructed to be particularly alert for any signal from the stranded schooner. At 8:00 P.M. the surfman on north patrol reported that the schooner, still only two hundred and fifty yards off the beach, could no longer be seen. Outside the station, nothing was visible; a gale force wind blew snow across the beach, and the surf broke higher and higher upon the beach. Still no distress signal was sent from the schooner.

Finally, the next report on the schooner came around 11:00 P.M. when the north patrolman returned with the startling news that the schooner's hatches and part of her small boat had been washed ashore. The alarm was sounded and the surfmen readied their equipment. The Inspector for the Fifth District, Lieutenant Failing, was on a regular visit to the Smith Island Life-Saving Station and helped the surfmen load the beach cart. Hauling the beach cart along the beach proved a laborious task—the three-mile distance to the schooner was made even more difficult by the snow and sleet which was driving into the faces of the surfmen by gale force winds. They dragged the beach cart through snow a foot deep which covered soft, wet sand. Furthermore, the snow hid tree stumps and washed-out roots which caught the wheels of the beach cart and delayed them even more.

When the surfmen finally reached the wreck scene sometime after 2:00 A.M., they were exhausted and suffering from the cold. All that could be seen of the sunken schooner were the dim outlines of her masts; the hull was already invisible. The sea had boarded the schooner so fast and with such fury that the men on board had no time to send a signal to the life-savers—they only had enough time to climb into the rigging. Six Coston lights burned on the beach to signal those on board that they would soon be rescued. The surfmen made several attempts to launch the surfboat, and after an hour they succeeded in getting the boat beyond the crashing shore breakers. Once away from the beach they were unable to locate the schooner and feared that they might be smashed to pieces in the darkness by the floating timbers; they returned to the shore.

The dawn came drearily and brought with it a terrible spectacle. In the dim early light of day only two masts with the spars could be seen in the surf. Those who stayed aboard the schooner could be seen aloft, lashed to the rigging where they had been for almost twenty-four hours, now only white, shapeless masses in the blizzard. The surfmen saw this devastating scene through a veil of sleet and snow, but lost no time in setting up the Lyle gun; their only hope was to get a line to the men in the rigging and set up the breeches buoy. The first shot fell short of its target—the men in the rigging could not get to it. The keeper ordered the line hauled back and fired a second time. Again the shot fell short in almost the same place, and the surfmen realized the men in the rigging were just too weak to secure the line. The third and fourth shots also failed their mark. With frustration fueling their energy, the surfmen grimly acknowledged the helplessness of the stranded men.

The only chance to rescue these men was with the surfboat, but the condition of the sea made a launch impossible. The wind was beginning to slacken and swing around to the west, which meant the storm was abating. The only thing the surfmen could do was to wait. Finally, near noon on 10 January, three days after the initial stranding, the surfmen launched the surfboat into a sea which was still running high and was littered with timbers and other bits of wreckage from the dying schooner. The surfmen's clothing, wet and frozen from their exposure during the long hours on the beach, literally cracked as they pulled at the oars. Despite all the skills of the surfmen in handling it, their boat was swept to leeward of the wreck and they had to put back to shore.

After a few minutes rest, the surfmen repeated their efforts, this time grabbing a length of line attached to the wreck. The fury of the storm won again, and the surfboat was once more forced to leeward, away from the wreck. The keeper ordered the men back out immediately after they landed the surfboat on the beach. "You are ordered out," was the surfman's creed, "but you have no orders to return." This time the surfmen reached the wreck and were able to hold on long enough to get four men out of the rigging and into the surfboat.

Lt. Failing, Keeper Hitchins, and others on the shore took care of the unconscious sailors, carrying them quickly to the station. Without pausing for more than a few minutes, the surfmen pushed the surfboat out into the breakers once more and pulled for the wreck. Perhaps with their energy renewed by success in rescuing four of the sailors, the surfmen struggled, finally getting their boat alongside the wreck, and took the remaining men into the boat and rowed for shore.

The relief and exultation of the successful rescue were shortlived, however, when it was learned that one of Mr. Cobb's crew died from exposure shortly after the boat landed. Also the schooner's steward had been washed overboard during the night and was not seen again. Of the eight men rescued, seven survived; two of those seven required hours of constant attention to revive them, all of which stands as a tribute to the diligent and courageous efforts of the men of the Life-Saving Service.

Mr. Cobb's survival of the wreck of the *Albert Dailey* requires more than just brief mention. In the early 1830s, Nathan F. Cobb, his wife, and three sons, Nathan, Warren, and Albert, put all their possessions on

Views of Cobb Island Life-Saving Station. Courtesy: U. S. Coast Guard.

board a schooner and sailed from their native Massachusetts, seeking a warmer and healthier climate. On their coastal voyage south they encountered a severe storm and were forced into an inlet not far from where the town of Oyster, Virginia, stands today. From their experience of near disaster, Nathan Cobb gained respect for and love of the sea. He also obtained a new home and a new occupation. Nathan Cobb became a reputable "wrecker," a waterman who salvages shipwrecks. (The Cobb Wrecking Company was typical of some of the smaller wrecking companies of this period. They might be said to have been the forerunners of the later salvage and tug fleets of today.) In March 1839, Cobb bought Great Sand Shoal Island and moved his family there. Soon the island was known as "Cobb Island."

The Cobb family worked hard, and, with their "Yankee ingenuity," not only developed a very profitable salvage business but a prominent resort business as well. The Cobb Island Hotel was known throughout the Eastern seaboard as a fine and gracious vacation spot with guests coming from as far away as Maine. By the 1880s its fame for fine hunting and fishing had spread to Europe. Duck hunting, however, brought the greatest acclaim to Cobb Island as the Cobb family hunted, cleaned, and shipped the ducks to the cosmopolitan restaurateurs of New York City.

Chapter 4

Ever Watchful

FEBRUARY 1883 – MARCH 1887

In 1883 there was but one incident on the shores of Virginia Beach, and it was the altogether unnecessary loss of the Italian bark *Figogna*. The 843-ton bark had sailed from Parma, Italy, bound for Baltimore with a cargo of one thousand tons of iron ore. She arrived off the coast of Virginia Beach at 8:00 A.M., 27 February, and was discovered by the Little Island Life-Saving crew shortly thereafter at anchor in six fathoms of water, a mile to sea, and a mile north of the station. The weather on that morning was cloudy with a strong northeast wind, high surf, and a powerful shore current. Little Island Keeper Abel Belanga ordered his crew to haul the surfboat north, along the beach above the position of the *Figogna*, to lessen the rowing distance. After launching the boat, the crew proceeded through the surf, rowing against the wind and current that held them almost stationary. It took an hour and a half to travel the one mile to the bark; after that struggle they found their troubles had only begun.

No one on board the *Figogna* spoke English and the life-saving crew was equally incapable of speaking Italian. After many attempts to communicate the life-savers and the bark's first mate wrote a telegram to the Italian Consul in Baltimore which the Little Island crew sent after returning to shore. Although Keeper Belanga and his crew erected a signal pole on the beach in front of the *Figogna*, they never received a response to their flags.

Fearing for the bark's crew, the life-savers again pulled their surfboat alongside the vessel. Keeper Belanga used his International Code of Signals to learn that the bark was leaking badly and had a considerable amount of water in her hold. He wanted to put his men immediately at the pumps, but the vessel's captain, fearing that the life-

48

savers might be salvagers, refused. Nevertheless, Captain Nicolini gave Keeper Belanga another telegram and the life-savers pulled for shore in order to send it.

Late that same afternoon a dispatch from the Italian Consul arrived in response to the first telegram announcing that a Baker Salvage Company steamer was on its way to help. Once more the life-savers took their surfboat out to the side of the distressed bark. This time they were able to board her and help man the pumps until after dark at which time they rowed back to shore in the surfboat. The weather had cleared somewhat and Keeper Belanga kept watch during the night, the moonlight making the bark clearly visible. At 4:00 A.M., 28 February, he saw the *Figogna* get under way.

But, at daybreak the bark again proved unmanageable and the Little Island crew rowed the surfboat to her for a fourth time. To their horror, they found the *Figogna* with her decks nearly level with the sea; she was slowly sinking. Belanga wanted to keep the vessel afloat, at least until the salvage steamer arrived, but by midmorning the only vessel near by was the revenue cutter *Hamilton,* to which he signalled for aid.

Unfortunately, the Italian captain appeared to have misunderstood any and all attempts to explain to him that his vessel was not being taken away from his authority. He refused all assistance and ordered everyone other than his crew off the *Figogna.* The wind began to blow harder from the west, pushing the bark, along with the Little Island surfboat, out to sea. In the meantime, the *Hamilton* left the bark to go to the aid of a dismasted schooner while Keeper Belanga, fearing for the lives of the fourteen crewmen on board, kept close to the side of the bark.

By midafternoon when the *Figogna*'s bow settled into the sea, the frightened crew finally left the vessel in their own boats, ignoring the life-savers offers of assistance. The captain and mate would not leave the flooded decks despite warnings from the life-savers and their own crew that stood by in the boats. It was not until the bark listed to port that the *Figogna*'s two officers made gestures to be taken off. Quickly,the men brought the surfboat into position, taking the two men aboard.

After the surfboats had gotten beyond the suction of the sinking vessel, the crew turned to watch the *Figogna* as she "made a plunge, bow first, and with a sickening clatter and throb, went down."[1] She sank ten miles to sea due east of the Little Island Life-Saving Station. It was obvious that in addition to the language barrier the actions and suspicions of the Italian captain resulted in the loss of his vessel. The life-savers appeared to do all they could to aid the bark and her crew but were rewarded, as we have seen, with nothing but frustration and exhaustion for their efforts.

The Life-Saving Service received national recognition for its efforts that resulted in increased aid both from the private and public sectors. At the beginning of the 1883-84 winter season for the United States Life-Saving Service, for example, WNRA, the charitable organization discussed earlier, supplied seventy-three stations with boxes of food and clothing to be used to aid shipwrecked mariners. In addition, Congress appropriated funds for and authorized the building of eleven new life-saving stations within all districts: two of them were Virginia stations, Wallops Beach and Parramore Beach.

During the 1883-84 season three schooners stranded on the shores of Virginia Beach; two of the schooners were total losses and the third was floated from her perch on the sandbar with only minimal damage a few days after she stranded. In contrast, twenty-two vessels came ashore between October 1883 and April 1884, on Virginia's Eastern Shore, keeping station crews there more than busy. The number of stations on the Eastern Shore grew to eight, and in 1889 the addition of another station made the total nine.

Fifth District Life-Saving Stations in Virginia

Station	Location
Popes Island	8.5 miles north of Assateague Light
Assateague Beach	1.2 miles south of Assateague Light
Wallops Beach	1.5 miles south of Chincoteague Inlet
Metomkin Inlet	southern tip of Metomkin Island (1889)
Wachapreague	southern end of Cedar Island (replaced Cedar Island station in 1882)
Parramore Beach	midway point on Parramore Island
Hog Island	southern end of Hog Island
Cobb Island	southern end of Cobb Island
Smith Island	at Cape Charles Light

In the same year there were no changes made in the number of life-saving stations along the coast of Virginia Beach on the western side of the Bay.

However, the area was being transformed in other ways. Around the Seatack Life-Saving Station an expanding real estate development was taking place. In 1878 a small group of Norfolk businessmen, who

Assateague Beach Life-Saving Station and crew.
Courtesy: U. S. Coast Guard.

Parramore Beach Life-Saving Station. Courtesy: U. S. Coast Guard.

formed the Seaside Hotel and Land Company, purchased approximately sixteen hundred acres of land, including nearly four and a half miles of oceanfront property beginning at Rudee Inlet and running north to present-day 75th Street. The company referred to its holdings as

"Virginia Beach," which can be interpreted as the unofficial birth of the city of Virginia Beach. The first hotel built along the oceanfront was erected in 1883 between present-day 14th and 16th streets. Also in 1883 a narrow-gauge railroad was built between the oceanfront and Broad Creek, then just a small village east of Norfolk. To ride this railroad one would board a small boat in Norfolk, ride to Broad Creek, and then transfer to the railroad. In 1885 a trestle was built across Broad Creek as the rail service was extended through to Norfolk.

The rail service between Broad Creek and Virginia Beach had been in operation for less than one year; however, when the coasting schooner *Lewis A. Rommell* stranded two miles north of the Little Island Life-Saving Station on 15 January 1884. The 334-ton schooner carried a cargo of phosphate rock from Charleston, South Carolina, to Baltimore, a cargo too heavy for a relatively small vessel. The schooner had seemed to be in trouble for some time; the crew from the life-saving station watched as she tried in vain to tack off shore, but she was unable to work against the heavy seas and northeast gale force winds. The surfmen followed Keeper Abel Belanga's instructions to the letter and made six trips in the surfboat and finally brought the crew of the *Lewis A. Rommell* safely to shore. The following day an attempt was made to remove some of the crew's personal effects, but without success. The schooner quickly broke up and, along with her cargo, became a total loss.

The three-masted schooner *Albert C. Paige*, like the *Lewis A. Rommell*, had loaded a cargo of phosphate rock at Charleston, but was bound for New York City. At 6:00 A.M. on 26 January 1884, the schooner was reported by the north patrol of the Dam Neck Mills Life-Saving Station as being ashore two and one half miles from the station. The schooner stranded while attempting to tack offshore, Captain Haley reported. On her way to New York City with her cargo, there had been a very strong wind from the north accompanied by heavy seas that had pushed the schooner from her coastwise course. Two life-saving stations responded with their surfboats. The Seatack Station crew came south on the long shore current, while the Dam Neck Mills Station crew hauled their surfboat on its carriage along the beach. The schooner, however, was not in any immediate danger; Captain Haley was taken ashore by the Dam Neck Mills crew to telephone from the station for assistance in getting his vessel off the sands.

The *Albert C. Paige* was still in good condition when Captain Haley and the Dam Neck Mills crew returned to the scene. A wrecking steamer had arrived by that time, but they were unable to get the schooner off because of the extremely high surf. The breeches buoy was set up and Captain Haley returned to his vessel. For two days the wrecking steamer made unsuccessfull attempts to save the schooner. After fifteen trips with the breeches buoy, the surfmen had been able to rescue all those on board the *Paige;* but the schooner was declared a total loss. In both the stranding of the *Lewis A. Rommell* and the *Albert C. Paige,* the heavy cargo was a contributing factor to their destruction.

The men of the Life-Saving Service trained constantly—their days were made up of training exercises and upkeep of their equipment. They had to keep themselves, as well as their boats and other equipment, in top form, for it was as uncertain as the weather itself when a ship would strand or wreck and require their skillful services. No two shipwrecks were alike, although the experiences the crew had from one rescue were learned and applied to later rescues. Keepers from neighboring stations also met and exchanged ideas, or just sat and told "sea stories" when their busy schedules permitted. For the most part, however, the lives of keepers and crews were lonely on these remote and desolate beaches along the coast of Virginia, even though there was growth along the beaches during the latter part of the nineteenth century. The summer visitors rarely stayed past September, which left the life-savers to patrol empty beaches in the winter months.

The life-saver's only chance for advancement within the service came when a vacancy occurred, either because of the death of a surfman or his release from the service. Both were common occurrences. Some men didn't have the proper outlook for such a lonely and life-threatening existence and were dismissed when, under tense and dangerous situations, they failed to do their job. Some found the Life-Saving Service not worth all the sacrifices they had to make. Their families suffered from their long absences—they had to live at the station during the entire winter season unable to help out at home when emergencies might arise. It was not uncommon, for instance, for Surfman Number Two to quit the service at one station and return to it a few months, or even a few years later as Surfman Number Six at another station along the coast. These hardy individuals made the Life-Saving Service their career and devoted their lives to saving the lives and property of others.

On 4 October 1884 the three-masted schooner *Sarah Shubert* stranded on the shoals off Little Machipongo Inlet and was gradually grinding towards the beach when she was discovered at 7:00 A.M., four

Crowd gathered on a Sunday afternoon to observe the life-savers in action at the Seatack Life-Saving Station, Virginia Beach, in the early 1880s. Courtesy: Virginia Beach Maritime Historical Museum.

and one-half miles south of the Parramore Beach Life-Saving Station. The surfboat was launched into the heavy surf and gale force northeast winds. It took the surfmen nearly two hours to reach the schooner which was only two hundred yards off the beach. When they reached the 157-ton schooner, the surf was sweeping over her decks, and her crew of five men had taken to the rigging after gathering as much of their personal gear as possible. When the surfmen arrived, they found the crew and gear lashed to the rigging.

In a later report on the rescue operations, the Keeper of the Parramore Beach Station explained that it was impossible to get the surfboat alongside the schooner for fear of swamping her since the *Sarah Shubert* had lost her steering gear during the night and had drifted, unmanageable, ashore stern first. The life-savers pulled their boat as close as they dared to the schooner to tell the sailors to climb down from the rigging to the bowsprit. The life-savers then rowed their surfboat for the shore, beached, and bailed it out. They carried the surfboat well to windward to allow for the strong current. As soon as they received a signal from the sailors on board the *Shubert* they shoved off again.

The sailors on the bowsprit failed to catch a line thrown to them, and the surfboat, pushed by the high winds, drifted past them to leeward. Again the surfmen beached the boat, bailed it out, and carried it back up the beach to windward. The third attempt was finally successful and a line was tied off, securing the surfboat to the schooner. It was a very difficult task to rescue the sailors from their position on the bowsprit— there was the danger that the surfboat would again be swamped. Furthermore, it was difficult to keep the surfboat steady alongside the schooner. Each of the five sailors had to wait and time his jump from the flying jib-boom into the bobbing surfboat. But, all the sailors and their gear were taken into the surfboat in this manner and safely returned to shore. All hands walked back to the station for warmth and rest. The next day the life-savers rowed more than twenty miles in two trips to Little Machipongo Inlet so that the rescued sailors could board a steamer and return to their homeport, since the schooner and her cargo of coal were declared a total loss.

The Norwegian bark *Lena* with her crew of ten men left Natal, Brazil, on 1 December 1884, loaded with a cargo of sugar bound for Philadelphia. The bark was driven off her course by strong northeast winds on 26 December in the vicinity of Hog Island. The south beach patrol from the

Hog Island Life-Saving Station saw both the red and green running lights of a vessel offshore about one mile and three hundred yards from the station at 3:45 A.M. on 27 December. The surfman ran quickly to his station and awakened the Keeper who rushed to the lookout tower. With the aid of his "marine glass" he spotted a square-rigged vessel heading for the shoal waters and ordered a Coston flare to be ignited.

In a statement made by one of the survivors of the wreck, the sailors explained they saw the bright red glow of the Coston light but mistook it for a pilot signal. The Keeper and crew watched the *Lena* as she plowed on through the surf and stranded on the shoal only a mile offshore directly in front of the station at 4:00 A.M.

Keeper Johnson ordered his Hog Island crew to haul out the surfboat. The night was cloudy and dark, the wind blowing moderately from the north. However, the sea which was only at quarter ebb, was extraordinarily high. The surf was much too violent for launching the surfboat, but it was hoped that this same surf might drive the bark closer to shore and within range of the Lyle gun. The *Lena* was, in fact, working towards shore as she was lifted and pushed forward with each surge of the surf on the shoal. The Keeper was convinced that this action would ultimately push the bark within their range; he and his men rushed back to the station to get the beach apparatus cart. The tide was falling fast away from the beach as the surfmen quickly set up the Lyle gun at the low water mark.

All this time the weather had been thick and dark, but at 7:00 A.M., when daylight appeared, the *Lena* was illuminated "leaping and staggering forward, like a thing maimed, in the immense area of broken foam."[2] The crewmen aimed the Lyle gun and fired towards the bark, but the distance was still too great, and the line did not reach her. By 8:00 A.M. it had begun snowing. The second shot from the Lyle gun also did not succeed as the *Lena* was still lurching towards shore. The third shot was fired a short time later only to fall short of its mark.

Two hours later, six hours after the bark had stranded, Keeper Johnson decided to launch the surfboat in an effort to rescue the crew on board, despite the appalling surf conditions. The chances of reaching the vessel were slim, but the Keeper had trained his crew well, and they had the reputation of being one of the best crews on the coast. They knew that the only chance of survival for those on board the bark would be rescue by boat, and they resolved that the effort must be made. The surfboat was launched and their battle with the sea began.

Hog Island Light Station, 1884. Courtesy: U. S. Coast Guard.

In the tumult of the shore breakers, the boat, swamped to her gunwales, drove seaward under the surfmen's powerful strokes only to be pushed back toward the beach with each swell. For over an hour the crew worked, trying to scale the walls of surf. Finally, the men were exhausted and the surfboat was full of water. They beached the boat, bailed it out, and carried it a mile down the beach to attempt another launch. After that desperate effort failed, the Keeper fastened a line to a barrel and had his crew carry it up the beach where they launched it into the surf in hopes that the current would carry the line within reach of the sailors on board the bark. The tide was then at its lowest, but the barrel failed to get beyond the breakers and another heroic effort ended in failure.

As night approached, Keeper Johnson ordered a bonfire built on the beach opposite the bark's position. This served as a signal to those still clinging to life on board the bark, as well as to keep warm the fifty or more people that had assembled on the beach to help in the rescue effort. With the darkness came increasing cold; the snow had turned to rain earlier in the day, but the drop in temperature turned it to freezing rain.

Many of the volunteers stayed on the beach with the surfmen all night despite all these adversities.

Around 11:00 P.M. on 27 December, a thick fog spread over the roaring surf and obliterated the *Lena* from view. Five hours later the Keeper saw a dark spot through the dense fog and launched the surfboat into the darkness among the wreckage which floated in on the breakers. With a great deal of difficulty the crew succeeded in reaching the dimly outlined mass and found that it was only a part of the *Lena*—the cabin and stern section. On it were two men, still alive and lashed to the wreckage, along with the lifeless body of the captain. The surfmen maneuvered the surfboat close enough to the wreckage to take the men off. Despite all their precautions, three holes were gouged in the hull of the surfboat.

Stranded on the shoal more than twenty-four hours, eight of the *Lena*'s crew died; only the bodies of the captain and the sailmaker were recovered, later to be buried on the island. The life-savers felt that they could have done more in the rescue attempt, but at no time was the bark closer to shore than eight hundred yards, which prevented the Lyle gun from reaching its mark. The dangerous and heavy surf hampered the rescue efforts by use of the surfboat—all conditions over which the surfmen had no control. The loss of life on board the *Lena* was, therefore, inevitable.

In contrast to the devastating loss of life and difficult rescue attempt of the *Lena* on the Eastern Shore was the stranding of the schooner *A. M. Bailey* one mile north of the Seatack Life-Saving Station in Virginia Beach on 22 March 1885. The *A. M. Bailey*, from Somers Point, New Jersey, was sailing light on her way to Hatteras Inlet, North Carolina, when she encountered a northeaster that drove the 66-ton schooner high up on the beach. Her four-man crew jumped from the schooner to the beach safely and required no assistance from the life-savers. The schooner's crew was sheltered for ten days at the Seatack Station while the surfmen tried every means possible to save what they could from the wreck. The *A. M. Bailey* was valued at three thousand dollars and became a total loss despite all efforts.

Every vessel that stranded in 1885 on the shores of Virginia Beach was a total loss. The year 1886, however, proved to be much more successful for the life-saving stations. They aided six vessels that stranded: three steamships, two schooners, and one bark. The three steamships, valued at $283,000 including their cargos, were towed off the sands undamaged, and sixty-five lives were saved. The three steamships were international traders. The *Serpho* and the *Clapyron* were carrying cargoes of iron ore from ports in Spain to Baltimore. The *Pirate* had loaded her cargo of lumber at Baltimore and was bound for Kingston, Jamaica.

The two schooners, however, were not as fortunate as the steamships that stranded in 1886. On 5 December there was a strong northerly gale so intense that a day patrol had been sent along the beach. At 1:00 P.M. the Seatack Station's north patrol reported a schooner heading directly for the beach. With a disaster imminent, the station crew was called together as the schooner passed their position. The surfmen pulled the apparatus cart and followed the schooner south. The 196-ton schooner *Pangusset*, struck the shores about half a mile south of the Seatack Station and seventy-five yards from shore.

The *Pangusset* carried railroad iron and fire bricks from New York City to Norfolk, and had weathered the northerly gale for two days until she lost her sails which left her unmanageable and at the mercy of the storm. Since the schooner stranded so close to the station, the sailors were soon taken off in the breeches buoy. The six survivors were aided by wreckers in stripping the schooner and saving her cargo, but the *Pangusset* was a total loss.

On the following day, 6 December 1886, the three-masted schooner *Annie F. Conlon*, sailing in ballast from Boston to Baltimore, stranded three miles north of the False Cape Life-Saving Station. This schooner had weathered the northerly gale much better than had the *Pangusset*. She was discovered in the surf by the beach patrol shortly after she stranded. The schooner worked her way shoreward; so a line was thrown from her to the surfmen standing on the beach. The breeches buoy was set up, but the schooner's crew of eight men was not in any immediate danger. The *Annie F. Conlon* remained stranded on the shore for eight days before a wrecking crew floated her and she was towed to Norfolk for repairs.

On 3 April 1886, the bark *May Queen*, with her crew of eight men, stranded two miles north of the Little Island Life-Saving Station about 8:30 P.M. The bark had loaded coconuts at San Andres, Colombia, and was on her way to Baltimore. The estimated value of the vessel was $4,000; her cargo of coconuts was valued at $7,700. The Little Island Station patrol discovered the wreck at 9:30 P.M. and rushed back to the

Schooner *Annie F. Conlon* in port receiving cargo.
(*Annie F. Conlon* is the three-masted schooner on the left.)
Courtesy: A.M. Barnes Collection, Mariners' Museum.

station to sound the alarm. By about 11:00 P.M. the patrol hauled the surfboat on its cart to the scene to find the Dam Neck Mills Life-Saving Station south patrol was there. By 1:00 A.M. the next day the surfmen had made two trips to the *May Queen* and brought four seamen and the bark's steward to shore on the first trip, followed by the captain and other officers on succeeding ones. During daylight, the station crew made several trips in the surfboat to land all the bark's stores. On the following day the bark began to break up, and the cargo washed ashore. Both the Dam Neck Mills and Little Island Station crews were engaged in saving coconuts that came within their patrols; a little over one third of the cargo was saved.

The remaining two-thirds of that cargo was discovered years later as the following story reveals. On 7 November 1950 a special meeting of the Virginia Beach Town Council was held to honor the first mayor of Virginia Beach elected in 1906, Mr. Bernard P. Holland. Mr. Holland was eighty-three years old at the time of the meeting. He was not the only one honored at this event, but he was the principal speaker. He spoke of the beginnings of Virginia Beach as a resort community, how it began around 1878 with Norfolk investors purchasing oceanfront property and farms. The first building erected by that group was a little clubhouse near the end of what is now 17th Street. Mr. Holland spoke about spending the winter 1885-86 in the clubhouse as a nineteen year old young man. He explained that he remembered his stay well and went on to describe how he and others had put out a net to catch fish but caught more than fish. They pulled in about five or six barrels of coconuts.

The area that was to become the nucleus of Virginia Beach was twelve miles north of the wreck of the *May Queen*, but the bark's cargo of more than two hundred and fifty thousand coconuts was scattered up and down the beach for miles. Mr. Holland described the situation:

> Everyone who could, gathered coconuts, sent them away to friends and so forth. There were so many they could not be taken care of so people walking along the beach would drink the milk and throw the coconuts aside. For several years coconut hulls were visible all up and down the beach at high tide.[3]

One of the Life-Saving Service's most perilous rescue attempts happened 2-4 March 1886 and involved the crew of the Hog Island Station on the Eastern Shore. The 3-masted schooner *Leona*, a 202-ton vessel, was on a coastal voyage from New York City to West Point, Virginia, when she sailed into the clutches of a wintery northwest gale. The schooner stranded at high tide on the outer shoals about three miles south of the Hog Island Station. Almost as soon as she stranded the patrolling surfman saw her and immediately raced to the station to sound the alarm. The keeper and surfmen hurried to a cove on the west side of Hog Island where they launched the surfboat. As it happened this station was equipped with a self-bailing, self-righting surfboat that carried a mast along with sails.

Since the temperature had reached zero and the bay was frozen, the surfmen had to break through ice for two miles to reach an inlet, and it took them three hours to reach open water. By this time the schooner was leaking—her heavy cargo of phosphate rock ripping holes in her bottom and the sea breaking over her fore and aft. All the exposed portions of the hull, including the masts and rigging, were sheathed with ice. The six men aboard were huddled in a lee created by the cabin, the only safe place they could find.

After leaving the inlet and entering the open ocean, the life-savers were hit with the full force of the icy northwesterly gale which actually aided them to reach the schooner. Keeper Johnson decided to remain by the schooner to take advantage of any lull the weather provided. As it turned out the same force that helped them reach the schooner would make it impossible for them to reach the inlet safely.

Keeper Johnson realized the longer he kept the surfboat alongside the schooner the greater the chances were of the surfboat being battered to pieces, thus preventing any rescue attempt and endangering the lives of both the life-savers and the crew of the *Leona*. Keeper Johnson and the Hog Island crew boarded the *Leona* and sought shelter with the sailors where they stayed for nine hours, their clothing soaked; the schooner crunched and groaned beneath them, and threatened to go to pieces at any moment. The temperature never rose above zero and there came no lull in the gale. Around 5:00 P.M. darkness closed in and the *Leona* broke in two, settling deeper into the sand. The life-savers and the *Leona*'s sailors were forced to make their escape in the surfboat.

Once in the surfboat the men pulled hard at the oars in their endeavor to reach the shore. It was of no use, however, for the boat steadily lost ground. The keeper put out the boat's anchor but it did little to hold the boat stationary. As a last resort the sails were set, close reefed, in the hope of getting under a lee of the island, then into one of the many inlets to the south, but the raging winds ripped the sails to shreds and pushed the surfboat farther offshore. In addition the heavy cloud cover prevented any moonlight from breaking through the dark night. The keeper had no alternative but to set the surfboat adrift. The self-righting, self-bailing surfboat (a larger and heavier boat that was a "new" piece of equipment only provided to those stations, like Hog Island, which had direct access to water from their boathouses) was safe enough, but the men inside had little protection from the freezing winds and were in constant danger of being washed overboard. They drifted in that condition throughout the night.

Shortly after daybreak on 3 March, the schooner *Elisha Gibbs*, which was riding out the gale at anchor some five miles southeast of Smith Island Life-Saving Station, spotted the surfboat. With great difficulty, the captain of the schooner maneuvered her into a position where the crew on board was able to toss a line to the drifting surfboat

The self-righting, self-bailing surfboat in action.
From the authors' postcard collection.

and take the men on board, some so exhausted and overcome by exposure that they had to be hoisted up the side of the schooner by rope. The master and crew of the *Elisha Gibbs* did all they could to make the life-savers and sailors comfortable.

After only six hours on board the *Elisha Gibbs,* the surfmen and the crew of the *Leona* boarded the surfboat and set off for Smith Island Life-Saving Station, which they reached safely and without further mishap. They stayed at the station throughout the night, leaving at dawn to sail up the coast to Hog Island. Because gale force winds still prevailed, their progress was slow. When they were three miles north of their destination, the steamer *Resolute* of Norfolk took them in tow to Hog Island where they arrived about 5:00 P.M.

The keeper and crew of the Hog Island Life-Saving Station had been gone for nearly sixty hours, drifting over twenty miles from the wreck of the *Leona* in horrible weather conditions. Of the thirteen men involved, only two suffered from exposure and exhaustion to the extent that they had to be hospitalized. The *Leona*'s crew remained at the Hog Island Station for two days during which time the surfmen went out to the wreck twice. They were able to recover only a small portion of the schooner's sails; the schooner and her cargo were a total loss.

The following letter sent to the General Superintendent of the Life-Saving Service, Sumner I. Kimball, speaks for itself about the heroism of Hog Island life-saving crew and keeper.

Dear Sir:
    I cannot find language to express my gratitude towards Captain J. E. Johnson and his brave crew in successfully, at the risk of their own lives, saving the lives of myself and crew of five men. The brave fellows, after toiling and battling for two hours through ice which had formed on the shore by the extreme cold, came to our rescue, and by their noble act, alone of any earthly assistance, we were saved. God bless, encourage, and reward the Life-Saving Service, that glorious institution of our coast. At the time, the weather was extremely cold and the vessel, stranded and waterlogged, lay several miles from the station, a complete iceberg. Had the life-saving crew not come to our rescue we should doubtless have all perished.

                    Garrett Lippincott
                    Master of schooner *Leona*
                    New York[4]

On 9 January 1887 the readers of *The New York Times* were greeted with the headline, "Twenty People Drowned." The sad truth was that twenty-seven people had lost their lives: twenty-two crewmen of the ship *Elizabeth* and five men from the United States Life-Saving Service. The wreck of this thirty-two year old ship was one of the most tragic and disastrous shipwrecks ever to occur on the coast of Virginia.

The ship had sailed from Hamburg, Germany, late in November 1886 with a cargo of manure salt and five thousand empty petroleum barrels. Her destination was Baltimore. The discovery of the wreck was made by the midwatch patrols from the Dam Neck Mills and Little Island Life-Saving stations. On south patrol from Station Three, Dam Neck Mills, George W. Stone waited at the halfway point on his beat to meet with Station Four, Little Island, north patrol James E. Belanga. The two men were to meet and exchange checks. The morning was bitterly cold with a fierce northeasterly gale and blowing snowstorm.

The *Elizabeth* stranded parallel to the beach with her bow to the north. Around 1:00 A.M. on the morning of 8 January the patrolling

The *Elizabeth*. Courtesy: Virginia Beach Maritime Historical Museum.

Captain Halberstadt of the *Elizabeth*.
Courtesy: Virginia Beach Maritime Historical Museum.

surfmen discovered the wreck and fired Coston flares to let the crew of the
ship know that she had been seen. Surfman Stone reached the Dam Neck
Mills Station, two and one half miles south of the *Elizabeth* at 2:00 A.M.
to sound the alarm. It took Surfman Belanga almost two hours traveling
into the force of the blizzard to reach the Little Island Station. The Little

Island Station crew, led by Keeper Abel Belanga, started traveling north into the storm, pulling along the cumbersome beach apparatus cart. Nearly one hour later, shortly after 3:00 A.M., the Dam Neck Mills crew reached the stranded vessel ahead of the Little Island crew; Keeper Barco of the Dam Neck Mills Station had his men push on southward to assist the Little Island crew with their equipment. After both crews arrived abreast of the *Elizabeth,* Keeper Belanga took command of the rescue operation. Fighting snowdrifts and gale force winds, the life-savers began the rescue attempt shortly before 5:00 A.M.

When the *Elizabeth* was discovered, she had begun sending signals to shore every ten to fifteen minutes. However, since the early morning was so dark, only a dim outline of the ship could be seen from shore some three hundred and fifty yards distant. The Lyle gun was used to fire a line to the vessel in an attempt to establish communication. A total of four attempts were made to fire a line on board before daylight, all unsuccessful. At daybreak for the first time the life-savers could identify the vessel as a large ship: the *Elizabeth* was registered at 1,239 tons. About the same time it could be seen that the crew of the ship had abandoned her. With the surf crashing into the starboard side, the ship's crew had launched a boat into the small lee on the port side. The sixth attempt to fire a line to the ship failed, using the last of the life-savers' firing powder. Therefore, Keeper Belanga decided to return to the Little Island Station for more powder and the surfboat. A total of eight shots had been fired from the Lyle gun; all fell short and the surfmen were unable to establish communication with the stranded ship.

By 11:00 A.M., ten hours after the discovery of the ship, the surfboat was in position. The tide rose and the ship was battered as waves washed across her decks. The temperature was cold enough to cause anything that got wet to freeze. Huge waves crashed on the outer sandbar where the *Elizabeth* was stranded, only to build again and come crashing headlong onto the beach.

Keeper Abel Belanga picked a boat crew from the two station crews assembled on the beach. They were George W. Stone, who had given the first alarm, John H. Land, John T. Etheridge and Frank Tedford from the Little Island Station, and Joseph Spratley and James E. Belanga from the Dam Neck Mills Station. (Joseph Spratley and Frank Tedford were Keeper Abel Belanga's brothers-in-law while James E. Belanga was his brother). The men positioned the surfboat to the north of the *Elizabeth* and launched it into the breakers.

Pulling desperately through the rough surf, the surfboat crew reached its destination; Keeper Belanga then saw that the *Elizabeth*'s boat contained twenty-two men. Captain Halberstadt and six of the *Elizabeth*'s crew transferred into the surfboat and were issued life preservers for the treacherous trip back to the beach. But as the surfboat was turning shoreward,

> suddenly an immense wave swept around the rear of the ship, combed over the two boats which had tailed somewhat astern without the notice of the surfmen, swamped them and turned them completely over and over.[5]

Twenty-nine men struggled for their lives in the icy water. The ship's boat remained tied to the side of the *Elizabeth* and some sailors managed to cling to life longer by hanging on to the boat until their strength failed. The surfboat was carried south with men holding on through the offshore breakers; they soon dropped off from exhaustion and exposure. Of the twenty-nine men who were alongside the ship only two, John T. Etheridge and Frank Tedford, survived. With the exception of Captain Halberstadt and one passenger called Hollmann, the names of the sailors who drowned were not known. As for the *Elizabeth*, only her empty barrels survived. She was a total loss. The weather and rough seas took a devastating toll of life and property in this disaster even though the life-savers had toiled relentlessly.

On 8 March 1887 the German steamship *Rhein* stranded on the outer sandbar three miles southeast of the Hog Island Life-Saving Station. The 3,705-ton steamship grounded early in the morning during a very thick fog. The seas were relatively calm. Had they not been, this could well have been the most disastrous wreck ever to occur on the shores of Virginia as the *Rhein* had 930 passengers on board and a crew of 93 men.

Although the surfman on south patrol heard the *Rhein*'s whistle before she stranded, he could not determine her position until the fog cleared somewhat. Through the morning the surfman waited; the winds shifted to the northeast, and heavy breakers loomed out of the thick fog and crashed ominously on the beach. It wasn't until midmorning, some five hours after the steamship stranded, that the surfmen were able to launch the surfboat. The sea was running very high, and the fog was thicker than ever. It took the surfmen hours to locate the steamship; she was pounding heavily on the sandbar with surf crashing all around her.

The passengers were very much alarmed by their situation but their fears were soon calmed by the Hog Island keeper when he assured them that they were in no immediate danger. The *Rhein*'s master, Captain Reman, was anxious to send a telegram to Baltimore for assistance. One of the surfmen was dispatched to the mainland for that purpose. In the meantime a passing steamer was signaled to stand by. The following day dawned with the information that a storm was approaching; the captain decided to transfer all the passengers to the steamer lying near. With the crews of both steamships assisting the surfmen, still it took all the remaining daylight hours to accomplish the transfer of passengers.

On the morning of 10 March the surfman saw a signal flag flying from the *Rhein* and once again the station crew set out in the surfboat, but the fog was still quite dense and they were unable to find her. After a search of several hours they located the steamship afloat, slowly moving away from the shoals. Most of her general cargo had been jettisoned and she was leaking badly. Without her passengers and cargo, however, the *Rhein* was able to complete her voyage, which had originated in Bremen, Germany, to Baltimore without further mishap. The *Rhein* could be considered one of the luckiest vessels to strand on the coast of Virginia—not one of her 1,023 passengers and crew was injured.

Chapter 5

The Toll Mounts

APRIL 1887 – APRIL 1889

On 5 April 1887 the schooner *Nellie Potter,* seeking shelter from a northeast gale on a coastwise voyage from New York City to Washington, North Carolina, darted into the safety of the Chesapeake Bay. But the schooner soon stranded six miles northwest of the Cape Henry Life-Saving Station, in Lynnhaven Bay, far beyond the normal patrol limits of that station. Tragically, the news of the disaster reached the surfmen in time only for them to assist in the salvage of the *Nellie Potter*'s general cargo.

The stranding of the schooner *Nellie Potter* was one of a very few instances where the life-savers had no way of knowing of the disaster beforehand, either because of lack of communication or the distance involved. Lynnhaven Bay afforded some degree of safety to vessels within the Chesapeake Bay but unfortunately was out of the beach patrol limits of the Cape Henry Life-Saving Station.

The Norfolk Virginian on 1 November 1887 reported that "Yesterday's Storm," a furious northeasterly gale, caused the telegraph lines between Norfolk and Cape Henry to go down and communications between Norfolk and the life-saving stations to be interrupted. The rain, driven by gale force winds, made the conditions on the beach so rough that the beaches were constantly patrolled during daylight as well as evening hours.

The newspaper only reassured its readers that despite the most severe storm since 1879, only one disaster had been reported from the oceanfront, that of the *Mary D. Cranmer,* which at the time was anchored close by the False Cape Life-Saving Station. The newspaper concluded that "she probably got off safely last night." *The Norfolk*

70

Virginian's statement was, however, quite removed from the facts. The fury of the vicious storm had caused the destruction of four vessels and cost the lives of two men.

Because the telegraph lines were down, it was impossible for the newspaper to know of the disasters which occurred on 31 October, and which involved not only the *Mary D. Cranmer* but the *Carrie Holmes*, the *Manantico*, and the *Harriet Thomas*. The crew of the *Mary D. Cranmer* was taken safely to shore in the breeches buoy by the Dam Neck Mills Station life-savers after the 214-ton schooner had parted her cables and stranded. Later that same afternoon the patrol of the Cape Henry Station discovered another stranded schooner about two miles south of the station. The *Carrie Holmes* was driven so high up on the beach that her crew jumped from the schooner and waded safely to shore. The 375-ton schooner's home port was Forked River, New Jersey, and she was on her way in ballast from New Haven, Connecticut, to Norfolk. Captain Holmes of the *Carrie Holmes* told the life-savers that he had sighted another vessel on the beach about half a mile beyond his schooner. The life-savers continued with their apparatus cart to the third wreck, the *Carrie Holmes* having become a total loss and her crew safely housed at the Cape Henry Station.

The keeper of the Cape Henry Station saw the 177-ton *Manantico* beyond the outer sandbar, gradually slipping toward shore. Her captain was George E. Emmons, and she was carrying a heavy load of lumber on her way to Richmond. Captain Emmons had lost his bearings while trying to make the relative safety of the Chesapeake Bay during the storm. When he sailed by Cape Henry he judged that he was off Cape Charles; his reckoning was reinforced when he saw a three-masted schooner riding at anchor just south of his position. The schooner that he saw was the *Harriet Thomas*, the fourth vessel to strand on 31 October 1887. The unfortunate decision made by Captain Emmons on that stormy October day would claim his life.

The Cape Henry Station keeper stayed by the *Manantico* and tried to assure the crew on board that help was on its way. The beach patrolman from the Seatack Station spotted the wreck and hurried back to his station to sound the alarm. The pace of events then quickened. The *Manantico* was boarded astern by the heavy seas that sent the schooner's only boat crashing into the wheel, smashing both to splinters. Suddenly, the captain and crew could hear the thunder of breakers. Their hope was to drop both anchors to prevent the vessel from shoaling, but the sea was running so fast along the coast that the anchors failed to hold. The sailors were forced into the rigging as the schooner slowly scraped toward the outer surf line. The schooner's cook, Henry M. Hedges, was crushed to death when the shifting deck load of lumber crashed into the aft cabin. With the surf sweeping over her, the *Manantico* passed over the outer sandbar. Once on deeper water inshore, "the crew changed from the main to the fore rigging for greater safety, the captain taking a position on the starboard side, quite high up with the mate directly below him."[1] The schooner was pushed toward the inner sandbar. The captain began to climb down to the deck, but as he reached the mate's side, the schooner screamed to a halt, flinging the captain into the churning surf. He did not make the shore alive. The remaining crew members were rescued by the life-savers using the breeches buoy; the schooner was a total loss as a result of the combination of the captain's error in judging his position and the ferocity of the northeast gale that was to claim a total of four vessels that day.

The fourth and final vessel to strand on the sands of Virginia Beach on 31 October 1887 was the 475-ton schooner *Harriet Thomas*. She had sailed light from New Haven, Connecticut, and was bound for her home port of Baltimore. Captain Edgell of the *Harriet Thomas* stated that "he had anchored in the afternoon some two miles north of the station, but the anchors would not hold against the northeast gale."[2] The vessel slid south and stranded one mile north of the Seatack Station. It is not known if the sailors observed the surfmen struggling with the apparatus cart, but the sailors floated a line ashore that was tied off by some local fishermen on the beach. They climbed hand-over-hand shoreward except for their captain, who was too "portly." The Seatack crew finally arrived, set up the breeches buoy and hauled the heavy skipper ashore. The *Harriet Thomas*, valued at $7,000, became another total loss on that stormy October Sunday.

The following month of November three vessels stranded between Cape Henry and False Cape. The first vessel to ground was the *Macauley*, a 1,038-ton ship with a crew of nineteen men. The *Macauley* was commanded by Captain Bennett who had his wife and son aboard. The ship had just crossed the Atlantic and ran aground at low tide one fourth of a mile north of Cape Henry on 9 November 1887. The Cape Henry Station's surfboat was manned and rowed out to the ship where Captain Bennett requested that his family be taken ashore, and also that a tug be sent for. With the help of the tug the *Macauley* was successfully refloated on the following high tide. The voyage had begun in Hamburg, Germany, and would end in the *Macauley*'s home port of Baltimore with the unloading of her cargo of manure salt and empty barrels. Captain Bennett's family stayed at the Cape Henry Life-Saving Station until 11 November when they continued on to Baltimore.

At 4:00 P.M. on 17 November 1887 the 425-ton schooner *Bessie Morris* stranded during a thick fog. The schooner was a "coaster" with a cargo of guano from Elizabethport, New Jersey, bound for Savannah, Georgia. She grounded on pebble shoals two miles southeast of the False Cape Life-Saving Station. The station surfmen launched their boat, rowed to the sinking schooner, and found the *Bessie Morris* full of water and in a hopeless situation. The vessel's master, Captain Wheaton, and his crew of six were all landed with some baggage in both the surf boat and the schooner's boat. The schooner along with her cargo was a total loss.

On 20 November, another ship from Hamburg, Germany, the 1,251-ton *Deutschland*, stranded two miles southeast by south of the Little Island Life-Saving Station. The *Deutschland*, like the *Macauley* before her, was bound for Baltimore with a cargo of salt and empty barrels. With the men in the surfboat taking soundings, the Little Island crew helped to refloat the ship in less than four hours after she struck without any injury to the ship or her crew of nineteen men.

Nine vessels stranded on the coast of Virginia Beach during 1887. Two of the vessels involved loss of life—the *Elizabeth* and the *Manantico*. Of the nine stranded vessels only two, the *Macauley* and the *Deutschland*, escaped burial in the sands. The other seven, six schooners and one ship, all remained to rot as ghostly hulks scattered along the Virginia Beach coast.

Nearly every foot of beach along the coast of Virginia was patrolled by surfmen. During the winter season, from the first of September through the end of April the following year, in all weather conditions, the surfmen were on the lookout for vessels that might be approaching shore or running toward reefs, shoals, or sand bars. During the winter season of 1888-1889 a total of 188 vessels were warned by the Life-Saving Service in Virginia Beach. The following is an excerpt from a report filed by the Keeper of the False Cape Life-Saving Station on 26 November 1888:

> Between sunset and 9 o'clock the keeper warned off two steamers that were in danger of stranding abreast of the station. During the same watch two steamers approaching the beach were warned off

by the north and south patrolmen. A blinding snowstorm prevailed at the time.[3]

These results are significant in explaining the benefits of the beach patrol system; they also testify to the watchfulness of the surfmen and the diligence with which they performed their duties.

In the year 1889, from 18 February to 17 November, no fewer than twenty-six vessels were stranded on the shores of Virginia. On 18 February shortly after 8:00 A.M., the Dam Neck Mills north patrol reported a vessel ashore two miles from the station. It was the bark *E. L. Pettingill*, on her way from Valparaiso, Chile, to Hampton Roads with a cargo of nitrate of soda. The value of the bark's cargo ($41,755) was more than the value of the bark itself ($30,000). Because of an unusually heavy fog, Captain White had lost his course during the early morning hours.

The Dam Neck Mills Station crew found the *E. L. Pettingill* grounded on the outer sandbar at low tide. The crew pulled the surfboat abreast of the vessel and launched out into the surf. There they directed and assisted the setting of anchors which prevented the vessel from working her way shoreward during the incoming tide, and the bark was floated off the sandbar successfully without the aid of a tug nor with the loss of life or property.

The *William B. Wood* was one of the largest 3-masted schooners built in the United States registered at 599 tons and manned by a crew of nine men, the normal crew for a 4-masted schooner. She had loaded a cargo of sugar valued at $60,000 at Saguala Grande, Cuba, and was racing towards Philadelphia in a strong southeasterly wind. Twelve miles southeast of Assateague Light she struck the spars of a sunken wreck which damaged her hull and caused her to leak.

Shortly after 6:00 P.M. on the evening of 3 March 1889 the south patrol of the Wallops Beach Life-Saving Station saw the huge schooner heading directly for the beach. At once he burned a Coston light and ran to the station to sound the alarm. The keeper hurried down to the beach and saw the schooner, still on course for the beach, lighted more Coston flares and ordered the surfboat out. The sea was very high, the worst he had seen that year, but the surfboat was sucessfully launched; the surfmen reached the schooner after a difficult and strenuous journey.

The *William B. Wood* sank in three fathoms (eighteen feet) of water, about one third of a mile from shore, a mile and a half from the Wallops Beach station. After struggling to keep the schooner afloat, her crew took to the bowsprit and jib boom when she sank; the sea was so

Flashing the Coston Signal, Cape Cod

Surfmen flashing the Coston flare.
From the authors' postcard collection.

rough that only five of the nine crewmen could safely be taken into the surfboat without endangering the lives of all of them. The surfmen safely landed the five men and hauled the boat up on the beach to empty it of water.

Darkness enveloped the surfmen and sailors on the beach. As the winds increased in velocity, nothing but a dim light could be seen in the vicinity of the wrecked schooner. When the surfmen launched the boat for a second time against the wind the driving rain blocked their view of the schooner completely. Captain Davidson, the schooner's master, had the presence of mind to trail a line which the lifesavers succeeded in picking up. The remaining four men—the captain, the first mate and two seamen—were taken from their perilous perches on the bowsprit and carried safely to shore in the surfboat. Had the lifesavers not acted with swift assurance there surely would have been loss of life.

At noon the following day, 4 March, the keeper and his men again pulled the surfboat to the sunken schooner, this time at low tide and in milder weather conditions. It was hoped that some portion of the schooner or her cargo could be salvaged but her decks were under twelve feet of water; the crew's personal gear was lost as were the schooner's log books, papers, and nautical instruments. On 5 March the Wallops Beach keeper conveyed the unfortunate crew to Chincoteague where he acquired transportation for them, free of charge, to Philadelphia. The keeper then reported to the U. S. Coast and Geodetic Survey the exact position of the submerged wreck which had caused the beautiful and stately *William B. Wood* to sink.

The wreck of the brig *Agnes Barton* on 14 March 1889 is an example of a wreck brought on by a triumvirate of reasons—vessel condition, captain error, and weather. The 400-ton brig was loaded with a cargo of phosphate rock bound from Navassa, West Indies, to Baltimore with a crew of ten men. The *Barton* had leaked constantly since leaving port on 20 February, forcing the crew to man the pumps to keep her afloat. She had been sailing for twenty-two days when, on 14 March, Captain H. B. Knight discovered that his reckoning was off; partly due to a northeast storm, the *Barton* was miles to the south off Currituck Beach, North Carolina, not coming nearer to Cape Henry as he thought. With this discovery, the deep water sailors, fearing they were in dire trouble, took the necessary actions. They took soundings to ascertain a navigable water depth (twelve fathoms), but as the *Barton* sailed northward under full canvas, she was driven to leeward and crept closer to the shore.

The *Agnes Barton* sailed north to a position opposite the Dam Neck Mills Life-Saving Station where the life-savers watched her from the lookout tower. The *Barton*'s crew hoisted the American flag flown upside down as a distress signal, which was answered by the surfmen as a command to open communications. Captain Knight mistook the life-saver's signal to mean that they knew the condition of his vessel as well as his intentions. This misunderstanding from ship to shore led to needless loss of life.

When he saw the answering signal from the life-savers, Captain Knight headed the brig under "all forward sail, squarely for the beach."[4] The gale force winds failed to clear the *Agnes Barton* over the outer sandbar, and she stranded two hundred and fifty yards offshore, one fourth of a mile north of the Dam Neck Mills Life-Saving Station. The brig was immediately attacked by the rough breakers bombarding the stern section. The crew quickly moved to the forecastle and watched as the surfmen pulled their beach cart abreast of the wreck. Hopes for rescue must have been high, for a line was immediately fired from the Lyle gun on the beach, only to fall short of its target. A second shot, however, was placed squarely in the rigging, and the sailors quickly hauled out the whip line and the hawser.

The brig was under constant siege from the surf breaking across her stern, and she began to break up. She slid nearer and nearer the shore with her stern swinging south until she finally came broadside to the beach, coming to rest shortly after 4:30 P.M. on 14 March. The brig's constant shifting combined with her shoreward movement had cost the rescue attempt valuable daylight time. The *Barton* was listing to port with her masts pointed toward the beach. The breeches buoy was finally sent out to be dropped into the surf and quickly brought out as the hawser answered the brig's movements by slackening and tightening the line. Once the breeches buoy reached the vessel, a sailor was helped in, and the surfmen hauled him ashore. As many as twenty people hauled on the line, but with the rolling of the vessel the line was either taut or slack. After the mate was hauled through the surf he informed his rescuers that a piece of rope had lodged in the tail block and jammed the sheave and line and that he had been trying to clear it when he was hauled ashore.

Quickly the breeches buoy was run back out, for with all the delays the night was swiftly descending. The brig's steward was landed in the buoy's second trip. The Dam Neck Mills Station Keeper had to detail someone just to keep the line clear because there was so much rope and wreckage adrift. Again the buoy was hauled back to the vessel as darkness prevented those on shore from seeing the buoy when it reached its outward end.

When the breeches buoy was hauled ashore for the third time, it was empty. Two of the survivors who testified during the investigation of the wreck stated that Captain Knight was "in a weak and helpless condition," and was "assisted into the buoy."[5] The captain had gotten into the breeches buoy wearing his long woolen overcoat which hung outside the buoy. A crewman, fearing that the surf would get between the coat and the captain, tried to cut the coattails away but the buoy was hauled back toward the beach before he could finish. One of the survivors watched helplessly as Captain Knight was washed out, and an empty breeches buoy was hauled shoreward. At that time the Life-Saving Service had been established for eighteen years and it was the first and only time in its history that anyone was washed out of the breeches buoy during a rescue attempt.

On the fourth trip the breeches buoy carried a sailor and the cabin boy to safety. In the darkness the buoy was hauled away again only to return empty. On the sixth trip the buoy failed to clear the beach; it had fouled and simply stopped moving in either direction. The Seatack Life-Saving Station crew arrived and assisted in attempting to free the fouled line and then decided to wait until low tide because the *Agnes Barton* would be steadier. A fire was lighted to signal the remaining sailors that they had not been abandoned. Around 11:00 P.M. the keeper of the Little Island station arrived and after some discussion a line was fired across the vessel, but none of the remaining five sailors could reach it.

When daylight came, the sailors could be seen clinging to the rigging. Efforts were renewed to fire a line on board. The second shot scored, but the sailors could not haul out the heavy line needed to run the rescue apparatus. The surf was too heavy to launch the surfboat. The surfmen watched helplessly as a sailor tried to make shore by climbing hand-over-hand on the shot line. He was in such an exhausted state that he soon lost his grip and fell to his death in the sea. Shortly thereafter the Agnes Barton "suddenly took three heavy rolls, and collapsed, the heels of her masts floating up. Those on board were instantly engulfed, and so far as could be seen, did not come to the surface again."[6]

The four survivors' names were unknown. The names and residences of those men lost on the *Agnes Barton* were: Captain H. B. Knight, Baltimore; Second Mate James Richards, Philadelphia; Seamen John Smith, Cape Charles, Virginia; Charles Hobbs, Suffolk, Virginia; Peter Florida, Panama; and Edward Forbes, Turks Island, West Indies. The *Agnes Barton* was valued at $10,000, and along with her cargo she became another tragic reminder of man's struggle with and loss to the sea.

The schooner *G. W. Bentley,* a small "coaster" of 113 tons, stranded one and one-fourth miles south of the Cape Henry Life-Saving Station on 15 March 1889. The schooner was under the command of Captain Doane who had sailed her from Provincetown, Massachusetts, to Fishing Bay, Virginia, where he misjudged his position upon entering the Chesapeake Bay. The Cape Henry surfmen arrived on the scene minutes after she stranded. The *G. W. Bentley* was less than one hundred yards from shore so the surfmen needed only one shot from the Lyle gun to put a line on board. The crew of six men were safely landed, for unlike the events that occurred during the rescue attempt of the wreck *Agnes Barton,* nothing interfered with the working of the breeches buoy.

Although it was with much success that the crew of the *G. W. Bentley* was saved from the sea the schooner was lost.

While the *G. W. Bentley* was going to pieces on the beach during the heavy northeast storm on 20 March 1889, another coasting schooner, sailing light from New York City bound for Norfolk, drove ashore south below the entrance to the Chesapeake Bay. Sometime during the early morning hours of 20 March, the *Benjamin C. Terry* anchored one mile north of the False Cape Life-Saving Station. The schooner's master, Captain Mathis, knew he could never reach the Bay in time, but was resigned to ride out the storm at his anchorage. Shortly after sunrise the next day the schooner's anchor cables parted and she stranded three fourths of a mile north of the False Cape Station. When the beach patrolman discovered the vessel, he made his way across the flooded beach to his station; the False Cape Station Keeper telephoned the Little Island Station keeper, then proceeded to the scene with the crew and apparatus cart. Only one shot was required to get a line on board and set up the breeches buoy.

By the time the apparatus was ready to land the first survivor, the Little Island keeper and four surfmen arrived. Without mishap Captain Mathis and his six crewmen were hauled ashore and taken to the safety and shelter of the False Cape Life-Saving Station. The *Benjamin C. Terry*, however, was declared a total loss and left on the beach where she wrecked.

Though less frequent than northeast storms, hurricanes were prevalent along the east coast of the United States and contributed to many of the wrecks along the shores of Virginia. Much more violent than northeasters, hurricanes destroyed life and property not only at sea, but on the shores and inland. Such a hurricane hit Virginia Beach on 6-7 April 1889.

> The wind was blowing at hurricane rate from the north-northwest at times exceeding one hundred miles an hour as registered at the Signal Service Station at Cape Henry, and the tide was over all the beaches in the vicinity.[7]

Because of this violent weather three schooners stranded on Virginia Beach near the Seatack Life-Saving Station. The station's midwatch patrols left on time; shortly thereafter, around midnight on 6 April, the north patrol reported a large vessel ashore about a fourth of a mile away. The beach was underwater, and the surfmen had to travel through the soft sand of the dunes to reach the scene. The vessel, the four-masted 1,155-ton *Benjamin F. Poole,* which sailed in ballast from Providence, Rhode Island, was light and landed high up on the beach.

It was 1:00 A.M. when the surfmen reached the *Poole,* only about seventy yards from the station. Quickly the Lyle gun was fired and nine crewmen were landed using the breeches buoy. The schooner's first mate realized that the vessel was not going to break up sitting as high as she was on the beach; so he went back on board with the captain.

The second schooner to strand during this hurricane was the *Emma F. Hart,* a 400-ton vessel on a voyage from Nassau to Boston. While the surfmen of the Seatack Station were working on the *Poole,* the south patrol from the Cape Henry Life-Saving Station discovered the *Hart* ashore a mile north of the Seatack Station. The patrolman continued south until he found the Seatack crew just landing the first sailor from the *Poole.* A quick trip was made to the Seatack Station where the surfmen obtained a "second outfit from the extra gear, procured a team and proceeded by road some distance back from the beach."[8] Even with the aid of the horses the surfmen had a very difficult time reaching the second stranded schooner. The wind had forced the sea over the beach, uprooting trees and making progress slow and hazardous.

The *Benjamin F. Poole* on the beach. Courtesy: Mariners' Museum.

When they reached the *Emma F. Hart,* the surfmen quickly set up the Lyle gun, fired a successful shot line on board, and rigged the breeches buoy. "The crew of seven men with their baggage was then landed, without mishap, by means of the breeches buoy, the last one reaching the shore about sunrise."[9] During the rescue of the crew of the *Emma F. Hart,* as with that of the *Benjamin F. Poole,* the blowing rain and sand almost blinded the surfmen. The return trip to the station with the wind at their backs was much easier. Although most of the *Hart*'s cargo of lumber was saved, the schooner was a total loss. One stop had to be made and that was to haul ashore the captain and first mate.

At last the exhausted surfmen could return to their station which was about 9:00 A.M. on 7 April, only to learn shortly after they arrived that a small schooner, a Chesapeake Bay oyster pungy, had drifted past the station riding very low in the water. Two waiters from the Princess Anne Hotel were following the craft south along the beach. The surfmen retraced their steps back to the two stranded schooners to retrieve sufficient gear to hurry south, following the two waiters. Since the beach was completely flooded, they hauled the apparatus cart along the railroad tracks which ran parallel to the beach beyond the dunes. Rudee Inlet stopped all progress south, and it was there that the Seatack crew learned from a fisherman that the small vessel had gone to pieces with only one survivor who, he said, had been cared for.

The oyster pungy was the *Northampton,* a small thirty-six ton schooner valued at only a thousand dollars. The day before she had parted her anchor chain and drifted from Cherrystone on the Eastern Shore out through the entrance of the Chesapeake Bay. Since she was light, having discharged her cargo, her captain, Elijah Lawson, feared she would capsize and so he cut both masts away. It was in that mastless condition that Captain Lawson and two sailors drifted south to their deaths. From the testimony of John Moody, who had jumped from the schooner seconds before she broke into pieces, a steamer had spent hours trying to get a line to the drifting schooner. The crew of the *Northampton* tried valiantly to hold on while the sea constantly battered and tossed their vessel, but the captain and two of the three crewmen were swept overboard by a huge wave only two hundred yards from the beach. The bodies of the sailors were not found, and it was several days before the body of Captain Lawson was recovered ten miles south of the stranding.

There were five incidents on the Eastern Shore of Virginia on 7 April, 1889. On that day there were more mishaps than on any other date on record along the shores of Virginia; the vessels, however, were much smaller than average, and there was no loss of life. At 7:00 A.M. the Cobb Island keeper watched as a sloop raced before the gale force winds; the *J. O. Fitzgerald* was driving directly toward Bone Island which was separated from Cobb Island by Sand Shoal Inlet. The *Fitzgerald* failed to make safe harbor and ran ashore near the northern end of Bone Island, three-fourths of a mile from the Cobb Island Life-Saving Station. The two crewmen on board took to the rigging as soon as their vessel hit the surf zone and easily made their escape when the sloop beached.

The gale had made surf conditions so rough in the inlet that it was impossible to launch the surfboat. But around noon that same day the gale subsided enough for the surfmen to launch the boat and pull across the inlet to Bone Island where they found the two sailors—cold, wet, and hungry. In the time it took the surfmen to successfully rescue the stranded crewmen, the storm again increased in strength which prohibited a return trip to the station.

About 4:00 P.M. that afternoon, while trying to recross Sand Shoal Inlet with the stranded sailors from the *J. O. Fitzgerald*, the surfmen observed another small sloop in trouble. The *Minnie Sylvia* was about three miles south and flying a distress signal while her captain frantically waved his arms to attract attention. The Cobb Island surfboat crew at once altered their course and pulled to the aid of the sloop. The owner-captain was on board and had been working all day to keep his sloop afloat.

The *Minnie Sylvia* had dragged her anchors during the gale and had been battered so hard that the caulking was working out of her seams and she was leaking badly. The Cobb Island keeper put two of his surfmen on board to assist the captain and they quickly got the sloop under way and followed the surfboat into New Inlet. The surfmen made several attempts to row back to their station but could not make headway. They put in at New Inlet where they were made comfortable for the night. The storm increased throughout the night and there was no doubt that but for the timely arrival of the life-savers, both small sloops and the three men on board would have been lost.

There were three other vessels that were assisted on the night of 7 April 1889. The sloop-yacht *Challenge* had eight persons on board, all of whom were safely landed by the Parramore Beach life-savers. The schooner *Levi Lewis*'s crew of three were assisted by the Smith Island life-savers when the schooner was driven high up on the beach in the storm that was also described as "a hurricane, with mountainous seas." Finally, the schooner *E. K. Rayfield*'s crew of three was saved, again by the Smith Island life-savers, and because of their aid the *Rayfield* safely rode out the storm at anchor and remained undamaged.

Chapter 6

Surfmen's Peril

JUNE 1889 – MARCH 1891

The USS *Constellation*, a former war vessel converted to use as a training vessel, was one of the most majestic vessels ever to strand on the shores of Virginia. She ran aground during a thick fog in the "off season" when the surfmen were not in residence at the Cape Henry Life-Saving Station. The large sailing ship stranded on 18 June 1889, one and three fourths miles northeast of the Cape Henry Station. The next day *The Norfolk Virginian* proclaimed that the ship had a "large number of naval cadets on their summer cruise on board," and that "the vessel may prove to be a total loss."[1]

The *Constellation* grounded on a sandbar three hundred yards off the beach where an all-volunteer crew of surfmen assembled and used the equipment from the Cape Henry station to fire a line successfully from the Lyle gun to the ship. The life-savers remained on the beach throughout the night, but the *Constellation*'s master, Captain Harrington, managed to get his ship off the sandbar on the following high tide after which she was towed to the Norfolk Navy Yard for inspection and minor repairs. Fortunately, the *Constellation* was certainly not a total loss.

Another storm and another vessel stranded while attempting to reach safe anchorage inside the Virginia Capes. Shortly before 8:00 P.M. on 12 September 1889 the British steamship *Godrevy* grounded about three-fourths of a mile northeast of the Cape Henry Life-Saving Station and several hundred yards offshore. The ship was sighted by both the keeper on watch and the north patrol. The sea was too rough for them to use the surfboat; therefore, the apparatus cart was dragged to a point opposite

84

The USS *Constellation* dockside (circa 1890).
Courtesy: Mariners' Museum.

the steamer, and four shots were fired from the Lyle gun—all unsuccessful. By midnight the sea had moderated somewhat, and the crew launched the surfboat. Although the crew found that the ship was in no immediate danger, Captain Jamieson requested that the life-savers take a message ashore for a tug to come to his aid. The telegram was sent to Norfolk shortly before 3:00 A.M. on 13 September 1889.

The *Godrevy* was bound from Santiago, Cuba, to Baltimore with a cargo of "minerals," probably iron ore. The steamer encountered a hurricane on the voyage and most of the ship's provisions had been spoiled by salt water. The crew of twenty-three men including the captain were in dire straits. A few hours after the telegram was sent a wrecking tug arrived, carrying provisions. However, it was not until noon on 14 September that the vessel was pulled free and continued on her way to Baltimore.

On the morning of 23 October 1889 the sloop *General Harrison* of Bridgeton, New Jersey, anchored in Fisherman's Inlet, Cape Charles, Virginia. Her crew feared an oncoming storm and went ashore in the sloop's boat. As the winds shifted to the northeast and increased to gale force, their fears were justified.

Around sunset the *Harrison* began to drag her anchor, and during the night she drifted south across the great mouth of the Chesapeake Bay before coming ashore three miles west northwest of the Cape Henry Life-Saving Station at midmorning on 24 October. The report was made to the Cape Henry Keeper and upon investigation of the *Harrison*, she was found to be high and dry on the beach.

Since there was the possibility that the sloop might be stripped and robbed, the surfmen stayed to guard her. On his return to the station the keeper stopped at the telegraph office and sent an inquiry to Norfolk in the hope of discovering the ownership of the abandonded sloop, but it was not until the *Harrison*'s Captain arrived to claim her on 28 October that her ownership became known. With the help of the surfmen, the sloop was launched on 31 October and, having sustained only minor damage, sailed on to Norfolk for repairs.

During this time, from the 23rd to the evening of the 27th of October, a storm raged without intermission—the winds gusting to hurricane velocity. Four vessels stranded along Virginia Beach's shores in addition to the *Harrison*. On 23 October, two three-masted schooners battled the easterly winds that blew and gusted violently. Both were coasting schooners: the 688-ton *Frank O. Dame* and the 648-ton *Henry P. Simmons*. At approximately 10:00 P.M. both schooners struck ground and stranded. The type of cargo they carried and their direction of travel played a very important role in the events that followed.

The *Frank O. Dame* was sailing light, in ballast, on her voyage south along the coast from Providence, Rhode Island, to Norfolk where she was to load coal at Lambert's Point. The schooner failed to make Norfolk; she stranded two miles north of the Little Island Life-Saving Station. The north patrolman from the Little Island Station reached the upper limit of his beat and observed the three-masted schooner as she drifted just offshore down the coast before the gale. The surfman at once ignited his Coston flare and turned back to his station, keeping abreast of the schooner. The south patrol, recalled by the fired flare, their signal to return, immediately readied the apparatus cart and in less than twenty minutes from the time "Vessel ashore!" was shouted at the station, the life-savers were on their way to rescue those on board the *Frank O. Dame*.

The *Henry P. Simmons* carried a crew of eight men and was deeply laden with a heavy cargo of phosphate rock, a commodity used in the manufacture of fertilizer. She was sailing from Charleston, South Carolina, to Baltimore when, during the storm, her heavy cargo caused her to plunge deeply and take on a great deal of water. By 8:00 P.M. on 23 October she was battered by the full force of the storm and had become unmanageable. What happened that night was best described by Robert Lee Garnett, the only survivor of the disaster, as reported in *The Norfolk Virginian:*

> We encountered stormy weather during most of our trip, but none like that of the 23rd. The wind blew like we had never seen it before and the sea was in an awful state of trouble. The waves broke over our vessel and she began to leak. All day long the wind blew and at night the weather became very thick and the sea higher. The captain lost his bearing and none of us knew where we were. At 10 o'clock the vessel struck and as she layed on her keel a big sea swept across her decks, washing away her cabin house and filling the vessel. She sank almost immediately and the captain and crew took to the rigging.[2]

The schooner sank on Pebble Shoals, one and one half miles offshore, northeast of the Wash Woods (North Carolina) Life-Saving Station and north of the Virginia-North Carolina state boundary. The 4:00 A.M. to sunrise patrolman from the Wash Woods station returned from his north patrol and reported to the keeper that he had seen a vessel sink sometime during the night well offshore.

Although the surfman passed the *Henry P. Simmons* at dawn, he had not seen any of the vessel's crew. The Wash Woods keeper dispatched another surfman, to view the wreck in the light of day, who reported that he had seen seven men in what remained of the rigging. The eighth crewman, steward John Warner, had fallen to his death from the rigging. The Wash Woods surfmen arrived at the wreck site about 10:00 A.M. with their apparatus cart. They fired the Lyle gun, but the shot reached only half way to the wreck. In the meantime, two more of the schooner's crew fell from the rigging. The remaining sailors bitterly condemned the life-savers for not getting aid to them; on the beach were highly skilled surfmen with the latest equipment available, but unable to rescue the sailors. They could do no more than watch and hope that the storm would abate, for no surfboat could survive in the extremely high and dangerous surf.

At noon on 24 October the False Cape Life-Saving Station crew arrived in time to witness one more unfortunate sailor fall exhausted from the schooner's rigging. The crew's arrival did no good, however, for the storm continued undiminished, and nothing could be done. The survivors could only watch as fires were lighted on the beach and blazed throughout the night. On the second day an effort was made to launch the surfboat at low tide, but even with their most highly trained surfmen on board the attempt failed because of rough surf conditions. Then toward noon another sailor fell from the rigging and disappeared into the sea. This left three men alive: Captain Grace, First Mate Vaughan and Robert Lee Garnett.

It seemed obvious that the only hope for these men would be a rescue attempt from the sea. The station keeper sent a message to Norfolk for a vessel, and the small revenue steamer *Lot M. Morrill* made an attempt, but was driven back by the rough sea outside the Capes. The storm raged throughout the day and into the night. Sometime during the night of 25 October, Captain Grace fell into the sea to his death.

> First Mate Vaughan was the only man left to keep me company on the morning of the 26th, and he had little or no strength left. He was watching all the time for a glimpse of a passing vessel, but he saw none, and at 12 o'clock that day dropped into the sea after having gone off into an unconscious spell.[3]

Three surfboat attempts were made on 26 October to reach the *Henry P. Simmons,* and each time the surfmen were driven ashore with their boat full of water. The wind changed to the southeast and blew constantly at hurricane force, making conditions even worse.

On Monday morning 28 October 1889, almost five full days after the *Henry P. Simmons* sank in shallow water on Pebble Shoals, the surfboat again was moved to the water's edge in readiness for launch. Keeper Malachi Corbel from the Wash Woods station and Keeper John R. O'Neal from the False Cape station picked the best surfmen from both stations to man the surfboat. With veteran Keeper Corbel manning the steering oar, "a bold and successful dash was made through the heavy line of breakers on the bar."[4] Once through the shore breakers, it didn't take the surfmen long to reach the sunken schooner.

> On the morning of the 28th I was rescued by the life saving crew while asleep in the crosstrees. I was very weak and had to be helped into the boat. They rowed me to land and gave me the first food I had tasted for five days and furnished me dry clothes.[5]

Garnett's incredible endurance kept him alive to tell of his shipmates and the horror of watching each of them die of exhaustion or perish by drowning. These men were, in addition to Captain Robert C.

Grace, First Mate Ward H. Vaughan, Seaman George Teach, Seaman Isaac Hollier, Seaman Kidd, and Steward John Warner.

The rescue of the *Frank O. Dame* was relatively simple compared to that of the *Henry P. Simmons*. On 23 October, shortly after she stranded, the *Dame* was dragged about one-half mile south, and around 2:00 A.M. on 24 October the surfmen arrived at the scene. With the unusually high tide and the vessel light, she was only about one hundred yards from the surfmen on the beach. The surfmen ignited their red Coston flare and held it high so that the light provided some illumination for the area and let those on board know that help was at hand. They then turned to the Lyle gun, putting it into position and quickly firing a line towards the schooner. But because the night was so dark, the crew of ten men on board the *Dame* had difficulty finding the line. Finally, the life-savers pulled the whip and hawser out through the surf with the rigged breeches buoy and got to the stranded sailors. They all reached the Little Island Life-Saving Station safely at 5:30 A.M. on 24 October. In this case the ease of the rescue of those on board was due in part to the schooner sailing light and to its landing so close to the shore that the life-savers had little difficulty reaching her.

During the time that the Wash Woods and False Cape station crews were standing by the sunken *Henry P. Simmons* and after the rescue of the *Frank O. Dame,* two more vessels became victims of the storm. At 8:00 P.M. on the evening of 24 October a large British steamship of 3,730 tons lost her steering while she tried to enter the Chesapeake Bay. She was driven ashore 900 yards northeast of the Cape Henry Life-Saving Station. The vessel was the *Baltimore* from Liverpool, England, bound for Baltimore with a general cargo. The ship was too far from shore to establish communication by firing a line from shore; therefore, the Cape Henry keeper telegraphed Norfolk for a wrecking tug. Unlike the *Henry P. Simmons,* the *Baltimore* was hauled off the sandbar, and her crew of forty-one men and ten passengers were on their way again within twenty-four hours of her stranding.

The fourth vessel to strand in this storm was the schooner *Welaka* and she was abandoned because of a collision. At daybreak on the morning of 26 October the keeper of the Cape Henry Station spotted a three-masted schooner ashore not far from where the *Baltimore* had been. The schooner was one hundred yards closer to shore and eight hundred yards northeast of the Cape Henry Life-Saving Station. Moments after sighting the schooner the keeper noticed a small boat containing, presumably, the schooner's crew, and by using signals, the keeper warned the men not to try to land for he feared the small boat would not make it through the rough and churning surf.

The *Welaka* was a 433-ton schooner from Union Island, Georgia, loaded with a cargo of red pine. While at sea, the *Welaka* had encountered what the crew thought to be a cyclone on 16 October during a storm which lasted for two days and left the schooner without some of her sails. The crew, under the direction of Captain Mahoney, tried diligently to repair the rigging and all went well until Wednesday evening, 23 October, when the heavy gale hit. The *Welaka* drifted north northwest in the storm; on Friday, 25 October, the captain saw Currituck Light and hoisted a distress signal. The British steamship *Spendthrift*'s captain sighted the schooner and came to her aid and agreed to tow her to port for two thousand dollars!

In rigging a tow line the two vessels collided, causing considerable damage to the schooner. At this point the *Welaka*'s captain and crew abandoned her and were taken aboard the steamship. The captain of the

The *Welaka* on a marine railway in a shipyard. Courtesy: Mariners' Museum.

Spendthrift placed his first mate and six of his crew on board and towed the schooner as far as Cape Henry, but the hawser parted and the schooner stranded where the Cape Henry Keeper discovered her. After an ineffectual effort was made to refloat the schooner, a tug from Norfolk arrived and tried to dislodge the *Welaka* from the sandbar. Wreckers later boarded her and threw the deck load of lumber overboard, but it was still impossible to budge the schooner. The crew landed on the beach safely in the small boat at the Cape Henry Life-Saving Station where they were housed until they could reboard the *Spendthrift*.

The fourteenth and final vessel to strand on the shores of Virginia Beach in 1889 presents an example of a wreck caused by captain error. The 825-ton British bark *Ordovic* sailed from the Lobos Islands off the coast of Peru where she had loaded her cargo of guano. When she reached the Virginia Capes on 16 November, Captain Austin, unable to secure a pilot so late in the evening, took it upon himself to pilot his vessel into Hampton Roads although the night was extremely dark and he admitted to being unsure of the channel. The inevitable occurred. The *Ordovic* grounded shortly after midnight on 17 November about two miles northwest of the Cape Henry Life-Saving Station. The beach patrol soon discovered the bark, stranded four hundred yards from shore, sounded the alarm, and quickly hauled out the surfboat. But all the life-savers needed to do was to send a telegram to Norfolk for a tug and the bark was hauled from her niche in the sand the next day without any apparent damage. Her captain, it was hoped, learned a valuable lesson from his experience and would, thereafter, leave the navigation of unsure waters to a qualified pilot.

The Life-Saving Service was constantly striving for improvement, both in technique and in equipment. As a result, the Service was an avid participant in the International Marine Conference held in Washington, D.C., during November 1889. Before attending the conference, delegates from twenty-six maritime nations gathered informaton from experts in all fields of shipping and its related industries and occupations. On 22 November Sumner Kimball read his *Organization and Methods of the United States Life-Saving Service* to the Committee on Life-Saving Systems and Devices. The United States had been one of the first nations to introduce a federally supported life-saving service and Kimball's reorganization of that service was of prime importance. Kimball gave the committee members a brief sketch of the Life-Saving Service, highlighting his talk with cost analyses of the equipment used.

For example, the gun devised by U.S. Army Captain D. A. Lyle was chosen for use rather than the Hunt gun or the Cunningham rocket as Kimball indicated;

> The cost of the Lyle gun and all its appurtenances, exclusive of the projectiles, is $87.33. The lowest cost of any efficient rocket with appurtenances that I know of is not much less. The only expense attending the use of the gun is the cost of the cartridge, say half a dime, except when occasionally a shot is lost, which can be replaced for $2.00. When a rocket is fired, several dollars are expended. These facts are of consequence when considered in connection with the utility of frequent drilling.[6]

Kimball related the glories of the service, in general, and of the floating life-saving station on the Ohio River in Louisville, Kentucky, in particular. This station had a scow-shaped hull on which sat a two-story frame house with a lookout tower, much the same as the coastal station houses. During the great floods of 1883-84 this station supplied food and other necessities to more than ten thousand stranded and homeless people. Kimball was also justifiably proud of the work of the service along the shores of Virginia, which was in the midst of its busiest year ever.

Although there were only two mishaps on the coast of Virginia Beach in 1890, there were eighteen on the Eastern Shore. On 8 February 1890, the Seatack Station keeper received a message via telephone from his counterpart at the Cape Henry station that a small sloop was seen running before a strong northerly gale. The Seatack north patrol was advised to keep a sharp lookout for the sloop. The patrolman had gone about two miles when he saw the sloop strand; the vessel went so high up on the beach that the crew jumped to safety. The vessel was the eight-ton oyster sloop *Wyandotte* of Norfolk, homeward bound from Fisherman's Inlet, whose sails were blown away in the gale. Her master, Captain Elliot, was looking for a place to beach her when she stranded. The *Wyandotte* was successfully refloated nine days later. The storm that drove the *Wyandotte* high on the beach also succeeded in breaking up what remained of the schooner *Welaka* that grounded near Cape Henry 26 October 1889.

The 174-ton schooner *Hattie Perry* stranded one mile south of Cape Henry on 29 September 1890. The schooner had loaded coal at Philadelphia and was to sail her cargo to New Bedford, Massachusetts, but when she left the Delaware breakwater a northeaster caught her and pushed her down the coast. Her captain tried to run into Hampton Roads to anchor and ride out the storm, but he made the same mistake that many other captains had made and hugged the shoreline too closely. The schooner ran very high up on the beach, and the Cape Henry life-savers had little difficulty in rescuing the seven-man crew in the breeches buoy.

The northeaster that wrecked the *Hattie Perry* brought the highest tides since the gale of April 1889. The large four-masted schooner *Benjamin F. Poole* was floated from the beach on 29 September 1890, seventeen months after she had stranded. The tides also floated the *Frank O. Dame* which had stranded during the hurricane of October 1889. Her freedom, however, was shortlived as the schooner parted her tow cable and was driven broadside on the beach by the northeaster. Since she sustained so much damage, she was left to go to pieces in the winds and weather on the shores of Virginia Beach.

One of the more significant disasters to occur along the stretch of Virginia Beach coast near the Seatack Life-Saving Station happened on 27 March 1891. Much has been written about the wreck of the Norwegian

The *Benjamin F. Poole* prior to being floated from the beach on 29 September 1890. Courtesy: Mariners Museum.

bark *Dictator* and there is still controversy concerning what happened during the rescue operations. The sad facts are that seven lives were lost including those of the captain's wife and young son.

The *Dictator* had been at sea for twenty-four days; she had left Pensacola, Florida, on 3 March, after loading a nine-thousand-dollar cargo of yellow pine, and was on the way to West Hartlepool, England. As she passed from the Gulf of Mexico to the Atlantic Ocean, the bark was battered by stormy weather and rough seas. The twenty-four-year-old vessel began to leak, and two of her boats were lost in the storm. Captain Jorgensen decided to have the *Dictator* repaired before he attempted the ocean crossing. The bark was headed toward Hampton Roads when she arrived off the coast on the morning of 27 March. Around 9:00 A.M. she was seen by the crew of the Dam Neck Mills Life-Saving Station about a mile off the beach, headed north.

The news of the bark's position was relayed north. Keeper Edward Drinkwater of the Seatack Life-Saving Station received the message and immediately posted additional lookouts. Captain Jorgensen had been sailing for days by dead reckoning—the storm had blotted out all traces of the sun. In the later investigation of the wreck, Captain Jorgensen stated that he thought he was near the Cape Charles Lightship and so when he saw surf east of his vessel, he turned more to the west. The wind was blowing a gale with heavy rain and whirling fog. Shortly after correcting his course, Captain Jorgensen spotted a solid line of shore breakers, "and before the mistake could be rectified, the bark's keel grated on the bottom."[7]

Captain Jorgensen's next action, observed by the lookouts at the Seatack Station, was to turn the *Dictator* to port and head squarely toward the beach. With a draft of twenty-nine feet, she skidded to a stop on the outer bar. Captain Jorgensen then ordered the mainmast cut away, and as it fell, it took the fore and the mizzen topmasts with it. The *Dictator* was stranded about one mile north of the Seatack Station. Because of the flooded beach it took the life-savers nearly an hour to reach a point opposite the vessel. Once in position, they fired the Lyle gun, only to drop the line short of the target. When the Cape Henry Life-Saving crew arrived, the two crews worked together throughout the operation. When they fired the Lyle gun again, this time using the smallest line, once more it fell short. Communication with the *Dictator* was not established until her crew tied a line to an empty barrel which the surf carried to the life-savers on the shore.

Quickly the crews rigged the breeches buoy, sending it out to the bark which slowly swung her stern south and became almost parallel to the beach. The seventeen people on board the bark must have felt some degree of relief when the first sailor was hauled ashore eight minutes after the breeches buoy had been rigged. Throughout the day the *Dictator* rolled and pitched uncontrollably, causing the breeches buoy to be "at one time under the water and the next minute or two sixty or seventy feet in the air."[8] Those words were spoken when Captain Jorgensen explained why he tied a line to the bark's only lifeboat to see if it would reach the beach. It had been his intention to haul it back and attempt to save his wife and son; his wife, in a state of near hysteria, refused to be taken ashore in the breeches buoy. When the sixteen-foot lifeboat reached the shore full of water with four sailors from the *Dictator,* Keeper Drinkwater refused to allow the boat to attempt a return to the bark. Drinkwater stated:

> The boat would have filled as soon as it left the beach. The current would have swung it broadside to the sea and it would have filled at once. It was utterly impracticable.[9]

By nightfall only eight men had been saved from the *Dictator.* She was rapidly breaking up; the stern had been completely swept away by the churning surf. The nine remaining survivors gathered together on what was left of the deck; their only hope of survival was placed on their own initiative. Captain Jorgensen tried to save his wife, Johanne Paulene, and his son, Carl Zealand, by tying one of the two life ring buoys to his wife and the other to himself with his son strapped to his back. The captain was knocked into the sea among the floating wreckage, but somehow managed to make the beach alive. His son, however, had been snatched from him by a towering wave that had surged the captain toward shore. Johanne was swept overboard and drowned. Even with the life ring buoy it would have been difficult for her to attempt to swim ashore because of her clothing. Her heavy woolen dress with its voluminous skirts soaked up water like a sponge and dragged her down to her death.

The final crush came to the *Dictator* around 8:00 P.M., ten hours after her well-intentioned captain beached her. It would be difficult to imagine a more complete and devastating wreck. "The broken timbers of the hull and the timber forming the cargo were scattered along the beach" for more than a mile.[10] The ten survivors were taken to the

Seatack Station and cared for. Besides Mrs. Jorgensen and her son, First Mate Cornelius Nilsen, Seaman Ole Olsen, Seaman Jean Baptiste, Seaman Andreas Isaacsen, and Steward St.Clair also lost their lives in this tragedy.

The official investigation by Lieutenant T. D. Walker, Assistant Inspector of the Life-Saving Service for the Sixth District, criticized Keeper Drinkwater, implying Drinkwater should have used the life car once he learned of the woman and child on board the *Dictator*. As quoted in *The Norfolk Virginian*, Lieutenant Walker explained:

> The life car is not an ornamental adjunct; it is for use and if ever there was an occasion which demanded its use, this was one.[11]

He went on to recommend to the Superintendent of the Life-Saving Service that there was no alternative but the severance of Keeper Drinkwater from the Service. When the Seatack keeper was asked to resign, he complied. Those who witnessed the disaster were divided: some felt the Service was fully justified in its action; the vast majority felt, however, that the action taken was unfair, and that Keeper Drinkwater was being made a scapegoat in a series of events over which he had little or no control.

The *Dictator* was an aging bark in very poor condition when she sailed from Florida, and Captain Jorgensen did a remarkable job in keeping her afloat for as long as he did. But it was his dead reckoning that had put her in such a precarious position. In defense of Drinkwater, had not the *Dictator*'s mainmast been cut away, he could have had the elevation necessary to run the breeches buoy apparatus properly. The *Dictator*'s deep draft plus her condition of constant leaking caused her to ground so far from shore, hampering the life-savers rescue attempts. The weather conditions—extremely rough surf and high tides, strong winds, heavy rains, and cold temperatures—prevented all but the most elemental rescue efforts.

In these modern times of high technology, it is difficult for us to imagine the primitive conditions under which the men of the Life-Saving Service had to operate. It is a chilling experience to stand on the shores of Virginia Beach in front of the old Seatack Life-Saving Station on a cold and blowy day in winter with the rain and sleet blasting your face and imagine seeing survivors stranded on a vessel in the icy, churning surf offshore. It is just as difficult to imagine pushing the surfboat through that roiling surf and rowing to their aid. Few people today could deal with the kind of work the surfmen did.

Because the United States Life-Saving Service was constantly striving to refine and improve, and perhaps in part because of the *Dictator* disaster, which was seen as avoidable, the Service adopted the life-saving signals recommended by the International Marine Conference of 1889. Every life-saving station was supplied with the necessary equipment. Among the changes adopted by the Service were the following:

> 1. Upon the discovery of a wreck by night, the life-saving force was to burn a red pyrotechnic light or fire a red rocket to signify, "You are seen. Assistance will be given as soon as possible."
> 2. The flying of a red flag by day or the firing of a red rocket or red roman candle at night was to mean, "Haul away."
> 3. Two flags, one red, one white, waved at the same time on shore by day, or two lights together, a red one and a white one by night was to mean, "Do not attempt to land in your own boats. It is impossible."[12]

These changes were made to secure a greater measure of safety for those who found themselves in danger from the perils of the sea.

Chapter 7

A Light in the Fog

FEBRUARY 1892 – OCTOBER 1896

Early in the morning of 23 February 1892 surfman J. R. Dunton saw the running lights of a steamship and immediately burned a Coston light to warn the ship of danger. The running lights soon disappeared in the thick fog which swirled and blanketed the beach. Dunton returned to the Hog Island Station in the "nor'easter" and reported the events to Keeper J. E. Johnson who quickly went to the lookout tower with his field glasses but saw nothing in the fog. The northeaster increased in intensity until the sea flooded the marshes, and the surf crashed in heavy waves upon the beaches. The gale pushed the surf in a southerly direction along the shore. Keeper Johnson kept his vigil in the tower and shortly after sunrise spotted the ship's masts over the top of the sand dunes and sounded the alarm—ship ashore!

The vessel, a twelve-year-old, 1,291-ton Spanish steamship *San Albano* of Bilbao, Spain, was on a voyage from New Orleans to Hamburg, Germany, with a valuable cargo of cotton, grain, and oil. She was to have stopped at the port of Hampton Roads for coal before her ocean crossing. For three days the captain had been unable to make an observation and his dead reckoning was off as his vessel passed by the entrance to the Chesapeake Bay. In retracing his wake along the coast he steered too far west, grounding the *San Albano* at approximately 9:00 P.M. on 22 February 1892. The ship, which had a draft of nearly twenty-one feet, stranded six miles northeast of the Hog Island Life-Saving Station on an outer sandbar. Gradually the ship scraped and bounced across the bar and was refloated on an inshore channel where the captain immediately dropped anchor.

The sea surged across the shallow water on the anchored *San Albano*, lifting her high, then running out from under her to crash the hull down upon the sand. Throughout the night the waves grew in size and strength, punishing the steamer for her captain's error. On board, the crew of twenty-seven men feared for their lives as the steamer slowly shattered beneath them. Their hopes of rescue soared when they saw the bright red Coston light only five hundred yards away, but a few moments later, the steamship's hull split. The heavy waves soon filled the ship with seawater, and she sank approximately five hundred yards from the beach, five miles north of the fog-shrouded Hog Island Station.

In the meantime the Hog Island surfmen fought their way northward pulling the beach apparatus cart across the flooded sands, a struggle which took them three hours before they reached the wreck, shortly after 9:00 A.M. on 23 February. They found the *San Albano* broadside to the sea and through the slowly clearing fog could see the ship's crew huddled near the deck house. The Spanish flag was flown at a halfway point in the main rigging as a distress signal. Keeper Johnson immediately ordered the surfmen to return to the station for the surfboat and the life car. With immense surf crashing over the ship, then racing on across the beach, it was a difficult rescue situation, to say the least. The keeper wanted at hand all the options open to him. The rescue effort took four hours as three horses hauled the additional equipment the ten-mile round trip across the flooded land. It was not until 2:00 P.M. that afternoon that the life-savers were once again opposite the wreck and able to begin their rescue operations.

The Lyle gun was placed in position and fired—the line parted twenty yards from shore. A second shot was quickly fired to the steamship and landed on the deck. The crew hurriedly hauled the line on board, and, because of their inability to read the instructions and in their eagerness to be rescued, tied it in a position in the main rigging that caused the line to chafe. This action against the rigging in addition to the great strain and friction created by the action of the sea soon broke the line.

At the same time the rising tide pushed the life-savers farther back on the beach, increasing the distance to the wreck. The northeaster raged on with even greater fury which caused the next five shots from the Lyle gun to fall short of the mark. Since daylight was drawing to an end, Keeper Johnson decided to launch the surfboat. Despite the gloom permeating the atmosphere among the experienced men on the beach, they dragged the surfboat windward and launched it. But, high surf, and the more than forty-mile-per-hour winds, and the strong currents were too much for the surfboat crew who were driven down below the wreck. It was with great difficulty that they were able to reach the shore, the surfboat full of water. The surfmen quickly hauled the boat north and made a second futile attempt to reach the *San Albano*. At this point seven members of the steamship's crew lowered the only remaining lifeboat and made what seemed a miraculous trip ashore. Shortly after their landing, the sun set, and those remaining on board faced yet another night aboard the sunken steamship.

The keeper learned from the sailors on shore that the *San Albano* was still solid and that her deck houses were dry. The keeper decided to return to the station with his exhausted surfmen. The Reverend J. R. Sturgis was left in charge of a group of volunteers to keep watch and maintain a fire on the beach. A horse was left at the scene so that the keeper could be quickly notified if the situation changed.

The surfmen arrived at the station for a few hours rest, and they again set out for the wreck, taking with them the last dry powder and shot line. When they reached the steamer, conditions had changed very little. Although the surf remained high, the tide was at its lowest. But, the steamship was the same distance from shore and still beyond the range of the Lyle gun. It should be noted here that Keeper Johnson was regarded as one of the best life-saving keepers on the coast of Virginia, and his ingenious actions during this rescue operation only enhanced that reputation. Lashing the Lyle gun to the top of the apparatus cart, he secured the shot line box to the forward axle of the boat carriage and in his words:

> We then waded waist deep out in the surf and fired after getting the gun as near the wreck as possible. The shot barely reached the wreck, falling over the ship's rail.[1]

This time, having learned their lesson, the crew of the *San Albano* kept the line clear. The surfmen were aided on the beach by some of the residents of Hog Island, and the connection with the wreck was finally made. The surfmen sent out the life car, successfully landing the nineteen remaining crewmen in eight trips. It was only at that point that those on shore found out that one of the *San Albano*'s crew had been lost. Against the advice of his shipmates, one man had tried to make shore by swimming with the aid of a plank. The Reverend Sturgis said he had heard a cry around 2:00 A.M. and had made a search along the beach, but found no one.

The crew of twenty-six including the ship's cat were cared for at the Hog Island Station where they were supplied clothing donated by the Women's National Relief Association. The crew remained at the station for seven days before they could be transfered to the mainland.

The rescue of the crew and cat of the *San Albano* was among the most notable rescues of the USLSS for that year. The inspector who investigated this remarkable case ended his report with the following:

> Great credit is due the Keeper and the crew of the Hog Island Station for their brave and persistent efforts, and every man did his whole duty. The people of the Island were prompt and ready to assist the life-saving crew in every way possible. This is the first time in the history of this station that the beach apparatus has been used, and demonstrates the great value of the life car as a means of landing men when the distance is great and the surf heavy.[2]

(Up to this point the Hog Island surfmen had found the need to use only the surfboat). The *San Albano*, along with her cargo valued at $120,000, became a total loss and was left to go to pieces on the coast of the Eastern Shore.

The *Edith Berwind,* a large four-masted schooner, sailed from Tampa Bay, Florida, on 22 December 1882, heavily laden with a 1,100-ton cargo of phosphate rock bound for Baltimore. Bad weather was a constant companion on her course following the Gulf Stream. Once off Cape Hatteras, North Carolina, the weather moderated, and the *Berwind* sailed a smooth sea. Her captain felt that all would go well, and that they would soon enter the quiet waters of the Chesapeake Bay.

Shortly after sunrise on 1 January 1893 those on board the schooner saw the Currituck Light and knew they were only thirty miles below Cape Henry. But by noon the *Berwind* sailed into a dense fog and her captain lost sight of land. Although the schooner sailed less than three miles offshore, past all five life-saving stations along the coast of Virginia Beach, no one on board saw anything, nor did anyone on shore see the schooner. When the wind picked up somewhat, Captain McBride was confident that his schooner made good speed. A veteran in coastwise navigation, he held his course, but took the precaution to furl his lighter sails.

The crew was anxious since no one knew the vessel's exact position. Guided only by Captain McBride's dead reckoning the crew remained quiet, waiting for the sound of the Cape Henry foghorn. As the schooner slipped noiselessly through the fog, not a sound was heard from the shore. By 3:00 P.M. the Captain estimated they had passed Cape Henry and made his turn westward to enter the Chesapeake Bay. The wind which had begun the day as a fresh breeze increased steadily and by midafternoon was blowing at gale force, carrying the *Edith Berwind* far beyond her captain's estimated position. They were well beyond Cape Henry—beyond Cape Charles as well—and when the turn to enter the Bay was made, the shoals of the Outer Middle Ground were southwest of the schooner. Suddenly, the crew saw breakers dead ahead, and the *Berwind* grounded with a shudder. The crew started to panic as the sea swept over the decks of the 815-ton schooner, but Captain McBride soon calmed them.

The three-year-old schooner pounded hard on the shoal as the swells lifted her. At last the heavy dead weight of her cargo split her bottom. The sails were still set in the hope that she would be forced across the shoal. She did slip across into deeper water, but sank in a matter of minutes. At that moment the crew cut the halyards and moved quickly to the forward house. The sea swept over the stern and raced towards the bow, forcing the crew into the forerigging.

An hour after dark the "donkeyman" (the crewman in charge of the auxiliary, or "donkey" engine used to raise and lower the sails on a large schooner), Charles Haines, descended from the crosstrees to the cook's lower position in the rigging. Haines was a large muscular man, but in the cook's description:

> As he stood alongside me in the rigging he appeared weak and discouraged. His hold upon the shrouds seemed to be feeble.[3]

In a gesture of comfort and reassurance, the cook put his arm around the big man, but Haines collapsed. He fell from the rigging into the water on the deck and without a sound was swept away into the sea. The masts shook and swayed with such violence that it took every bit of strength the surviving crew members had to hold on. The fog continued throughout the night and with their precarious positions in the rigging, it was impossible for the crew to signal for assistance.

One of the duties of the morning patrol of the Smith Island Life-Saving Station was to climb the light tower near the station and look in all directions for any sign of a distressed vessel. Surfman Wilkins walked the gallery along the outside of the tower three times and was about to climb down when he saw a vague shape through his field glasses in the vicinity of the Outer Middle Ground. Wilkins shouted to the keeper who bounded to the tower gallery. Together they scanned the area until the keeper was sure he had seen men in the rigging of the ship nearly six miles away.

Although the *Edith Berwind* was six miles to windward of the station and the seas were treacherous, the men wasted no time in launching the surfboat. At regular intervals the huge waves filled the surfboat but just as quickly the self-bailing surfboat emptied itself of water, leaving the surfmen drenched. They were more than halfway to the schooner before the men in the rigging spotted them. Captain McBride's son saw the rescuers first and shouted to his father that he could see a black speck far off in the water.

The crew's hope faded in the fog-enshrouded early morning as two vessels passed by the sunken schooner and their cries for help went unanswered. The young McBride shouted that he could see "a boat with six men at the oars and one standing up steering." With that the exhausted sixty-year-old captain exclaimed, "Thank God, it is the life-saving crew. We are saved at last!"[4] The sailors were fortunate indeed, for although it was January, the night had not been extremely cold and they had survived nearly sixteen hours of exposure. They were taken ashore in the surfboat and given shelter at the Smith Island station. Unfortunately, the *Edith Berwind* was a total loss, and nothing of her hull or cargo could be salvaged.

If the *Edith Berwind* had not made such a fast run around Florida and up the coast, her crew would undoubtedly have perished had they stranded a few weeks later. As far south as Big Kinnakeet, North Carolina, the coast was locked in a deep, bitter freeze. The surfmen at the Big Kinnakeet Station aided a sloop that was frozen fast in the ice on 20 January 1893. At the same time five men, comprising the crews of two small oyster sloops frozen in the ice, walked to Metomkin Inlet seeking shelter from the cold. The next evening four men reached the Wallops Beach Life-Saving Station and asked the keeper to help in the search for the one man they had left behind. He was found three miles from the station asleep on the ice, nearly frozen to death. He was taken to the station and well cared for by the surfmen.

On 20 April, 1893 during a fierce northeaster, the schooner *North Star* stranded and wrecked near the Little Island Life-Saving Station. Her crew of ten abandoned her and were soon taken aboard the surfboat coming to their rescue. The surfmen safely landed the men through the breakers and cared for them at the station, providing warm, dry clothing, food, and their own beds. While the rescued sailors were resting at the station, the surfmen returned to the surfboat and again rowed through the treacherous breakers to recover what they could of the crew's personal effects. They paid little heed to the danger of taking the surfboat so near a wrecked vessel, where broken timbers could damage the surfboat and smash it to pieces. Their duty was implicit—to save lives and property, and they did so with unselfishness and courage.

On 4 October 1893 two three-masted schooners stranded on the beach near the Seatack Life-Saving Station. A northeast gale battered the waterlogged *Wm. Applegarth*. In immediate danger, Captain Younger decided to beach his vessel to save the lives of his crew. The Seatack Station crew watched the schooner as she ran shoreward and stranded two hundred yards offshore. The surfmen rolled out the beach apparatus cart and quickly set up the breeches buoy and safely landed the six-man crew. The Dam Neck Mills life-savers came five miles north to offer assistance, for they too had followed the distressed schooner. But, by the time they arrived the Seatack crew had already completed landing the sailors. The *Wm. Applegarth* was declared a total loss.

As the Seatack crew was busy with the *Wm. Applegarth* near their station, another schooner was overpowered by the heavy wind and seas. The *C. C. Davidson*, from New Bern, North Carolina, bound for Atlantic City with a load of lumber, grounded two and one half miles north of the Seatack Station early in the evening of 4 October 1893. Bystanders on the beach helped two of the crew as they made their way to shore. The remainder were aided by the Seatack life-savers and all were taken to the Seatack Station to rest. The following day the Cape Henry Life-Saving Station crew helped in stripping the schooner. The *C. C. Davidson* became another total loss, and left to go to pieces on the sands of Virginia Beach.

Keeper J. E. Johnson of the Hog Island Life-Saving Station had spent many years on the island and had witnessed hundreds of small boats on their way through the inlet to deeper fishing waters. On 9 October 1893 several small boats came from the mainland through the passages and inlets that threaded the Eastern Shore's barrier islands. The sea was slowly building up even though there was only a moderate wind blowing. Johnson stood at a point on the inlet so that he could signal the small fishing fleet of the dangerous passage over the bar and through the line of heavy surf. Some of the small boats turned back, but a number continued on their journey. Keeper Johnson hurried back to his station tower to keep an eye on the boats while at the same time alerting the rest of the station crew for a quick call to action. The small fleet passed out over the bar without incident.

Throughout the morning the wind and sea increased in strength and by early afternoon the surf line extended nearly three quarters of a mile offshore. The Hog Island station lookout watched as the seven small boats moved toward the inlet and lined up outside waiting their turn to cross the bar. With more luck than skill the first two boats successfully navigated the surf to reach the calmer waters. The third vessel was the small sailboat *J. B. Denton* from Red Bank, Virginia, manned by a crew of four. The *Denton* attempted to come in without any sails set, using only oars. The men tried to ride upon the crest of a wave, but their boat plunged ahead of the wave into the trough "and pitchpoled, flinging the occupants into the water."[5] The station lookout at once notified Keeper Johnson who had his men launch the surfboat and pull towards the sailboat.

The four fishermen, dressed in oiled clothes and heavy rubber boots, mangaged to swim back and hang on to the overturned sailboat. The surf rolled the *Denton* over again and again. William F. Bool and James E. Sharpley rapidly lost the strength to hold on to the boat and sank beneath the breakers. Both Obed G. Goffigon and C. A. Burton kicked free of their boots and held on.

The surfmen reached the *Denton*, a distance of about four miles, in less than thirty minutes and found her upright with her grapnel hook anchoring her. When the small sailboat had "pitchpoled," everything had been thrown out; the hook had lodged in the boat and held fast and in that way had acted as anchor. Burton was able to pull himself back into the boat, but each time a wave crashed, he had to bend down as it swept over him—at times he was under water ten feet deep.

The surfmen pulled their surfboat to a point above the sailboat then dropped down alongside her and picked Burton up as the current carried them by. Burton quickly explained how both Bool and Sharpley slipped away from the side of the sailboat; he last saw Goffigon drifting away holding on to the mast. The surfmen rowed after Goffigon and safely pulled him into the surfboat. The two rescued men were taken to the station, and the surfmen launched the surfboat again to look for the missing men. The remaining four fishing boats turned south to Sand Shoal Inlet, south of Cobb Island, after they saw the surfmen row to the sailboat in distress. The bodies of the two drowned men were not found.

The following is an excerpt from a letter written by Obed G. Goffigon to General Superintendent Kimball of the United States Life-Saving Service:

> I was one of the crew of the fishing boat capsized off Hog Island on October 9 and I unhesitatingly say that Captain Johnson and crew did all that men could do to rescue us. I left the boat on a mast; my three companions stuck to the boat. Captain Johnson reached the upturned boat as soon as it was possible for a mortal man, but not soon enough, alas! to rescue two of my companions. But, thank God, one was saved, and he today owes his life to the prompt action and undoubted bravery of Captain Johnson and crew. I am a sailor and have been connected with the Life-Saving Service, but never in my life have I seen a surfboat driven faster, more skillfully handled, or in a worse sea.[6]

On 3 March 1894, the schooner *Fanny Arthur* stranded in the early morning hours less than one mile northeast of the Cape Henry Life-Saving Station. The account of the incident as it appeared in the Life-Saving Service's *Annual Report* stated simply, "Ran out anchors and hawsers, carried dispatches between vessel and shore and assisted in every way possible until afternoon."[7] The *Fanny Arthur*'s captain, John Douglass, however, was so impressed with the work of the life-savers that he took time to write to the Collector of Customs in Norfolk:

> Quick and efficient assistance was rendered by Captain Johnson of Cape Henry Life-Saving Station; anchor and hawser run, and all assistance that could possibly be rendered, which was cheerfully given. Captain Johnson deserves great praise for his good judgement and assistance at such a time.[8]

There was always one or more surfmen at a typical Life-Saving Station on constant alert. In fair weather a watch was kept in the tower from sunrise to sunset. Each of the surfmen in turn stood the daytime tower watch. At sunset two surfmen started out, one in each direction from the station, and patrolled the beach until they reached the end of their beat or the boundary. The boundary was either a post, an inlet, or a small hut which afforded the men some degree of shelter from the weather. At the boundary the surfmen met his counterpart from the adjacent station and exchanged checks (see Chapter 1). Throughout the night the checks of the stations to the left and right were collected and returned by the first watch the following night. This method was continued during the active season. At more isolated stations where the adjacent stations were not close enough to facilitate an exchange of checks, a patrol clock was used to register the time when the end of the patrol was reached.

During the season of 1893-94, the life-saving stations were manned by crews of between six and eight men. With the exception of the Hog Island station, all the Virginia stations had six surfmen from 1 September 1893 to 30 April 1894. One additional surfman was added on 30 November to finish the season. The Hog Island station, one of the busiest stations on the Atlantic coast, had eight surfmen during the season. During their employment period the surfmen received an average of sixty dollars per month. The keepers were employed at all stations during the entire year; those who lived at their stations received an average salary of about nine hundred dollars per year or seventy-five dollars per month.

Before the 1893-94 season began, the Metomkin Inlet Life-Saving Station had to be moved to a new location, three hundred yards inland and away from the encroachment of the sea, a problem not unique to this period. Every few years the stations were repaired and painted; some were renovated and improved to reflect new and innovative designs; and in some instances, new stations were built to replace ones that had burned or had been destroyed by hurricanes or floods. Such was the case in 1882 when the Wachapreague Life-Saving Station was built to replace the Cedar Inlet Life-Saving Station.

At the close of the fiscal year 1893-94 there were 247 Life-Saving Stations in the United States, divided into 12 districts. The largest was the Fourth District on the coast of New Jersey with 41 stations. The smallest was the Eighth District along the Gulf coast with 8 stations. There were 182 stations on the Atlantic and Gulf coasts and 51 on the shores of the Great Lakes. There was 1 station on the Ohio River at Louisville, Kentucky, and 15 stations on the Pacific coast.

As we have noted, the mouth of the Chesapeake Bay divided Virginia into two districts; the Fifth District to the north and the Sixth District to the south. The number of stations in Virginia (14) was 5.7

Metomkin Inlet Life-Saving Station after it was moved to
its new location. Courtesy: U. S. Coast Guard.

percent of the national total, while the number of disasters along the
Virginia coast (596) was 3.4 percent of the total number of disasters
which compares quite favorably to other states: Massachusetts had 9.7
percent of the total number of stations and 7.9 percent of the total
number of disasters, New Jersey 16.6 percent and 10.5 percent respectively.

    Studying of the figures in the *Annual Report* of the United States
Life-Saving Service for the fiscal year ending 30 June 1894 and compiled
below indicates that the stations in Virginia were extremely watchful
and diligent in their efforts.

Vessels Warned by Night Signals

	Warnings of All Stations	Warnings of Virginia Stations	Percent of Total
1893 July	5	0	—
August	5	0	—
September	12	4	33.3
October	23	3	13
November	25	5	20
December	46	13	28
1894 January	25	8	32

February	22	6	27
March	30	6	20
April	32	9	28
May	4	0	—
June	6	0	—
Total	235	54	23

Typical examples of entries in the Annual Report are the following:

Nov. 13, 1893, Cape Henry. The second patrol north from the station discovered a large steamer heading for the beach and very close in. He instantly flashed his signal, where upon the vessel reversed her engines, backed off into deep water and anchored. As the weather at the time was thick and foggy she would no doubt have stranded but for his promptness.

Dec. 2, 1893, Assateague Beach. About an hour after going on duty

Surfman warning a vessel of danger. Courtesy: The National Archives.

the first night patrol[man] flashed his signal and warned a vessel away from the beach.

Jan. 8, 1894, Hog Island. The surfman patrolling north from the station discovered before dawn a steamer's light very near the shoals. He flashed two Coston signals in quick succession, but they appeared to be unnoticed by those on board, and the vessel held her course down the coast. The south patrol[man] next saw her, and burned his signal seeing which she hauled broad off, but grounded on a shoal a few minutes before finally getting clear.

There could be no better evidence of the value of the beach patrol than the above examples. There were nine total documented warnings during daylight hours for the 1893-94 winter season, and the Virginia stations were responsible for preventing the stranding of three of the vessels. Still, the number of vessels actually saved from destruction cannot be precisely determined, but many of them had become uncertain of their position during foggy and stormy weather. When most of the vessels were warned they were already headed toward shoals or directly toward the beach. The saving of lives and property cannot possibly be determined in relation to the number of vessels warned, but nowhere could it have been greater than on the shores of Virginia.

On the night of 16 May 1895, the 940-ton barkentine *Josephine* stranded in the fog one and one half miles south of the Little Island Life-Saving Station. The vessel had loaded a cargo of coffee valued at one hundred eighty thousand dollars in Rio de Janeiro, Brazil, and was on her way to Baltimore. The Little Island beach patrol discovered the barkentine; the False Cape and Dam Neck Mills stations were summoned and the surfmen hauled the beach apparatus cart to the wreck. A line was fired which reached the vessel but the crew tied the line too low for use with the breeches buoy. Instead of wasting time firing another line, the False Cape crew launched the surfboat and reached the stranded vessel. All the *Josephine*'s crew were rescued without mishap. A great effort was made to float the *Josephine* off the beach, but unfavorable weather conditions prevented it. For two days the Merritt Wrecking Company of Norfolk worked on the vessel; only one third of her cargo was salvaged, and the barkentine became a total loss.

Around 6:00 P.M. on the evening of 9 February 1896 the keeper of the Hog Island station received a telephone message from the keeper of the Smith Island station that the Number Two Surfman was overdue, having left Hog Island the day before in his small boat. At once the Hog Island keeper sent three of his surfmen out to look for him in a sailboat.

The surfman had been drifting upon his capsized boat after it overturned sometime during the evening of 8 February. Unable to right the boat, he simply drifted about while clinging to its keel. Because dense fog rolled in and nothing could be seen, the three surfmen returned to the Hog Island station after a search of three hours. The beach patrols were instructed to keep a sharp eye for the capsized boat and their vigilance paid off when at dawn on 10 February the boat was discovered four miles southwest of the Hog Island Station. The surfman was exhausted, cold, but very happy to be rescued from the sea. He was given warm clothing and taken to the mainland for a few days rest. His small boat was badly damaged, but the *Annual Report* stated that it could be repaired for use again.

The men of the Life-Saving Service were sworn to aid anyone in distress from the perils of the sea without regard to their race, and did so willingly. On 7 October 1896, the Parramore Beach station lookout spotted a small sailboat in distress, drifting aimlessly, her sails blown away. The surfboat was launched and the surfmen pulled out to her. They found five, inexperienced "colored men" on board, and their "fish boat" the *Hungry Negro* was in grave danger of swamping. The five fishermen were taken into the surfboat and landed safely on shore. The surfmen then made a return trip through the surf and brought the *Hungry Negro* back under tow. The boat was hauled up on the beach, and her crew was given a hot meal and shelter at the station. Upon recovering from their ordeal they were taken to the mainland.

The *Hungry Negro* surely must have been destroyed shortly after it was hauled up on the beach, for on 11 October a violent hurricane pushed an angry sea across Virginia's barrier islands and down the coast, endangering many lives. At False Cape eight fishermen, whose clubhouse near the station had been carried away by the surf, were sheltered at the station. On Cobb Island the surfmen rescued two women who were almost swept away by heavy swells. They, too, were sheltered at a life-saving station for two days until the weather abated and the flooding subsided. Most of the reports from stations included narratives of the removal of families residing close by the stations. The high tides over the islands, driven on by the force of the hurricane, involved much loss of property.

Not all aid provided by the surfmen of the Life-Saving Service was the result of shipwrecks, storms, or fire. On 28 January 1897, some fishermen burst into the Seatack Station requesting help. They had found a man lying on the beach, apparently drunk, and had carried him to their camp where they thought to let him "sleep it off." But after six hours the man showed little signs of life. The fishermen became alarmed and raced to the station to report to the keeper. Immediately, the keeper and three surfmen took the rescue cart and went to the fishermen's camp where they worked on the man constantly for three hours until he was sufficiently revived to be taken back to the station. One of the surfmen kept a close watch on the man throughout the night until all danger was past. It appeared that while lying in a drunken stupor, the man had begun to freeze to death. It was fortunate that through the efforts of the fishermen, the Seatack keeper, and his men, another life was saved.

Chapter 8

Tragedy on the Coast

DECEMBER 1900–OCTOBER 1903

At 6:30 A.M. on Friday 21 December 1900, John H. Carroll, a 32-year-old surfman at the Dam Neck Mills Life-Saving Station, reported to Keeper Bailey T. Barco that a wreck was ashore about five hundred yards north of the station. The *Jennie Hall* was a three-masted, 412-ton schooner from Machias, Maine. The seventeen-year-old schooner was valued at ten thousand dollars and carried a cargo of 550 tons of asphalt.

This voyage of the *Jennie Hall* began on 12 November 1900 from Port of Spain, Trinidad, to Baltimore carrying the bulk cargo and crew of seven, including the captain. Upon sailing from Trinidad a stowaway, Ben Mall, was discovered. The crew of the *Jennie Hall* consisted of Captain Daniel H. Lamson of Westcogns [sic], Maine; First Mate Benjamin T. Bragg of New Jersey; the steward-cook, Fred Percival of British Guiana; Seaman Richard Coombs of Newfoundland; and Seamen Joseph Crosby, John Moore, and John Johnson of Gloucester County, Virginia.

The voyage was smooth and uneventful until the schooner reached the latitude of the Bahamas on 2 December 1900. From that time on heavy weather prevailed from the north northeast with "strong gales and high cross seas," as First Mate Bragg recalled during the investigation that immediately followed the wreck. The weather was the main concern as the crew worked to repair damages. "She carried away her sail repeatedly, hardly giving us time to repair her before they would be blown away again."[1] When the wind became so heavy that it blew away her foresail and mainsail, the vessel was forced south. The schooner was obliged to run before the wind, completely at the mercy of the wind and sea. The weather kept up, as Bragg stated, "until the 18th (December)

113

when we were in the latitude of Ocracoke (North Carolina) but out in the Gulf Stream."[2] The weather was so bad that no observation had been made for several days and no one on board knew the *Hall's* exact longitude.

On the morning of 19 December at 7:30 A.M. the *Jennie Hall* reached the Diamond Shoals Lightship at Cape Hatteras, North Carolina, and received supplies. Bragg stated that the crew had been out of provisions except bread for ten days. The schooner then continued north for the rest of the day. Late during the night of 19 December the wind slacked somewhat and remained so until midnight on 20 December when it began to blow hard from east northeast. Bragg calculated the vessel was making over six knots an hour under full lower sail, except for one reef in the mainsail. As the night grew longer, the rain began, and the weather was, again, quite threatening.

John H. Carroll, Surfman Number Six, left the Dam Neck Mills Life-Saving Station on horseback at 4:00 A.M. to patrol the beach north of the station until sunrise. Weather on the beach was "very stormy, thick fine rain, wind northeast and blowing" fifty miles per hour, Carroll stated.[3]

On board the *Jennie Hall* the crew saw a light through the rain at about 4:00 A.M. Immediately the lead line was cast to make a sounding. The line registered eight fathoms of water beneath the hull, so the schooner sped on; the crew concluded that the light was the Cape Henry Lighthouse. The course was then set north northwest, as the vessel made eight knots. Fifteen minutes after the first sounding, a second sounding showed eight fathoms. Everything seemed to be going well, and the schooner would be in sheltered waters soon; but the light the crew saw must have been in a dwelling on the beach, for within minutes the schooner stranded about ten miles south of Cape Henry.

The schooner was heavy with her load of asphalt and the breakers were soon washing across her deck. When the vessel skidded to a halt, all hands rushed on deck. They let go all the halyards but the main. Without making any signal of distress the crew and the stowaway took to the mizzen rigging. The master and mate tried to retrieve the vessel's documents, as well as any of their personal effects they could gather. This attempt was cut short by the icy water swiftly filling the cabin. The captain, sensing his vessel's imminent loss, wanted to give up. As Bragg stated:

He didn't seem to want to live; asked me what I had to live for. He said he was too old to live (about sixty). The only way I got him to leave the cabin was to tell him I would not go without him.[4]

Lamson and Bragg left the cabin; Bragg reached for the mizzen rigging and pulled himself into it, Lamson following. Bragg described trying to help Lamson into the relative safety of the rigging:

I took him by the coat collar to help him and called for help, but before anybody could reach us a big sea boarded the vessel and tore him from my grasp—tore his coat collar right off. He called for help a couple of times and in a few seconds was swept overboard.[5]

It was about 5:00 A.M. when the *Jennie Hall*'s captain was lost. For the next hour and a half the crew and their unwanted passenger remained in the rigging, ignorant of their whereabouts. Surfman Carroll was then making his way south, back to the station. Peering out into the heavily blowing mist at 6:20 A.M. he spotted the schooner with her bow straight towards the beach and the rough seas sweeping over her. With dawn fast approaching, Carroll did not see any men on board until he had ridden abreast of the vessel on his mount and spotted men in the rigging. Without making any signal to the vessel, Carroll rode to the station, about five hundred yards south, and reported the wreck ashore about 6:30 A.M. The station crew dressed and manned the beach cart. Keeper Barco telephoned the Seatack Station for assistance, then headed for the wreck. The crew of the Dam Neck Mills Station were at the wreck site less than thirty minutes after the alarm was sounded.

The weather was still stormy and the high surf rolled in, casting up wreckage thirty to fifty yards above the high water mark. The schooner rolled and pounded heavily on the outside sandbar less than three hundred yards from the beach; she was so heavily laden with asphalt that she did not lift much, but was, nevertheless, working her way towards shore. The sails of the *Jennie Hall* were blown to tatters with the exception of the mainsail which still drew and forced her higher and higher upon the sand.

At daybreak the shipwrecked sailors could dimly make out the shoreline through the driving rain and sleet and the spray from the breakers. Their hopes must have risen with the dawn, for minutes after daybreak they saw the Dam Neck Mills crew coming to their rescue with the beach apparatus cart. Keeper Barco noticed that the tide was just beginning to ebb and the long shore current still ran with torrential force before the northeasterly gale. To launch a boat under those conditions would have been completely out of the question. The only hope of a successful rescue lay in the use of the Lyle gun and the breeches buoy.

Since the *Jennie Hall* had stranded while traveling straight toward the beach, her bow-first position presented the life-savers with an extraordinarily difficult task. Thus, Keeper Barco fired the gun to windward. This quick action allowed the shot line to fall across her weather rigging, fore and aft. The first attempt had to be abandoned after the sailors hauled the line in and the block tangled in the headstays. The schooner's stern slid slowly toward the beach as the pounding surf constantly battered her. After the surfmen had hauled back the line, the movement of the vessel allowed them a much better angle to fire a line within the sailors' reach. The Lyle gun was mounted atop a large box to keep it above the water. A second shot was fired, but the line parted.

By this time the crew of the Seatack Life-Saving Station and a few bystanders had arrived. No time was lost in moving and loading the Lyle gun once more. The third shot was fired and passed between the main topmast and its backstay, which, to set up the breeches buoy, would have made it necessary for the sailors to cross from the mizzen to the main rigging. Keeper Barco quickly aborted the third effort to reach the vessel. The *Jennie Hall* was still sliding south and Keeper Barco, drawing upon his twenty-two years of experience, knew that little time could be lost. Once more the Lyle gun was moved; this time Keeper Barco aimed it with ten degrees elevation just as close as he dared to the men in the rigging. This shot was fired and it passed through a triangle formed by the mizzen topmast, the topmast stay, and the spring stay. The line slipped into the hands of the exhausted sailors. The sailors then had to haul the line out through the rushing long shore current. The shot line had a heavier line tied to it; the surfmen hauled the line up the beach windward, creating some slack in the line which was hauled out toward the schooner. By repeating this process it took about two hours to set up the breeches buoy.

The strenuous activity of hauling the line and setting up the gear on board the *Jennie Hall* exhausted what little strength the sailors had left. John Johnson and Ben Mall both lost consciousness and fell from the rigging to the deck and were "almost immediately swept overboard and carried off by the swift current."[6] They were not seen again. About the same time, the steward Fred Percival, must have felt as if he, too, would lose consciousness. He tied his feet to the rigging then slumped down between the crosstrees.

After the rescue gear was completely set up, the breeches buoy was sent out. Bragg had Crosby and Moore climb into the breeches buoy together. They were pulled ashore without further mishap, and the buoy was immediately sent back to the schooner. Bragg felt his strength ebbing, but climbed into the breeches buoy where he quickly lost consciousness.

> I suppose it was exposure. I hadn't felt cold until the two men were being landed. Then I felt a severe chill, but did not feel weak. I knew, however, that I couldn't hold on much longer.[7]

He did not remember anything until four hours later when he regained consciousness at the Dam Neck Mills station.

Once Bragg had been landed, the breeches buoy was sent back, and Richard Coombs was brought to shore. He told Keeper Barco that there was still one sailor left on board. The buoy was sent out again, but Fred Percival ignored it. Brought back to shore, the breeches buoy was voluntarily manned by thirty-seven-year-old John R. O'Neal, Surfman Number Three, and sent back to the vessel. O'Neal worked to free Percival from his position in the rigging until, "I began to feel numb. I signalled to be hauled back. I was drenched going out by the slackening of the hawser on account of the rolling of the ship."[8] When O'Neal reached the beach, he informed the crew that Percival couldn't be pried from his perch by one man. O'Neal again volunteered to return to the schooner if someone would go with him. Several men from both stations volunteered. O'Neal, in dry clothing, and another surfman made the breeches buoy ready. Keeper Barco then decided to use the surfboat, as the *Jennie Hall* had swung around enough to make a lee. It was decided that the two men would be put in the surfboat, in addition to the regular crew, and the boat would be held alongside the schooner until Percival could be extricated from his position and lowered into the surfboat.

It was nearly 11:30 A.M. when the surfboat pushed off and headed toward the *Jennie Hall*. John R. O'Neal and Horatio Drinkwater (a former surfman) positioned themselves in the bow of the surfboat and made ready to board the schooner. Keeper Barco manned the steering oar while William H. Partridge, George W. Whitehurst, and John H. Carroll (all from the Dam Neck Mills station), and John W. Sparrow, and Benjamin Simmons (from the Seatack Station) made up the rest of the crew. This was a very dangerous rescue attempt because the surf was still pushed by fifty-mile-per-hour winds, and the "current was running like a mill race."[9] The surfboat reached the schooner with little trouble and O'Neal and Drinkwater sprang onto the deck at the first opportunity.

The crew in the surfboat realized that the wreckage in the lee of the *Hall* could damage the surfboat; they could not stay long beside the schooner. Keeper Barco tried to keep the surfboat in the lee, but the strong current pushed the boat from the protection of the schooner into high rolling surf. A large wave struck the surfboat and threw Sparrow overboard and pushed the surfboat fifty feet away before Sparrow came to the surface. Sparrow grabbed the long safety line, and the crew hauled him back aboard the surfboat. Keeper Barco waited for his chance and deftly turned the boat and safely landed it on the beach.

When O'Neal and Drinkwater reached the deck of the *Jennie Hall*, Drinkwater moved up the mizzen rigging on the lee side while O'Neal moved across the deck and climbed up the rigging on the weather side. They found that Percival had so efficiently wedged himself between the crosstrees that they could not move him. As O'Neal explained:

> We put a piece of whipline, which we had taken off with us, around Percival's body just under his ribs and hauled it taut, making fast with a square knot and two hitches over the standing part of the rope. Then we made the rope fast to the neck of the buoy, right up close to the block. Then I got down under the crosstrees and got my head and shoulders under Percival's seat. I had my feet on the rat lines and clung to the backstays with my hands. In this way I was able to lift him out of the hole."[10]

Percival's unconscious body was launched into the air. The line caught on a cleat on the forward side of the topmast and it took ten more minutes to clear it. Percival was hauled to the beach and taken in a waiting cart to the station where they began resuscitation immediately. There were vital life signs, but Keeper Barco feared that the man might have suffered internal injuries; he telephoned for Dr. P. J. F. Miller. O'Neal and Drinkwater were landed safely in the breeches buoy, and the rescue operation was completed. Steward Fred Percival regained consciousness within a few hours of his rescue, none the worse for wear.

The stranding of the *Jennie Hall* was so unexpected and so sudden that it was only the excellent work of the Dam Neck Mills and Seatack Life-Saving crews that held the loss of life to a minimum. The *Jennie Hall* was a total loss. The body of Captain Daniel H. Lamson was recovered by the crew of the Little Island station on 22 December 1900, four miles south of the scene of the disaster. The bodies of the stowaway Ben Mall and Seaman John Johnson were never recovered.

The fog remained after the wrecking of the *Jennie Hall*. It blanketed the Virginia coast for days. On Christmas Eve the steamer *Ocean King* with two schooners in tow, stranded on Ship Shoal, eight miles northeast of the Smith Island Life-Saving Station at 3:30 A.M. The two schooners were the 1,381-ton *Astoria* and the 815-ton *Rondout*, being towed from New York City to Baltimore. Both schooners were manned by crews of four men while the *Ocean King* carried a crew of ten.

The keeper of the Smith Island Life-Saving Station was notified about 8:00 A.M. by telephone of the strandings and he, in turn, phoned the Cobb Island Station and then started for the scene with his crew in the surfboat. All three vessels pounded on the shoal, the high surf lifting them and crashing them down with a vengeance. The vessels leaked badly, and the keeper saw that there was little that could be done to save them. The two life-saving crews boarded the vessels and stayed for several hours. Before nightfall the crews landed nine men from the steamer and all four men from each schooner safely on shore. Captain Chase of the *Ocean King* refused to leave his vessel and stayed on board until a tug came and took him off. Some of the rescued men stayed at the Smith Island Station, the others stayed at the Cobb Island Station until all could be provided transportation to the nearest railroad station. All three vessels were listed as total losses and were left to go to pieces on Ship Shoal.

On 30 June 1900 the Life-Saving Service reorganized the districts. The Fifth District along Virginia's Eastern Shore became the Sixth District and what had been the Sixth District along Virginia Beach became the Seventh District. Further changes were made in 1903, and the winter season was expanded to cover 1 August to 31 May. Many of the life-saving stations along the Atlantic coast were replaced and repaired at this time. The new Virginia Beach Life-Saving Station replaced the old Seatack Station. Construction began on 2 April 1903 on the two-story building which stands today as the Virginia Beach Maritime Historical Museum. This life-saving station was originally erected for the sum of seven thousand five hundred dollars and was formally commissioned on 1 August 1903 at midnight when the surfmen officially went on duty.

At about 2:00 P.M. on 16 December 1902, John D. DeWald, Surfman Number Two, was on lookout at the Hog Island Life-Saving Station and observed two vessels as they approached the bar four miles distant. The day was ushered in by a strong gale blowing from the south southeast accompanied by heavy rain squalls. The occasional bursts of rain made it difficult to see anything on the sea at any distance. As the day progressed the weather conditions grew more threatening, causing Keeper J. E. Johnson to advise his lookouts to be especially watchful. Surfman DeWald, using the station's "marine glasses," watched the movements of the two small vessels as they approached from seaward. The sea was heavy and the surf rolled in, enveloping the entire bar and shoals in a whirling mass of foam and flying spray.

The surfman watched as the two vessels worked into a position to cross the bar. The sloop, sailing under reduced canvas, successfully coped with the huge waves which broke all around her. A very experienced captain, who was aware of every movement of his vessel, was sailing the sloop; the captain reacted to each changing condition as he crossed the bar. The surfman then turned his attention to the schooner that followed in the wake of the sloop.

The schooner was the *Lillian Russell* whose captain attempted to duplicate the maneuvers of the sloop, but "it was blowing a two-reefed gale, and the *Russell,* having taken in her foresail, stood on, under a whole mainsail and jib."[11] In the investigation that followed the incident, Surfman DeWald described what he saw next:

> I kept the glasses on the *Russell.* As I got a good look at her, she was in the wind, her mainsail and jib shaking, and it looked to me as if she was trying to come about . . . and immediately capsized. I saw the whole length of her keel. Did not see the men.[12]

In an instant the *Russell* had succumbed; she rolled over and was at the mercy of the relentless pounding waves.

The lookout rushed down from the tower to report to the keeper what he had seen. The keeper at once ordered the heavy lifeboat lowered, but it was low tide and the lifeboat only grounded on the mud flats that

The new Virginia Beach Life-Saving Station built in 1903. Courtesy: Carroll Walker Collection, Virginia Beach Maritime Historical Museum.

The old Seatack Life-Saving Station, built in 1878, in the foreground, and the new Virginia Beach Life-Saving Station in the background. Courtesy: U. S. Coast Guard.

surrounded the Hog Island Station. Quickly the life-savers moved to the Monomoy surfboat (smaller than the Race Point surfboat, and lighter) and started out to the bar. They met the powered launch *Christine*, a mail boat, and asked the captain and a former surfman on board to lend his boat in pulling the lifeboat off the mud flats and into action. With lines to the *Christine* and the surfboat, the surfmen made one last attempt to pull and push the larger lifeboat free but failed, and they abandoned their effort for the time being.

The mail boat took the much smaller Monomoy boat in tow and headed directly into the gale towards the bar The crew aboard the sloop *Romer,* which had successfully navigated the bar, in passing by, gave the rescuers the name of the vessel wrecked on the bar. It was getting late and much time had been lost in trying to free the lifeboat from the mud. The *Christine*'s captain refused to tow the boat close to the breakers on the bar. Since no one could see the broached schooner or any bodies, a decision was made to return to the station.

During the late afternoon the tide came in and the surfmen got the lifeboat successfully floated off the mud flats and took it out to the bar to continue the search for any victims or survivors. Once more the surfmen were forced back from the bar by the fierce storm which caused tremendous surf to smash upon the bar and swell again once inside the bar. This violent action forced the keeper and his men to abort their efforts, and reluctantly return to the station.

At 2:00 A.M. on 17 December, only twelve hours after the schooner wrecked, the surfmen manned the lifeboat for a third try. By this time the storm had passed and they reached the bar as the first streaks of dawn showed in the eastern sky. So complete was the destruction of the *Lillian Russell* that not one piece of the wreck was discovered. The sea refused to give up its dead; after a search along the bar, offshore and inshore, not one body was found. The Assistant Inspector of the Sixth District stated in his report:

> There were but two men on board the wrecked craft . . . George Parson, white, aged 24, and a colored man, name unknown. The vessel was from Norfolk, Va., bound to Hog Island with a load of oysters.[13]

The official investigation into the events surrounding the wreck of the *Lillian Russell* indicated that the life-savers did all that was within their power to come to the aid of the stricken schooner. However, this was not enough for Frank Parson, Jr., the brother of the dead sailor, George Parson. Frank Parson conducted his own personal investigation, and, in a letter to Keeper J. E. Johnson, he stated he had doubts that all was done to "rescue my brother on that fatal day." He was still confused as to why the proper boat could not be used in the search for his brother.

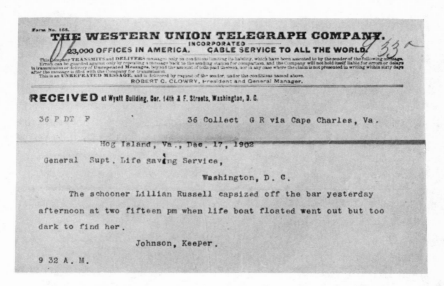

Telegram sent by Keeper Johnson to the Life-Saving Service headquarters in Washington, D. C. Courtesy: The National Archives.

> We beg to say, however, that should we ask an investigation, we shall at the same time commend you and your crew for your efforts to save their lives, and but for the negligence on the part of somebody that your boat is almost worthless to you in case of immediate need.[14]

Perhaps his confusion can best be explained by the fact that the station site had been secured years earlier, long before the Life-Saving Service initiated the use of the heavier powered lifeboats. In any event, there should have been precautions taken to avoid the situation that occurred during the wrecking of the *Lillian Russell*. Although it is doubtful that the two men could have been saved, it would have saved the Life-Saving Service some degree of embarrassment.

By the early twentieth century Virginia Beach had become a resort community for sportsmen and was developing as a seaside resort for vacationers. The milder winter climate along with both fresh and salt water fishing helped spread the community's fame along the north Atlantic seaboard. The area had supported such fine establishments as the Princess Anne Hotel for more than twenty years, but now oceanside property was developed by the area's more affluent people. One such property was a cottage completed 1 July 1903 for fifty-five hundred dollars as the summer retreat for the president of Chesapeake Transit Company, J. Edward Cole, and his family The Cole Cottage was two and one half miles south of Cape Henry, on the oceanfront.

At 2:00 A.M. Saturday morning 19 September 1903 as Surfman Barnes was on south patrol from the Cape Henry Life-Saving Station to meet Surfman Barco of the Virginia Beach Station, they discovered a fire as they were exchanging their patrol checks. They rushed to the cottage. The surfmen's loud cries woke the family, enabling an escape from the burning building unharmed. The cottage was of wood frame construction throughout and burned very quickly. Had the two surfmen not awakened the family, J. Edward Cole stated, "they would undoubtedly have been burned [to death]."[15] In less than one month, close by the charred ruins of the Cole Cottage, one of Surfman Barco's crewmates earned the Gold Life-Saving Medal (the highest honor for bravery a surfman could receive, akin to the Medal of Honor) in recognition of his heroic conduct in saving two men from drowning off Virginia Beach on 10 October 1903.

On Thursday 8 October the oceangoing tug *Richmond* of the Coastwise Steamship Company left Newport News with two schooner-rigged coal barges in tow. By late evening the *Richmond* was outside the Virginia Capes battling a northeast gale with winds reaching forty miles per hour. Because the tug was unable to hold her own against the gale winds and heavy seas, she was gradually forced astern, still holding to the schooner barges.

Schooner coal barges in tow. Courtesy: Mariners' Museum.

Around 9:00 A.M. on 9 October the tug, which had spent the entire night under steam, signaled to the barges to come to anchor. For the rest of the day they remained safely at anchor. During the night, however, the schooner-barge *Georgia* parted her cables and the *Richmond* went to her assistance, leaving the other schooner-barge, the *Ocean Belle*, on her own. Since the tug was unable to take the crew of the *Georgia* off, the *Georgia* drifted ashore near the Virginia Beach Life-Saving Station.

The *Ocean Belle* remained at anchor for the next twenty-four hours, but as the storm increased and reached hurricane force, the cables could not hold her and at 10:30 A.M. the cables broke. The *Ocean Belle* was attacked by huge waves which washed across her deck. With 2,605 tons of coal in her hold, the schooner-barge quickly filled with water. Her captain gave orders to the four-man crew to put the vessel before the wind on a south by west course that would bring her ashore. Shortly afterward, the *Ocean Belle*'s steering gear was carried away by the sea and she turned broadside to the beach, leaking badly.

Seeing that their once-proud schooner was doomed, the crew put on their life belts and huddled in the forerigging. The *Ocean Belle* grounded a mile offshore and immediately began to break up. In less than one hour after she stranded all of her masts had broken and her

deck house, boat, and decks were washed away, the foremast, where the crew had congregated, alone remaining, and the rigging had become so slack that the men held on with extreme difficulty.[16]

Captain Adams could do no more than wish each man good luck. The *Ocean Belle* was smashed by the surf and scraped slowly toward the beach. Captain Adams lost his hold in the rigging and was the first to fall into the sea.

It was evident to the surviving sailors that to stay on board the schooner-barge meant certain death, for she was likely to break up completely at any moment. Their chances for reaching shore, however, seemed equally hopeless, but after some discussion, they decided that it was the only option open to them. Peter Lopes, Manuel Pina, and Joseph and Charles Peters all jumped overboard and swam toward the beach.

At 2:00 P.M. Surfman J. W. Barco, on north patrol, returned to the Virginia Beach Station and reported to his keeper that he had seen a vessel stranded two and one-half miles from the station. Keeper Partridge ordered Walter N. Capps "up the beach to look out for anyone who might be in the surf or on the beach."[17] The remainder of the crew then followed a short time later. They had not gone far when they came upon a man in the sand dunes. Keeper Partridge detailed two of his men to help the survivor back to the shelter of the station. Capps, half a mile ahead of the party, spotted a man struggling in the surf.

> He plunged in and pulled him out and took him to a place of safety behind the hills and ran back to the surf to look for others as the man told him there were five on board.[18]

Capps saw another man in the surf; he took off his oilskin outerwear before he ran into the surf. Fighting the pounding waves, he pulled the man from the sea and dragged him about two hundred yards before he found a sheltered place to leave him. The surfman who followed Capps up the beach found the first survivor and escorted him back to the station. Capps, exhausted and drenched, started south back to the station. He soon encountered surfmen and volunteers who helped him and the other shipwrecked sailor. Surfman Capps, the keeper testified, staggered back to the station barefooted, half-clothed, and nearly exhausted. Keeper Partridge stated that "I gave him a glass of whiskey from the medicine chest to revive him."[19] In recognition of Capps' heroic conduct the Secretary of the Treasury awarded him the Gold Life-Saving Medal of Honor.

The *Ocean Belle,* like the *Georgia,* went to pieces. On 10 October 1903, the *Ocean Belle*'s captain, George H. Adams of Philadelphia, and Seaman Charles Peters had lost their lives trying to reach the shore. The body of the captain was found the next day two miles south of the station.

Keeper John W. Partridge received a letter from Providence, Rhode Island, dated 21 October 1903, which said, in part, how happy the writer was

> to see my friends, whom I never expected to see again, for which all thanks are due you and your brave crew, who saved us from destruction by the angry seas. With my best regards to your wife and three cheers for Captain Partridge and his crew, from one who will never forget Virginia Beach and the heroes of the Life-Saving Service.[20]

The letter was signed Peter Lopes, Mate, schooner barge *Ocean Belle.*

While the sailors on board the *Ocean Belle* were struggling for their lives, another three-masted schooner, the *Nellie W. Howlett* was offshore about a mile; she, too, had become unmanageable. The Dam Neck Mills Station's north patrolman that morning (10 October 1903) reported to his keeper that the schooner would surely strike the beach. Keeper James E. Woodhouse ordered the beach apparatus cart readied. The surfmen, acccompanied by several volunteers, followed along on the beach as the schooner sailed south past the station. The *Nellie W. Howlett* stranded three miles south of the station and three hundred fifty yards from the beach. The surf immediately began to break over her. Within fifteen minutes the surfmen were at the scene and fired five shots from the Lyle gun, the last shot within reach of the vessel's crew. Captain W. W. McGheen and his crew of seven were rescued in the breeches buoy. The schooner was bound north from Jacksonville, Florida, with a cargo of hard pine, most of which washed ashore near the Dam Neck Mills and Little Island stations and was salvaged. It was reported in *The Public Ledger* that the stranding of the *Nellie W. Howlett* was the worst wreck ever seen on this coast in so short a time after the vessel struck. The schooner was a total loss.

The hurricane that raged up and down the coast of Virginia on 10 October 1903 caused not only shipwrecks but property damage along the shore as well. The Assateague Beach life-savers had to rescue eight fishermen, not because their vessels had stranded, but because their house had been swept away by the high water. The fishermen were supplied with clothing provided by the Women's National Relief Association.

At the Wallops Beach Life-Saving Station a more conventional rescue took place, as again eight fishermen were taken to the safety of the station. The life-saving crew at Wachapreague was forced to abandon their station because the hurricane caused the ground floor of the station to be completely underwater. The life-savers left the station in the surfboat and while they were crossing to the mainland they rescued four men who themselves were in danger. The oyster shanty belonging to the four men was surrounded by the sea and was being attacked by violent waves.

The hurricane caused high seas and turbulent surf not only on the Eastern Shore but along the beaches at Virginia Beach as well. At False Cape the high water threatened all the dwellings near the station. The life-savers had to man the surfboat and transport nine women and seven children to a clubhouse which was on higher ground and better able to withstand the weather. Evidence of the hurricane's fury drifted up on shore as the storm passed. Along the sands of Virginia Beach were the remains of the vessels *Ocean Belle, Georgia,* and the *Nellie W. Howlett.* The residents of the area scurried about, gathering wreckage from the beach to repair their battered dwellings.

On 12 October a body was found on Smith Island by the station crew. There was not a clue as to the identity of the man and the surfmen performed a proper burial. At 3:00 A.M. the next morning, the north beach patrol from the False Cape Life-Saving Station found a man's body on the beach. A positive identification was impossible, but it was believed to have been the body of Seaman Charles Peters of the *Ocean Belle.* A coffin was made, and the station crew buried the body behind the dunes.

Although the surfmen's most rigorous duties involved saving lives and property during the violent storms which battered the coast and caused many shipwrecks, they also faced the difficult task of battling fire. During this era of wooden construction, cottages and homes were built close to each other and were tinder for fires which swept from one building to another with a diabolic swiftness. For example, during the early morning hours of 25 October 1903, a fire raged out of control near the Virginia Beach Life-Saving Station. The surfmen from the Cape Henry and Dam Neck Mills stations answered the alarm and arrived to help the Virginia Beach crew extinguish the blaze. A total of five closely grouped dwellings were destroyed by the fire which doubtless would have extended to several more as well as a large hotel nearby had the life-savers not acted quickly and efficiently.

Chapter 9

Farewell to Sail

FEBRUARY 1904 - DECEMBER 1913

The majority of vessels which stranded, grounded, or wrecked on the shores of Virginia were schooners, coasting vessels which carried the bulk cargoes needed along the eastern seaboard. However, there were wrecks involving a few of the larger ships, or deep water traders—those vessels which made trans-Atlantic crossings. One of these was the *Henry B. Hyde,* a full-rigged downeaster, closely related to the famous clipper ships. The *Hyde*'s lines were not as extreme as those of the clipper ships since she was designed for the bulk overseas cargo trade. The commodities that she carried on her long journeys were of the sort that would not deteriorate in transit: granite, lumber, case oil, coal, and grain. The *Hyde* was a wooden ship launched on 5 November 1884 at Bath, Maine with a registered tonnage of 2,583, and at that time the largest ship built in the state of Maine. Sturdily constructed and reinforced, she was 290 feet at the keel; her beam was 45 feet, and her hold was 29 feet deep. She was framed from heavy, well-seasoned oak, and her decks were made of 5-inch yellow pine planking. Over two hundred tons of iron went into her as she was braced with iron struts throughout. Above decks she was a sight to behold; her 6 yards ranged symmetrically from 90 feet in length on the lowers to 40 feet on the skysails. She was a fully-rigged ship carrying 3 masts and a full complement of square sails, staysails, and jibs.

The *Henry B. Hyde* was not built to break records, but neither was she slow in the water. She was built for trade between the eastern ports and San Francisco and the Pacific islands. These trips were made around Cape Horn from New York to San Francisco; her average trip was 124 days with some passages of 105, 108, and 112 days. Four voyages from

The *Henry B. Hyde* before her launching. Courtesy: Mariners' Museum.

San Francisco to New York were made in 88, 94, 110, and 135 days. On the trip of 88 days she carried a full cargo of 60,791 bags of refined sugar. Her log shows that in 241 days she traveled 35,000 miles while transporting 8,800 tons of various cargo. From the standpoint of persistent good qualities and in all weather and seas, some naval architects have judged the *Hyde* the best class of vessel ever produced in America.

Early in February 1904, the *Henry B. Hyde* was towed from the port of New York by the tug *Britannia*, which was under the command of Captain Dunn. On board the ship was a partial crew of thirteen men including the captain of the *Hyde*, Fred H. Pearsons, as well as one passenger, the captain's wife. The ship was to be towed south through the Atlantic to the Chesapeake Bay and then northwest to Baltimore where she was to receive her cargo of coal. Her full crew of twenty-eight men was to have been completed in Baltimore.

During the evening of Friday, 10 February 1904, the two vessels were off the Virginia Capes in a raging northeast blizzard. The weather conditions were such that Captain Dunn of the *Britannia* stated that he was driven south because he could not make out the Cape Henry Light in the driving snow. By midnight they were off the coast of Virginia Beach about ten miles south of Cape Henry, pushed by the fierce northeast blizzard that swept the coast. Between midnight and 12:30 A.M. Captain Dunn made the decision to cut free from the *Hyde* but only after the ship had grounded twice. It was the second grounding which caused Captain Dunn to realize that the ship was dragging the tug ashore, and he was compelled to cut loose from her to save his own vessel. The *Hyde* stranded two and one half miles south of the Dam Neck Mills Life-Saving Station at 12:30 A.M. 11 February 1904.

As soon as the ship struck bottom, the surf lifted the nineteen-year-old vessel only to crash her back down hard. A veteran of thirty-one years at sea, Captain Pearson stated:

> It seemed that the wind whistled with the strength of a thousand demons. The ship at once began to pound and it looked as though she would be beaten to pieces. The snow was a foot thick on the deck and every piece of rigging was solid ice. Our boots froze to our pants, and our fingers were numb with the cold.[1]

After the *Hyde* struck, the crew managed to fire an emergency rocket flare. Surfman W. H. Partridge from the Dam Neck Mills Station was on south patrol, from midnight to 4:00 A.M., when he sighted the emergency signal and the wreck near shore about 1:00 A.M. Surfman Partridge burned his Coston flare to let those on board know that help was at hand. He then rushed against the gale force winds that pushed sleet and snow in his face, and made his way two miles back to the station. Dam Neck Mills Keeper James Woodhouse was notified of the wreck and at once called Little Island Keeper Otto Halstead for assistance. Both station crews headed toward the scene of the wreck.

Keeper Woodhouse hired a horse to haul the beach cart, and with the wind at their backs, his Dam Neck Mills crew arrived first. Shortly after 2:00 A.M. the life-savers fired a line to the ship which was two hundred and fifty yards from shore. On board the *Hyde* it was much too icy and dark for any of her crew to climb into the rigging and secure the shot line. The *Hyde*'s crew answered the shot by firing another rocket, and all on board moved forward to the forecastle to await daylight. Captain Pearson stated:

> The wind was now blowing at a gale and as we crossed the deck for the forecastle some of the upper spars came down with a crash that sent us spinning against the forecastle house. None of us, however, was injured. You see, the reason we went forward is that the masts, when falling, always crash to the deck in the after part of the ship.[2]

At 4:00 A.M. Keeper Halstead and the Little Island crew arrived at the wreck site. The two station crews waited as Keeper Woodhouse's later laconic report explained, "First shot at 2:00 A.M. Crew on board could not go aloft. So had to wait for daylight."[3] Actually, the station crews waited in the gale and blowing snow until just after 7:00 A.M. when they fired the Lyle gun for the second time; this shot landed square on target, and the line was tied to the upper rigging. Captain Pearson and his crew had to decide who would be the first to get into the breeches buoy. The largest crewman, two-hundred-and-fifty-pound Seaman Sullivan, climbed into it and went sailing through the surf. The line was not quite taut and he got his feet wet. He was the only one, however, that did get wet during the rescue operation. Captain Pearson had complete confidence in the breeches buoy, helping his wife get into a pair of his trousers and into the buoy. Unlike Captain Jorgensen's wife who met death in the wreck of the *Dictator*, Mrs. Pearson rode safely to shore in the face of raging seas and gale force winds. Mrs. Pearson had sailed with her husband for years and was quite accustomed to life aboard ship as well as to taking orders in time of peril. The following day, rested and warm at the Granby Hotel in Norfolk, Captain Pearson recalled:

> Mrs. Pearson went shoreward with great speed and landed high up on the beach. She was not even wet. Then we followed one by one and all were safely landed. I cannot praise the life-savers too highly.[4]

The *Hyde*'s First Mate, Frank Rhodes, was sheltered at the station for a week while he waited to see how the weather would affect the condition of the ship. The sturdy *Hyde* was left high on the beach. The ship's owners, however, decided that nothing could be done for her, and she was left to go to pieces as wrecking steamers had been unsuccessful in their attemps to tow the ship off the beach.

During the spring of 1904 the beached *Henry B. Hyde* still displayed the high quality of workmanship that had gone into her construction some nineteen years before. There was hope that she could be refloated; in June the owners put a crew of four on board to see if she could get off the beach on the next flood tide. At 7:45 P.M., 10 June 1904, two crewmen employed to work on the stranded ship went to the Dam Neck Mills Life-Saving Station and asked Keeper Partridge to come to the aid of four men on the *Hyde* who wished to be taken off. There was a fierce northeast gale blowing at the time and heavy surf was pounding

The *Henry B. Hyde* aground at Virginia Beach, 1904.
Courtesy: Mariners' Museum.

against the ship, and the men were terrified. Once again the life-savers rescued the crew of the *Hyde*. For the rest of the summer, visitors to the vacation hotels at Virginia Beach would stroll along the beach to view the once-proud ship, lying on the sand like a beached whale.

On 21 September 1904, another attempt to refloat the *Hyde* proved successful, if shortlived. The very next day the *Hyde*'s tow cable broke, and once again she stranded on the beach. For the third and final time, surfmen from the Dam Neck Mills Life-Saving Station set up the breeches buoy and rescued the crew. Eight men were taken ashore safely. On 4 October 1904 the *Henry B. Hyde* broke in two, the life of a gallant and beautiful ship had ended.

On 1 December 1905 the *Pendleton Sisters,* a three-masted 798-ton schooner, sailed from Port Arthur, Texas, loaded with a cargo of square pine timbers bound for Noank, Connecticut. It had taken the schooner two weeks to reach Assateague Light; early on 15 December she

The *Henry B. Hyde* going to pieces in the surf.
A 1903 White automobile is in the foreground.
Courtesy: Mariners' Museum.

encountered a heavy "nor'easter." Captain John Davies decided that since his schooner carried a heavy deck load (1,100 tons overall) he would run back and anchor off Chincoteague in seven fathoms of water. Through the early hours of the fifteenth the storm increased in strength and Captain Davies dropped a second anchor to keep his schooner under control. The schooner tugged so hard at the anchors that she soon dragged them south; all during that day the schooner scraped southward just off the flooded coastline.

The anchors had kept the *Pendleton Sisters'* bow into the gale and she was better able to withstand the force of the heavy seas. Unfortunately both anchor cables finally broke, incapable of withstanding the constant stress any longer. The schooner was completely at the mercy of the northeaster. Captain Davies realized the only way to save his vessel was to beach her. He ordered his eight-man crew to raise sail, but the deck load of lumber was loosened by the constant battering and

The *Pendleton Sisters*. Courtesy: A.M. Barnes Collection,
Mariners' Museum.

pounding and made it impossible for the crew to work on deck. The
schooner stranded three hundred yards offshore, five and one half miles
north of Metomkin Inlet, three miles beyond the Life-Saving Station's
normal limits.

The northeaster was at its peak when the schooner stranded; the
weather was so bad that the flooded shore only three hundred yards away
could barely be seen. Captain Davies had no idea of his location or the
fate of his vessel and crew. The surf broke over the schooner and soaked
everything which made it impossible to ignite a signal flare. The crew's
only hope was to hold on while the waves relentlessly pounded and
smashed the schooner. During the night the temperature dropped below
freezing and the sailors shivered as they found what shelter was available
and waited for daylight.

Because this northeaster was so fierce and had completely flooded
the beaches the life-savers could not walk their normal patrol. As a
consequence, they did not discover the *Pendleton Sisters* until after

daybreak on 16 December. Keeper L. F. Taylor of the Metomkin Inlet Station hitched the station's horse to a cart and rode north along the beach behind the dunes. The veteran life-saver first noticed the debris strewn along the beach about a mile from his station; he rode on, looking for the source, knowing that there must be a vessel ashore. An eerie, thick fog hung over the beach as Keeper Taylor urged his horse on through the water and sand. Soon he saw the top masts of a vessel above the fog, apparently stranded. The keeper went far enough to assure himself that the vessel was aground then quickly turned and headed back to the station.

Since the flooded beach kept the crew from pulling the 1,500-pound beach apparatus cart to the wreck site, Keeper Taylor decided to launch the surfboat on the western shore and pull into what was known as the "inside passage." But it took them three hours to pull the surfboat across the narrow peninsula which separated the ocean from the bay. Finally, the life-savers arrived abreast of the *Pendleton Sisters*—it was near noon.

Heavy breakers crashed around and upon the schooner and huge timbers were tossed like so many matchsticks in the churning surf, a dangerous area separating the surfmen and the crew on the stricken schooner. The keeper hesitated to launch the surfboat, but immediately sent for the beach apparatus cart. He feared that the surfmen would be unable to haul the cart to the scene even with the aid of the horse; with the remainder of his crew Keeper Taylor made three unsuccessful attempts to launch the surfboat. Fortunately four volunteers arrived on the beach in time to assist the surfmen. They brought the surfboat again to the water's edge and launched it with the volunteers taking the places of the absent surfmen. Keeper Taylor skillfully maneuvered the surfboat out through the breakers and past drifting timbers. Once alongside the schooner, William H. Lang, a volunteer, stood in the bow of the surfboat and threw a line to the wreck. Very quickly the surfmen and volunteers took the schooner's mate and three other sailors into the twenty-six foot surfboat, turned, and rowed for the beach.

The storm increased in intensity as the surfmen landed the four sailors on the beach. By this time the surfmen from the station arrived at the wreck site with the apparatus cart, pulled by the station horse. They immediately set up the Lyle gun, faking box (a deep wooden box, and a lid with wooden spikes around which line was wound in preparation for firing from the Lyle gun), and sand anchor; only one shot was needed to land a line on board the schooner, less than three hundred yards from shore. Quickly Captain Davies and the three remaining sailors were hauled ashore in the breeches buoy. It was then that they learned that one of their crewmen, the black cook, W. W. King, had died of exhaustion from his battle with the elements. All of the survivors were indeed in a pitiful state; two of the sailors were unconscious. They were taken to the Metomkin Inlet Life-Saving Station where they remained for three days. As for the *Pendleton Sisters*, she was beyond saving, and soon went to pieces. Keeper Taylor's report to Washington specifically commended the four volunteers who risked their lives to aid the surfmen in their rescue operation. The four men were "Major" Jones, himself an ex-surfman, William H. Lang, John Webb, and Charles Sleigh.

On 9 January 1906 another terrible storm swept out of the north and hit the coast of Virginia with fifty mile-per-hour winds. It was during the height of this storm that the graceful five-masted, 2,258-ton schooner *Fannie Palmer* stranded three-fourths of a mile north of the Little Island Life-Saving Station, about two hundred yards offshore. The surfman on north patrol sighted her and fired two Coston flares to alert the schooner's crew that they had been seen and help was at hand. The schooner answered the signal with a blast from the whistle of her donkey engine. The surfman then made his way back to the station to sound the alarm. Keeper Partridge notified the adjacent life-saving stations by telephone; he and his crew transported the beach apparatus cart abreast of the vessel and quickly set up the Lyle gun. They fired one shot at the large schooner, and the line all but fell into the hands of the waiting sailors.

The crew of the Dam Neck Mills Life-Saving Station arrived and assisted in the rescue operation, hauling off the lines and securing the hawser. Captain Nash of the *Fannie Palmer* and his eleven-man crew were brought ashore without mishap in the breeches buoy. The schooner, however, remained stuck on the sands until 6 April 1906, when she was floated off the beach and towed to Norfolk for twenty thousand dollars worth of repairs.

As unusual as were the three strandings of the *Henry B. Hyde*, none was perhaps as dramatic as a collision which occurred along the shores of Virginia on 22 March 1906. At that time the four-masted schooner *Harry T. Hayward* collided with the German steamship *San Miguel* eight miles south of Cape Henry. The schooner was on her way

The schooner *Fannie Palmer.* Courtesy: Mariners' Museum.

from Punta Gorda, Florida, to Baltimore with a cargo of phosphate rock. The collision left a gaping hole in the bow of the 1,020-ton *Hayward,* and leaking badly, the schooner was driven ashore by her captain, A. C. Calcord, four miles south of Cape Henry. The crews of both the Cape Henry and Virginia Beach Life-Saving stations rendered valuable assistance to the schooner as well as to the wreckers which were summoned. It was the combined efforts of the station crews and wreckers that proved successful in refloating the *Harry T. Hayward.* She was then towed to Norfolk for repairs.

Another interesting shipwreck was that of the *Antonio,* an Italian bark, which stranded at Cape Henry Point on 31 March 1906 in a heavy northeast gale. The bark was first sighted southeast of the Cape Henry Life-Saving Station about one mile offshore. The *Antonio* tried to round Cape Henry in the gale and started to head straight for the beach. The Cape Henry Station lookout hoisted a signal to warn the bark of danger; the signal was recognized, and the bark began to tack away. But unfortunately she lost the wind and drifted shoreward, stern first.

The rescue of the crew of the *Antonio* by the Cape Henry life-savers was performed without error even with winds of forty miles per hour and

The crew of the Dam Neck Mills Life-Saving Station.
Courtesy: Virginia Beach Maritime Historical Museum.

an extremely heavy surf. The eleven-man crew was taken to shelter at the Cape Henry Station while the surfmen returned to the bark four times to retrieve the personal belongings of the *Antonio*'s crew. There was little that could be done to save the bark, and within five days she began to break apart where she had stranded.

The crew of the *Antonio* became anxious about their unpaid wages. One evening during their stay at the Cape Henry Life-Saving Station, the sailors, "crazed with too much grog," began to argue and then to fight among themselves about their lack of pay. The free-for-all got out of hand, and the surfmen summoned the police. The scrappy seamen were separated by the surfmen and police and put in individual rooms at the old Cape Henry station which served as a storage building. The crew's fears were calmed when the Deputy United States Marshal arrived from Norfolk and accepted their applications for compensation. According to law if the wages were not paid, the federal government libeled the vessel. It was the duty of the deputy marshal to secure the libel notice on the mast and place a watchman on board until the owners provided bond. The owners of the *Antonio*, however, were in Castle-

The launching of the schooner *Harry T. Hayward*.
Courtesy: Mariners' Museum.

mare, Italy, and the amount in question was only $208, or about $26 for each sailor. The owners ignored the libel notice. The captain, first mate, and steward also had claims, but had not filed them as of 6 April 1906.

For the first time in the history of the port of Norfolk the Deputy United States Marshal served libel on a vessel that was being battered to pieces in the surf off Cape Henry. The Cape Henry surfmen took Deputy Miller in their surfboat to the wreck of the *Antonio* where he tacked the libel notice on the mast. Since the bottom of the bark was covered with copper sheeting, it was stripped and the copper sheeting sold for salvage, settling the crew's claims.

Steamships were more prevalent in the early twentieth century; but even with their improved design and better control, they often suffered the same fate on the shores of Virginia as had the many sailing vessels. One such disaster was the wreck of the steamship *George Farwell* on 20 October 1906. At 7:15 P.M. Surfman Number Five, C. C. White, on

A postcard picture of *Antonio.* Courtesy: Mariners' Museum.

lookout at the Cape Henry Station, reported that he saw a light beyond the breakers which he thought to be too close to the beach for the safety of the vessel. With visibility impaired by a dense fog, Keeper Nelson Holmes immediately burned a red Coston flare to warn the vessel and then instructed two of his men to patrol the beach to see if the vessel had, in fact, stranded. The surfmen started out across the flooded beach with northeast gale force winds at their backs and discovered the 977-ton *George Farwell* approximately two hundred and fifty yards off the beach. The surfmen ignited another Coston flare and Keeper Holmes immediately dispatched the apparatus cart to the scene. He telephoned the Virginia Beach Life-Saving Station for assistance at 7:30 P.M., then chased after his men who were pulling the beach cart south.

In conditions that were far from ideal, it took the surfmen twenty-four hours to initiate and complete the rescue of the sixteen-man crew of the *Farwell.* The northeaster and dense fog presented difficult handling of the rescue equipment and extremely limited visibility. At one point

The wreck of the *George Farwell*, in foreground, and the *Antonio*, in background. Courtesy: Mariners' Museum.

during the rescue attempt, the hauling lines became fouled, and the operation had to be delayed until daylight.

The *George Farwell* was on a voyage hauling a cargo of lumber from Jacksonville, Florida, to New Haven, Connecticut. Most of the cargo was salvaged by the life-savers; the steamship, however, became a total loss. (The *George Farwell* became a landmark for strollers along the north end of Virginia Beach until she finally went to pieces, and a section of her boiler is now exhibited on the lawn at the Virginia Beach Maritime Historical Museum.)

From 20 October 1906 until the *Arleville H. Peary* drifted ashore on 31 October 1908, a total of six vessels stranded along the coast of Virginia Beach. Over $196,000 worth of vessels and known cargoes were endangered as a result of the strandings, but the total losses sustained were less than $600. During this same period along the Eastern Shore of Virginia, a total of eight vessels stranded with a total worth of $127,200;

of that amount $83,100 was lost. Of the eight vessels, three were total losses.

The thirty-four-year-old three-masted schooner *Arleville H. Peary* was in an extremely waterlogged state when she drifted ashore early in the morning of 31 October 1908. The schooner had been spotted by Clayton B. Ewell, Surfman Number Five, on south patrol from the False Cape Life-Saving Station. The *Peary* was offshore when Ewell saw a distress signal burning; Ewell returned the signal by igniting his red Coston Flare and quickly returned to the station. Keeper O'Neal and Surfman Ewell followed the drifting vessel south. The north patrolman from Wash Woods Life-Saving Station had also discovered the vessel in distress and rode his horse to his station to sound the alarm. The Wash Woods crew hauled their apparatus cart abreast of the stranded schooner and were joined by the False Cape crew. Quickly the crews set up the breeches buoy and took off the schooner's six-man crew. By this time the boat wagon from the False Cape Station had arrived, and the life-savers launched the surfboat to board the *Peary* for the crew's clothing and personal effects. As the seventy-two-year-old Keeper William H. O'Neal wrote in his report, his crew "did not save much owing to the vessel being sunk and sea washing over her and (her) breaking up."[5]

On 12 November 1908, the last shipwreck occurred involving loss of life on Virginia Beach under the jurisdiction of the United States Life-Saving Service. The cause of the wreck of the forty-one-year-old schooner-barge *Florence Shay* can be attributed to a fierce northeast gale combined with the deteriorating condition of the vessel itself. On this her final voyage from Norfolk to New York the *Florence Shay* carried a cargo of creosoted paving blocks. An old schooner, she had been reduced to that of a schooner-barge, and was in tow behind the barge *Nichols*, both in turn towed by the tug *Asher J. Hudson*. The *Shay*'s deteriorating condition was the result not only of her age but damage sustained a few weeks prior in a storm off Cape Henry, after which she had been towed to Norfolk for repairs.

Late in the afternoon of 11 November 1908, the *Asher J. Hudson* had left Hampton Roads with her tows; around 9:00 P.M. that night they reached Cape Henry. A northeast gale had begun to blow as the tug towed the barge and the schooner-barge north to a point off Hog Island on the Eastern Shore. It was at that position that the tow line or cable to the schooner was either cut, or due to the heavy laboring of the vessels

John Woodhouse Sparrow, surfman at the Virginia Beach Life-Saving
Station, early 1900s. Courtesy: Barbara M. Gietz,
photo by Charles A. Harbaugh.

The U. S. Life Saving Station, Virginia Beach, Virginia

This postcard, written by Mr. Charles A. Harbaugh to a friend in Washington, D. C., shows the 1903 Virginia Beach Life-Saving Station with crew. Mr. Harbaugh's daughter, Mary Campbell, is a volunteer at the museum which now occupies the old Virginia Beach Life-Saving Station. Courtesy: Virginia Beach Maritime Historical Museum.

under the strain of the storm, broke. Captain Gilbert of the *Shay* heard the tug blow and stated that "suddenly the tow line was cut by those on the barge, and the schooner was left to the mercy of the gale."[6] For whatever reason it seemed that the tug was unable to pass another line to the schooner. To make matters worse, the *Shay*'s steering broke and she was leaking badly.

The *Florence Shay* was to have been towed the entire distance to New York. She did not have all her sails and had only one small anchor on board. When left behind, she was helpless and in no condition to wage a successful battle with the strong gale force winds that pushed her down the coast. Sunrise on 12 November found the vessel three miles north of the False Cape Life-Saving Station and one mile offshore. She was discovered at 7:00 A.M. by Leonard E. Eaton, Surfman Number Five, from the Little Island Station. The surfman on lookout called to Keeper John W. Partridge to come to the tower where they both saw the *Shay* offshore with her sails all furled except the jib. Her flag was in the starboard mizzen rigging, union down. She appeared to be full of water and unmanageable.[7]

Keeper Partridge judged the schooner would strand between his station and the False Cape Station to the south. He called Keeper O'Neal at False Cape and informed him of the events. They agreed as to who would take what equipment, and both keepers led their crews toward the sinking schooner.

The *Florence Shay* with her crew of six, struck the outer sandbar less than three hundred yards from shore, three and one half miles south of the Little Island Life-Saving Station. Once the vessel grounded, the surf swept across her decks with increasing fury. Two of the crew, exhausted from their all-night battle with the raging sea and suffering from exposure, died shortly after the stranding.

The Little Island crew was abreast of the *Florence Shay* at 8:20 A.M.; the False Cape crew arrived within a few minutes. Three shots from the Lyle gun were fired. But the first two shots, while landing a line on board, failed to place a line within reach of the crew. The third line was successful, but the lines became tangled and twisted with other lines and debris from the vessel, and the surfmen were unable to get the breeches buoy working properly. They sent for the surfboat from the False Cape Station; by the time it arrived the tide was at mean low level and the surfboat was launched more easily.

With Keeper O'Neal in charge a boat crew was chosen from the two station crews. Launching the boat one hundred yards up current from the schooner, the crew pulled strenuously to the lee side of the vessel. The surfmen found four of the *Florence Shay*'s crew alive, and they successfully landed Captain Charles W. Gilbert, Mate John Jonson, and Seamen Frank Gotfoid and Martii Hukka. The surfmen made a second trip through the pounding surf to retrieve the bodies of the rest of the crew members. At the request of Captain Gilbert, the body of one sailor was buried on the beach. The body of the cook, Charles Molllinauk, was never recovered. (It was a common practice during this time to quickly bury those dead from injuries in a shipwreck especially if there were no known relatives nearby and if the bodies had been grotesquely mangled. More often than not, burial was on the beach where the bodies were found, in graves dug slightly above the dune lines. Transportation from the beach areas being what it was, quick disposal was advantageous, in addition to the fact that no refrigeration was available.)

The old vessel quickly broke up. Pieces of the wrecked schooner and portions of her cargo were strewn along the beach for miles, silent reminders of the *Florence Shay*'s final struggle with the sea. The life-savers had done all that was humanly possible in the saving of lives under the circumstances. The question of the cut or parted cable was never resolved. That, to be sure, contributed to the wreck of the *Shay* as much as did the weather conditions prevalent at the time and the condition of the vessel itself.

A six-year-old tramp steamer stranded close to the rotting hulk of the *Florence Shay* three and one half miles south of the Little Island Life-Saving Station at 3:30 A.M. on 7 March 1911. The 2,997-ton British steamer *Manchuria* was en route to Tampico, Mexico, from Newport News when she lost her rudder and drove ashore. The surfman on south patrol from Little Island discovered the stranded steamer and burned a Coston flare. The surfman on lookout at the station saw the signal and by the time the patrol returned to his station, the surfmen were ready.

The *Manchuria* had come ashore during a severe winter storm. With a draft of over twenty-one feet, she struck the outer sand bar six hundred yards offshore. The life-savers made two attempts to fire a line over the steamer, but were unsuccessful because of the great distance between them and the steamer. By dawn communications were established through International Signal Code, but all offers of assistance to the steamer were declined by Captain Taylor. The surfmen from Little Island and False Cape stayed by the vessel all day, ready to take action if the occasion demanded it. At sundown the wind increased and reached gale force. A hard stinging rain began, and the seas reached higher, breaking over the 330-foot ship from bow to stern.

As the night wore on the storm increased; the winds and seas rose together to frightening heights; fifty-mile-per-hour winds accompanied the 4:00 A.M. high tide on 8 March 1911. The beach flooded, and the rain turned to snow. Shortly after daybreak, those on board the *Manchuria* signaled that they desired to be taken off. The force of the storm had pushed the vessel two hundred and fifty yards closer to the beach so that a third firing from the Lyle gun placed a line across her. At that time the crews of the Dam Neck Mills and Wash Woods stations arrived, and all of the surfmen worked to set up the rescue apparatus.

> This was a task that required them to work in the water up to their waists, and taxed them to the utmost the strength of the twenty-seven men now on the beach.[8]

After eight men were landed safely in the breeches buoy, the rocking motion of the steamer snapped the line, putting the gear temporarily out of commission. When the storm suddenly lessened, the remaining crew on board the *Manchuria* became more assured, and signaled that they didn't want to be taken off after all. The two life-saving crews, having been on the beach for thirty-six hours and suffering from exhaustion and exposure, were more than happy to return to the safety and warmth of their station. The steamship remained stuck on the bar for ten days until she was successfully floated off by wreckers. The *Manchuria*'s crew was reunited 9 March when the life-savers took back on board those of the crew they had rescued during the blizzard.

One of the headline stories in the Norfolk newspaper on 8 March 1911 concerned the stranding of the *Manchuria*. It was noted that the captain of the steamship had made a mistake in declining the aid of the Life-Saving Service, thinking that tugs would haul his ship off immediately. The significance of the headline story was that it pointed out just how far a captain might go in endangering the lives of his crew as well as those of the rescuers. Captain Taylor was definitely wrong in his actions. He should have accepted the aid of the life-savers. By reversing that decision, he did a disservice not only to his crew but to the men of the USLSS.

On the morning of 2 March 1913 a small schooner left Chincoteague bound for Albemarle Sound, North Carolina. Most of the coastal residents on the Eastern Shore knew the schooner—the sixty-four-year-old coaster *Laura Tompkins*. The two-masted schooner only had a crew of two, Captain Dennard M. Merritt and his helper, a black man named Samuel Holden. The captain charted his course to Norfolk, the shortest but not the safest route. Instead of staying close to the beach until they reached any one of several inlets to the south, Captain Merritt took the old sixteen-ton schooner directly out into open sea. He planned to bypass the Cobb Island Inlet sea buoy three miles seaward. The weather cooperated for most of the day until late afternoon when the winds increased from the northwest. As the winds grew stronger, the *Laura Tompkins* moved farther away from the shelter of the land, and the heavy seas began to batter the old schooner more and more.

The Cobb Island Life-Saving Station lookout saw the *Tompkins* and recognized her on the afternoon of 2 March. She was last seen about sunset tacking northward and shifting her sails. Since there was no signal of distress, the lookout could only assume that she was still on her northeast heading as darkness came. While everything appeared normal to the station lookout, what actually happened was indeed a different matter. Captain Merritt himself wasn't sure exactly what caused the schooner to sink, but he knew it happened fast. Merritt figured he was about five miles from the Cobb Island Station. "I could see the buildings, but can't say I could see the beach."[9] He knew he hadn't struck anything that would cause the schooner to sink. In the formal investigation conducted by Assistant Inspector J. C. Cantwell of the U.S. Life-Saving Service's Sixth District, Merritt described what took place on board the *Laura Tompkins* while they were under observation from the Cobb Island Station:

> I floated a batteau off the deck, which was now careened over about forty-five degrees, and at this moment the air in the schooner blew off the hatches and a flood of water capsized the batteau. I called to Sam to get to the masthead, as the vessel quickly settled to the bottom. We swam to the main rigging and climbed to the crosstrees, where we lashed ourselves. The Negro was so frightened he was of very little aid to me and I had to lash him and myself also.[10]

Fortunately for the two men, the water was so shallow that as the *Tompkins* rested on the bottom, the masts were still several feet above the surface. Although the temperature was above freezing, the "chill factor," with a strong wind blowing had to be well below freezing. Merritt was lucky to have had his oilskins on, but Holden had on no outer garments. He was clothed only in his shirt, pants, and shoes. The two men were drenched as the schooner pitched and rolled, dipping them into the icy winter Atlantic. Merritt said that Holden died within three hours; Merritt remained in the rigging throughout the night, and the following day and night until about 10:00 A.M. on the morning of 4 March. Hanging on to the spreaders of the main rigging, he was able to stay alive for nearly forty hours. During this time he had no food or water and was constantly drenched.

Early on the morning of 3 March the Cobb Island lookout discovered a strange object at sea which none of the life-savers could identify. They decided it was either a buoy adrift or a piece of a floating navy target. The Cobb Island Keeper, called to the lookout tower, examined the object through his field glasses, but was unable to further identify the object which was, in fact, Captain Merritt lashed to the mast of the *Laura Tompkins*. The next day was the station's regular boat drill day, and Keeper Andrews took the motor surfboat out to look at the object in the water. At 7:30 A.M. on 4 March Keeper Andrews rescued Captain Merritt, his forty-hour ordeal over at last.

Keeper Andrews sent a telegram to the Life-Saving Service headquarters in Washington, stating simply that the schooner *Laura Tompkins* had sunk ten miles southeast of his station, that the Captain had been taken off the masthead, and that one man had drowned. This prompted the Assistant Inspector of the Sixth District to make an official investigation, as was the case in any shipwreck in which there was loss of life. However, a news item appearing in the *Washington Post* on 10 March 1913 indicated that perhaps the life-savers had not done all that was possible or had not responded quickly enough to the plight of those on board the schooner. Another investigation was ordered and again the Assistant Inspector returned to the Cobb Island Station and interviewed the keeper and his crew.

The results of the official investigation were that there was no evidence which showed any neglect or inattention to duty at the time of the foundering of the schooner. The Cobb Island life-savers were powerless to know of conditions on board since no signal of distress was visible. The vessel was under observation until darkness fell, and there were no signs of unusual activity. However, the investigation found that Keeper Andrews was guilty of not acting in the best interest of the service when he failed to investigate the strange and suspicious object in the water on 3 March. His action showed a lack of initiative and his failure to act promptly added to the suffering of Captain Merritt. Also, since Keeper Andrews failed to notify the Revenue Cutter Service of a sunken wreck in the path of navigation, the investigation found Andrews in direct disobedience to United States Life-Saving Service Regulations. Keeper Andrews also ignored Captain Merritt's request to have the revenue cutter *Onondaga* called to haul his schooner into shoal waters.

For both his failure to act more promptly and for the infractions of the regulations, Keeper Andrews was censured. At the same time, Assistant Inspector Cantwell asked for leniency on Keeper Andrews's behalf. He stated that Andrews's long, thirty years of an honorable career were unblemished, and his age of sixty years could very well have contributed to his lack of initiative. To defend Andrews's actions further, a study of the testimony in the investigation revealed no evidence that connected the mysterious object in the water to the schooner sighted the night before. And in defense of Andrews, it must also be stated that the aging *Laura Tompkins* carried no distress signal of any kind, not even flares, which by this time were standard aboard any vessel. Since the *Tompkins* did not strike any object in the water, it could be concluded that her very old planking loosened or her seams opened because of the extreme stress which caused her to sink as quickly as she did. The sad fact remains that one man lost his life, needlessly, notwithstanding the actions of the men of the Life-Saving Service.

At 6:00 P.M. on 23 December 1913, the lookout at the Little Island Life-Saving Station reported to Keeper John W. Partridge that he thought there was a steamer ashore about one and one half miles south of the station. With fog so thick and the night so dark it was impossible to be sure if the vessel were stranded or simply at anchor. Keeper Partridge decided to wait until the south patrol returned to the station. The patrolman reported he had seen nothing of a stranded vessel, but the fog lifted a short time later to reveal the lights of one. The keeper immediately burned a Coston flare and sent a message to the Revenue Cutter Service requesting assistance. Keeper Partridge also sent a telegram to the General Superintendent of the Life-Saving Service in Washington explaining the situation (see illustration). The Little Island surfboat was hauled to a position abreast of the distressed steamer. Because the surf was extremely rough, the keeper decided to wait until daylight before attempting to launch the boat. High tide came shortly after daylight and allowed the steamer to float free before the surfboat was launched. The crew returned the surfboat and equipment to their station as the steamer proceeded under her own power, apparently undamaged. There had been no communication between the surfmen and the steamer.

A short while later William J. Stevens, the surfman on lookout at the Little Island Station, saw a steamship just to the south of the station at 6:00 A.M. on 24 December 1913. The ship ran so close to the shore that the lookout fired a Coston flare to warn her of danger. At 7:00 A.M. the north patrol from the False Cape Station, Thoms J. Barnes, returned and reported that a steamer was ashore more than three miles north of the station. The surfboat was launched and the False Cape crew went to the vessel's assistance. The steamer was the *Frieda*, the same steamer that had stranded the evening before near the Little Island Station. The

WESTERN UNION
TELEGRAM
THEO. N. VAIL, PRESIDENT
Form 168

RECEIVED AT Wyatt Building, Cor. 14th and F Sts., Washington, D. C. ALWAYS OPEN

205N CV 22 COLLECT AND D H GVT

LITTLE ISLAND L S S VIA CAPE HENRY VA DEC 23 1913

GENL SUPT LIFE SAVING SERVICE

WDC

UNKNOWN STEAMER ASHORE ONE HALF MILE SOUTH OF STATION CREW GOING TO

RESCUE   PARTRIDGE

1214AM24TH

Telegram from Keeper Partridge to Life-Saving Service headquarters
in Washington, D. C. Courtesy: The National Archives.

surfmen arrived at the steamer by 8:30 A.M. to find that a revenue cutter
and a tug were within sight. With the aid of those two vessels, the *Frieda*
was hauled out into deep water on the next high tide.

While this action took place in Virginia Beach, the reaction in
Washington, D.C. deserves mention. Keeper Partridge had sent an
initial telegram to the general superintendent, but had sent nothing
else—he had not followed the telegram with the required wreck report. It
was not until January 1914 that General Superintendent Kimball found
out exactly what had happened at Virginia Beach on the night of 23
December 1913. Kimball wrote to Keeper Partridge formally requesting
that Partridge submit the missing wreck report. Kimball stated:

> This office was in ignorance of the seriousness of the casualty
> reported (in the telegram) and of what the Service did, if anything,
> in the way of rescue or relief work.[11]

This was the first time that a formal report, i.e., a wreck report,
station log entry, or other required information, had to be requested
from a life-saving station keeper. The stranding of the *Frieda* was a
confusing incident but not as serious an infraction as that of the *Laura
Tompkins*. It can be assumed that the Little Island keeper failed to send

the wreck report because there was no direct involvement on the part of the Little Island crew. Had he not sent the telegram to Kimball in the first place, the wreck report filed by the False Cape Life-Saving Station the following day would have been sufficient.

In 1915 the United States Life-Saving Service merged with the Revenue Cutter Service, and the United States Coast Guard was formed. In the year following the wreck of the *Frieda* in December 1913 there were only six incidents reported on the coast of Virginia: three on the Eastern Shore and three on the coast of Virginia Beach. Of these six vessels three were schooners and two were steamships; one was a United States Navy destroyer. No lives were lost, and none of the vessels were total wrecks. The vessels required little assistance from the men of the Life-Saving Service.

The *Riversdale*, a 1,785-ton steamship which ran aground
half a mile north of the Little Island Life-Saving Station on
20 February 1914. Courtesy: Mariners' Museum.

The USS *Paulding*, a 742-ton destroyer which ran aground in Lynnhaven Inlet, about six miles west of the Cape Henry Life-Saving Station on 27 October 1914. Courtesy: Mariners' Museum.

Chapter 10

Conclusion

The United States Life-Saving Service meant more to Virginia than only the saving of lives and property. Within the five Life-Saving Stations on the coast of Virginia Beach lived the area's first full-time winter residents of any number. The Seatack/Virginia Beach Station was a hub of growth for what is now known as the Oceanfront, and it was from this hub that the isolated shore was transformed into the resort city of today by investors seeking to take advantage of the area's many natural resources. Shortly after the life-saving stations were built, hunt clubs were constructed which attracted the more adventuresome to be sure, but these clubs also introduced newcomers to the beauty and solitude of the shore as well as the varied and extensive wildlife. During the 1880s and 1890s, people from all points along the eastern seaboard and beyond were enjoying the seashore, which led to the construction of summer cottages by society's elite. The proximity of Virginia Beach to the population centers of the northeast quickly led entrepreneurs to build large hotels in the grand manner of the day. Those who built along the shores of Virginia Beach knew that even during the harsh winter weather their property would be secure under the watchful eyes of the patrolling surfmen.

The development of the Eastern Shore of Virginia, on the other hand, has not grown in proportion to that of Virginia Beach. The areas surrounding the life-saving stations were more desolate and inhospitable and more subject to extreme damage by harsh winter storms and the fall and spring hurricanes. The population centers along the Eastern Shore are on the Chesapeake Bay side of this rather large peninsula, where the fishing centers are located. It is a more protected area than that of the barrier islands where there is little to guard the land and the residents from winds and weather. The interior land of the Eastern Shore has long been dominated by farms which produce much of the fresh vegetables and poultry consumed by residents of the eastern seaboard. The barrier islands, still desolate and windswept, are now controlled for the most part by the National Park Service in order to conserve wildlife and to protect the beaches from erosion caused by the interference of the human population—its careless construction of homes and condominiums—and the contamination such interference brings with it.

The United States Life-Saving Service was devoted to the saving of property as well as lives. The surfmen did all that was within their power: they warned vessels of danger; they aided damaged vessels by manning the pumps, and sending for towing tugs; and they hauled cargo and personal belongings from wrecked vessels. The life-savers sometimes had to deal with stubbornness and lack of understanding on the part of the captains and crews of ships in distress. The Italian bark *Figogna* is a clear example of an inexcusable loss due to misunderstanding. Her captain would not agree to any assistance offered by the Life-Saving Service or the Revenue Cutter Service. Even with the language barrier taken into consideration, it is still hard to imagine any captain of a sinking vessel unwilling to accept aid. The life-savers were forced to watch the *Figogna* for two days before they were allowed to make trips to the bark to take the sailors to safety, rowing nearly twenty miles in the process, clearly showing their devotion to duty. Of the 184 disasters that occurred along the shores of Virginia Beach from 1875 to 1915 only 46 vessels were declared total losses. The *Figogna,* due to the actions of her captain, is included in that total. Of the 383 incidents recorded on the Eastern Shore during that same period, 174 were total losses.

In some instances it mattered little what action was taken by the life-savers. The weather played a vital role in all but a very small number of incidents. The main weather condition which caused the majority of vessels to wreck was the northeaster, a combination of heavy seas, high winds just below hurricane force, and rain accompanied sometimes by blinding sleet or snow. In Virginia Beach alone there were 68 incidents in which a northeaster was the primary cause of the wreck. Fog was second only to the northeaster in the number of wrecks caused. The fog at times was so dense that it completely obliterated any and all navigational aids, and captains had to sail on their dead reckoning, which more times than not put them in danger of stranding their vessels.

Today it is difficult to imagine the perils seamen had to deal with during the late nineteenth and early twentieth centuries. The coastal merchant fleet as well as deepwater traders carried their cargoes to ports along the eastern seaboard of the United States and to ports all over the world throughout the year. They sailed with little technical knowledge of weather changes, without updated or reliable charts, and with few navigational aids on board. The Atlantic seaboard was well covered with lighthouses during this time; still, most crews and vessels depended upon the dead reckoning and experience of their captains. Many of the vessels that stranded along the shores of Virginia were "coasters" that hugged the shore when sailing south to avoid the northerly flowing Gulf Stream. These vessels sailed dangerously close to shore and when weather conditions changed abruptly, a large number of these vessels were found grounded or stranded on the shore.

The vast majority of the surfmen of the USLSS performed their duties flawlessly and were well trained in the use of equipment at hand. Whether it was warning a vessel of danger, serving as station lookout, patrolling the beaches in all weather conditions, or launching the surfboat into heavy breakers in a raging snowstorm these men courageously served humanity. As the population along the coastline of Virginia grew so did the responsibilties of the surfmen. They reported fires and helped put them out, kept a watchful eye on the community in general, and also acted as lifeguards along Virginia Beach in the summer season.

Over the forty-year time span of this study, stranded steam-powered vessels came to outnumber stranded sailing vessels. Unlike the sailing vessels, there was no loss of life on any steam-powered vessel wrecked or stranded on the shores of Virginia.

The waning years of the age of sail also witnessed the gradual decline in the need for the Life-Saving Service. In 1915 when the Life-Saving Service merged with the Revenue Cutter Service to form the United States Coast Guard, there were few sailing vessels to be seen from the shores of Virginia. Their majestic and graceful lines became only memories in the minds of some of the first rugged and resolute residents along the coast of Virginia—the men of the United States Life-Saving Service.

Appendix

The following tables provide an index of the vessels that wrecked or required the assistance of the United States Life-Saving Service between the years the USLSS began operations and the United States Coast Guard was established. Each listing included has been thoroughly documented from the Annual Reports of the United States Life-Saving Service and from the United States Coast Guard records in the National Archives (see Bibliography).

The first table, presented in chronological sequence by year, month, and day, indicates where the wreck took place in relationship to a particular lifesaving station. It also indicates the name and type of vessel, the number of lives lost/saved, and the value in dollars of the vessel and cargo lost.

The second table, presented in alphabetical order by name of vessel, provides the date of the wreck, tonnage, master, home port, origin and destination of voyage, cargo, and the dollar value of the vessel and cargo. (All unnamed vessels are placed at the beginning of the alphabetical listing.)

Abbreviations used in the tables are listed below:

Vessels

Bg	Brig	Sb	sailboat
Bgtn	brigantine	Sch	schooner
Bk	bark	Schbg	schooner barge
Bktn	barkentine	Sl	sloop
Dest	destroyer	SS	steamship
Lch	launch	Yl	yawl
Mtrl	motor launch	Yt	yacht
S	sailing ship		

Stations

As Bc	Assateague Beach	Pa Bc	Parramore Beach
Cb Is	Cobb Island	Po Is	Popes Island
Cd Is	Cedar Island	Setk/Va Bc	Seatack/Virginia Beach
Cp Hn	Cape Henry		
DNM	Dam Neck Mills	Sm Is	Smith Island
Fs Cp	False Cape	Wa Bc	Wallops Beach
Hg Is	Hog Island	Wach	Wachapreague
Lt Is	Little Island	Ww	Wash Woods (North Carolina)
Me In	Metomkin Inlet		

159

Year/Mo/Day			Vessel	Type	Station	Location	Lives lost	Lives saved	$ value of vessel and cargo lost
1875	1	8	San Marcos	Ss	Fs Cp	4 mi S	0	66	All saved
1875	1	22	C. E. Scammell	Sch	Fs Cp	3 mi N	0	8	27,000
1875	2	17	Aurora Mills	Ss	Cp Hn	100 yds E	0	6	11,000
1875	12	7	N. C. Price	Sch	As Bc	.25 mi S	0	4	?
1875	12	18	Anthony Kelley	Sch	Hg Is	S Hog Island Shoal	0	4	Total loss
1876	1	12	Aeolus	Sch	Hg Is	E Hog Island Light	0	3	?
1876	2	18	William H. VanName	Sch	Sm Is	Smith Island Point	0	6	?
1876	2	20	Ralph Howes	Sch	Sm Is	Isaac Shoal	0	6	200
1876	3	28	S. E. Barnes	Sch	Cd Is	.25 mi SE	0	5	?
1876	3	28	Angie Predmore	Sch	Hg Is	E. Hog Island Light	0	6	?
1876	6	30	George F. Wright	Sch	As Bc	Assawoman Inlet	0	5	All saved
1876	12	9	Fannie K. Shaw	Sch	Cp Hn	100 yds E	0	9	4,500
1877	1	17	Carpione	Bk	DNM	1.25 mi N	0	14	9,800
1877	1	20	Delphin	Sch	Cb Is	Cobb Island	0	7	200
1877	1	20	Lilla	Bk	Cp Hn	?	0	13	Total loss
1877	1	24	H. Prescott	Sch	As Bc	Ship Shoal	0	6	230
1877	1	27	George L. Treadwell	Scj	As Bc	Chincoteague Shoal	0	5	Total loss
1877	2	18	Alice Ida	Sch	Cd Is	Outer bar Metomkin Inlet	0	6	300
1877	3	22	Winchester	S	Cp Hn	"Near" Cape Henry	0	27	?
1877	3	26	Pantser	Bk	Cp Hn	"Off" Cape Henry	0	27	All saved
1877	3	26	Galathea	Bk	Sm Is	S end Myrtle Island	0	12	Total loss
1877	5	20	Armenia Bartlett	Sch	Hg Is	Little Machipongo Bar	0	6	Total loss
1877	5	24	Mary Wood	Sch	Hog Is	Rose Island Bar	0	4	Total loss
1877	11	18	James Anderson	Sch	Cd Is	1 mi ESE	0	3	Total loss
1877	11	25	Ossipee	Bg	As Bc	7.5 mi S	2	7	Total loss
1877	11	25	Frank Jameson	Sch	Sm Is	100 yds E	5	1	Total loss
1877	12	1	Jacob T. Alburgher	Sch	Cd Is	1.5 mi SE	0	7	7,000
1877	12	3	Winged Racer	Sch	Cb Is	1.75 mi ESE	0	8	Total loss
1878	1	4	Montevue	Sch	Cb Is	S end Wreck Island	0	7	Total loss

Year/Mo/Day			Vessel	Type	Station	Location	Lives lost	Lives saved	$ value of vessel and cargo lost
1878	1	4	Osborn Curtis	Sch	As Bc	1.25 mi SW	0	4	500
1878	1	4	Francisco Bella Gamba	Bk	Cp Hn	.5 ьi N	0	11	Total loss
1878	1	6	J. J. Spencer	Sch	Hg Is	1.25 mi SE	0	19	Total loss
1878	1	23	Southern Belle	Bk	DNM	1.5 mi S	0	19	11,000
1878	1	24	West Wind	Bk	Cb Is	SE end Carter's Shoal	0	10	?
1878	2	4	Jennie Sweeny	Bktn	Cd Is	.75 mi SE	0	11	20,000
1878	2	9	Guiseppe Messone	Bk	Cp Hn	100 yds N	0	14	?
1878	2	27	Mary A. Harmon	Sch	Sm Is	9 mi W	0	8	?
1878	3	7	North Point	Ss	As Bc	.75 mi S Ragged Point	0	20	Total loss
1878	3	25	Julius Webb	Sch	Cd Is	2 mi SE	0	6	?
1878	3	28	Nipote	Bktn	DNM	3 mi N	0	10	?
1878	5	22	Antonia	Ss	Cp Hn	.5 mi N	0	27	All saved
1878	10	22	A. S. Davis	S	Setk	1.5 mi N	19	1	Total loss
1878	11	17	Franklin	Bk	Fs Cp	6 mi N False Cape	0	?	?
1878	12	1	Peerless	Sch	Sm Is	5 mi WSW	0	8	Total loss
1878	12	2	Flora Curtis	Sch	As Bc	3 mi	0	6	Total loss
1878	12	23	Emma G. Edwards	Sch	As Bc	2 mi S Turner's Shoal	0	8	Total loss
1878	12	28	Tunis	Ss	Cp Hn	1 mi S	0	0	All saved
1879	1	28	Water Witch	Bgtn	?	4.5 mi NE	0	8	?
1879	3	2	Admiral	Bk	Fs Cp	1 mi S	0	14	Total loss
1879	3	11	Hattie Mary	Sl	As Bc	New Inlet Bar	?	0	200
1879	3	31	James M. Vance	Sch	Cp Hn/ Setk	2.5 mi N	0	6	Total loss
1879	10	13	(Unnamed)	Yl	Cd Is	.5 mi N	2	1	?
1879	10	20	Ellie Bodine	Sch	Sm Is	4.5 mi S	0	6	?
1879	11	2	Hansa	S	Cp Hn/ Setk	1 mi N	0	21	All saved
1879	11	3	W. E. Heard	Bk	Cp Hn	"off" Cape Henry	0	13	All saved
1879	11	13	James Ford	Sch	Sm Is	8 mi S	0	9	?
1879	11	24	Ellie	Sch	As Bc	.75 mi S	0	3	?
1879	11	26	Jason	Bk	Hg Is	1.5 mi SE	0	12	Total loss
1879	12	25	Ellie Bodine	Sch	As Bc	.25 mi S; .25 mi offshore	0	?	?
1880	1	8	Alice Lea	Bgtn	Cd Is	3.5 mi S	0	9	Total loss
1880	1	11	Ada M. Hallock	Sch	Hg Is	?	0	4	Total loss
1880	2	1	J. F. Knapp	Sl	As Bc	2.5 mi SW	?	0	?
1880	3	11	Osborn Curtis	Sch	As Bc	3 mi S	?	0	All saved

Year/Mo/Day			Vessel	Type	Station	Location	Lives lost	Lives saved	$ value of vessel and cargo lost
1880	4	13	Charles H. Malleson	Sch	As Bc	3.5 mi S; .5 mi offshore	?	?	?
1880	4	16	Hannah Morris	S	Fs Cp	1 mi N	?	?	?
1880	5	9	Swiftsure	Ss	Sm Is	4 mi SE	?	0	?
1880	8	18	North Carolina	Bk	Lt Is	.5 mi N	0	17	All saved
1880	9	25	Woodruff Sims	Sch	Setk/ DNM	1 mi S Setk	0	6	Total loss
1880	10	22	Giambattista Primo	Bk	HgIs/ Cb Is	SE Hog Island Shoal	0	13	Total loss
1880	11	5	Sandringham	Ss	Cp Hn	250 yds S	0	18	5,000
1880	11	7	Sallie Coursey	Sch	Sm Is	4 mi SW	0	6	Total loss
1800	11	14	John S. Higgins	Sch	Cd Is	1.5 mi S	0	3	Total loss
1880	11	22	Maggie E. Gray	Sch	Sm Is	E end Isaac Shoal	0	8	All saved
1880	12	7	Robert W. Brown	Sch	Cb Is	2.5 mi E	0	7	Total loss
1880	12	19	Madora Francis	Sch	As Bc	3 mi SW Fox Shoal	0	5	All saved
1880	12	29	Elizabeth White	Sch	Cb Is	Carter's Shoal	0	5	Total loss
1880	12	29	Elysia A.	Sch	Cd Is	Dawson Shoal	0	7	2,700
1881	1	2	J. Ricardo Jova	Sch	Cd Is	2 mi SE	0	7	Total loss
1881	1	11	Nettie Murphy	S	Cp Hn	100 yds N	0	20	5,000
1881	1	20	Kwasind	Bk	Cd Is	N end Parramore Beach	0	17	Total loss
1881	1	26	John Eills	Bk	Cb Is	Carter's Shoal	0	12	All saved
1881	1	28	D. Ellis	Sch	As Bc	Turner's Shoal	0	4	Total loss
1881	2	8	Rosalie Starita	Bg	Cp Hn	1 mi N	0	12	All saved
1881	2	10	Joanna H. Cann	Bk	Cp Hn/ Setk	2.5 mi S	0	17	Total loss
1881	3	2	L. S. Levering	Sch	Cp Hn	?	0	7	400
1881	3	3	Henrietta	Sch	Sm Is	Isaac Shoal	0	6	300
1881	3	10	William Allen	Sch	As Bc	SW side Ship Shoal	0	7	All saved
1881	3	28	Mabel Thomas	Sch	As Bc	Turner's Shoal	0	7	100
1881	4	21	Dictator	Bk	Lt Is/ Fs Cp	Halfway between stations	0	13	?
1881	5	23	David F. Keeling	Sch	Cp Hn	100 yds E	0	7	3,000
1881	8	7	William Allen	Sch	Cd Is	Cedar Inlet	0	9	Total loss
1881	9	4	Scindia	Ss	Hg Is	Outer bar Hog Island	0	33	800
1881	10	5	Adelia F. Cohen	Sch	Sm Is	Smith Island	0	5	150
1881	10	9	Mary Ann	Sl	Cb Is	Cobb Island	0	2	All saved
1881	10	19	Zulu Chief	Sl	Hg Is	Hog Island Bar	0	6	50
1881	10	22	G. B. Claxom	Sl	Cd Is	New Inlet Bar	0	3	Total loss

Year/Mo/Day	Vessel	Type	Station	Location	Lives lost	Lives saved	$ value of vessel and cargo lost
1881 10 30	Katie Collins	Sch	As Bc	Assawoman Beach	0	8	8,500
1881 11 4	John McDonnell	Sch	Cb Is/ Sm Is	Carter's Bar	0	6	Total loss
1881 11 16	Dauntless	Sch	Cb Is	Halfway between Cobb Island and Bone Island	0	3	All saved
1881 11 23	James W. Brown	Sch	Cp Hn	7 mi W	0	7	Total loss
1881 12 9	J. H. Chapman	Sl	Hg Is	4.25 mi N	0	3	Total loss
1881 12 14	Agostino C.	Bg	Sm Is	Smith Island Beach	0	10	Total loss
1881 12 15	Ocean Star	Sl	Cb Is	Cobb Island	0	3	All saved
1881 12 22	Carrie Hall Lister	Sch	Cd Is	1.5 mi S	0	7	All saved
1882 1 9	Sagitta	Bk	Cb Is	Cobb Island Inlet	0	12	?
1882 1 17	Nederland	Ss	Cp Hn	200 yds N	0	34	All saved
1882 1 29	Elizabeth A. Baizley	Sch	Cb Is	Carter's Bar	0	7	17,300
1882 1 31	Dolly Varden	Sch	As Bc	3.5 mi ENE	0	3	Total loss
1882 2 21	Dauntless	Sl	As Bc	3.5 mi SW	2	1	Total loss
1882 2 24	Pearl Nelson	Sch	Fs Cp	"Off" False Cape	0	6	All saved
1882 3 1	Memento	?	Hg Is	Outer bar Hog Island	0	2	600
1882 3 1	Alvira	Sch	As Bc	Hammock Beach	0	5	All saved
1882 4 27	Mary C.	Sch	Hg Is	Hog Island	0	5	All saved
1882 5 5	Maggie Bell	?	Wa Bc	Wallops Beach	0	2	Total loss
1882 7 17	Annie E. Moore	Sch	Sm Is	1.25 mi NE	0	5	8,350
1882 8 7	B. H. Jones	Sch	Sm Is	8 mi SW by S	0	10	250
1882 11 20	George White	Sch	Wach	1 mi NNW	0	4	All saved
1882 12 4	Maddalena Seconda	Bk	Wach	1 mi NE	0	12	2,000
1882 12 7	Pecora	Sch	Wach	2 mi SW	0	6	800
1882 12 7	Anthea Godfrey	Sch	Cb Is/ Sm Is	3.5 mi SE Cobb Island	0	6	1,000
1882 12 17	Gertrude T. Browning	Sch	Sm Is	5.5 mi SW	0	5	300
1882 12 30	Boston	Sch	Fs Cp	1.5 mi S	0	5	4,050
1883 1 7	Albert Dailey	Sch	Sm Is	3 mi NE by E	2	7	Total loss
1883 1 12	Shekinah	Sch	Cb Is	SW end Cobb Island	0	5	All saved
1883 2 3	Carrie Hall Lister	Sch	Wach	2 mi SE	0	5	All saved
1883 2 28	Figogna	Bk	Lt Is	1 mi ENE	0	14	?

Year/Mo/Day			Vessel	Type	Station	Location	Lives lost	Lives saved	$ value of vessel and cargo lost
1883	3	7	*Wolverton*	Bktn	As Bc	5 mi SE	0	10	Total loss
1883	3	11	*Jane Emson*	Sch	Cb Is/ Sm Is	Myrtle Island	0	7	Total loss
1883	3	13	*H. J. Bishop*	Sl	Hg Is/ Cb Is	S Hog Island Inlet	0	3	All saved
1883	3	21	*Vienna*	Sl	Hg Is	SE Rogue's Island	0	3	All saved
1883	4	30	*Edith Fowle*	Sl	As Bc	2.5 mi SSW	0	4	50
1883	8	19	*Amaryllis*	Ss	Cb Is	N end Carter's Bar	0	22	?
1883	10	6	*A. M. Payne*	Sch	Sm Is	Isaac Shoal	0	5	Total loss
1883	10	18	*Madora Francis*	Sch	Hg Is	SE bar Hog Inlet	0	3	All saved
1883	10	18	*Henry Doremus*	Sch	Wach	Metomkin Bar	0	4	1,400
1883	11	1	*Ella T. Little*	Sch	Hg Is	Hog Island Inlet bar	0	7	?
1883	11	11	*Two Sisters*	Sch	Cb Is	Halfway between Cob Island and Bone Island	0	3	All saved
1883	12	1	*Undine*	Sl	Wach	Dawson Shoal	0	2	All saved
1883	12	16	*Lena Hunter*	Sch	Sm Is	Isaac Shoal	0	6	All saved
1883	12	20	*T. W. Wiltbank*	Sl	Hg Is	SE bar Rogue's Island	0	3	?
1883	12	21	*Olga*	Bk	Hg Is/ Cb Is	Outer bar Hog Island	0	13	All saved
1883	12	21	*Chiswick*	Ss	Hg Is	Hog Island Shoal	0	22	500
1883	12	23	*Frank*	Sl	As Bc	E Assateague Beach	0	4	All saved
1883	12	23	*Lillie A. Warford*	Sch	As Bc	S Shoal Chincoteague Bar	0	6	All saved
1884	1	5	*William T. Elmer*	Sch	Hg Is/ Cb Is	Hog Island Shoal	0	5	Total loss
1884	1	10	*Lizzie Jane*	Sl	As Bc	.75 mi E	0	3	Total loss
1884	1	15	*Lewis A. Rommell*	Sch	Lt Is	2 mi N	0	6	Total loss
1884	1	26	*Albert C. Paige*	Sch	DNM	2.25 mi N	0	7	Total loss
1884	2	28	*Samuel Fish*	Sch	Cb Is/ Sm Is	Carter's Bar	0	7	Total loss
1884	3	30	*Celia*	Sch	Cb Is	2 mi ENE	0	5	Total loss
1884	3	30	*Daniel S. Williams, Jr.*	Sch	Cp Hn	2.25 mi WNW	0	9	5,000

Year/Mo/Day			Vessel	Type	Station	Location	Lives lost	Lives saved	$ value of vessel and cargo lost
1884	4	4	Anne Dole	Sch	Wach	Dawson Shoal	0	6	Total loss
1884	4	4	H. M. Somers	Sch	Pa Bc	Cheesewreck Shoals	0	3	All saved
1884	4	10	Ocean Star	Sch	As Bc	Ship Shoal	0	3	300
1884	4	27	Fred	Sl	Wach/ Pa Bc	NE Parramore Beach	0	0	300
1884	5	26	B. L. Burt	Sch	Sm Is	Isaac Shoal	0	8	All saved
1884	5	26	Helen Hasbrouck	Sch	Sm Is	Isaac Shoal	0	7	All saved
1884	6	17	Jas. B. Johnson	Sch	As Bc	Chincoteague Beach	0	10	All saved
1884	7	8	Bateau Sharpley	?	Pa Bc	.5 mi N	0	2	12
1884	7	23	Bradshaw	Sl	Wa Bc	Assawoman Inlet	0	2	Total loss
1884	8	18	Ida C. Schodcraft	Sch	Wach	Metomkin Inlet	0	17	All saved
1884	8	23	Flying Scud	Sl	Wach	Metomkin Inlet	0	3	Total loss
1884	9	17	J. H. Crittenden	Sl	Sm Is	Little Inlet	0	3	Total loss
1884	10	10	Lizzie	Sch	Wach	Parramore Beach	0	5	All saved
1884	10	14	Sarah Shubert	Sch	Pa Bc	Stingray Point	0	5	Total loss
1884	10	24	Lillie A. Warfield	Sch	Sm Is	4.5 ENE	0	5	550
1884	11	6	John M. Rogers	Sl	As Bc	.5 mi SE	0	2	50
1884	11	15	A. D. Scull	Sch	Hg Is	Outer bar Hog Island	0	7	Total loss
1884	11	26	Thomas and William Dickerson	Sch	Wach	Metomkin Bar	0	5	All Saved
1884	12	9	Joseph J. Comstock	Sch	Sm Is	Cape Charles Point	0	3	2,170
1884	12	15	Peter J. Hart	Sch	As Bc	1.5 mi SW	0	4	2,800
1884	12	15	Bedabedee	Sch	Wa Bc	Williams Shoal	0	6	2,000
1884	12	27	Lena	Bk	Hg Is	SE bar Hog Island	8	2	Total loss
1885	1	9	Ivanhoe	Ss	Wa Bc	Chincoteague Inlet	0	8	All saved
1885	3	22	A. M. Bailey	Sch	Setk	1 mi N	0	4	Total loss
1885	4	12	R. B. Leeds	Sch	As Bc	Chincoteague	0	3	200
1885	5	21	Rescue	Sch	Wa Bc	Chincoteague Bar	0	4	Total loss
1885	7	1	Emma D. Endicott	Sch	Hg Is/ Cb Is	Outer bar Hog Island	0	8	5,600
1885	9	20	Sallie Solomon	Sch	Sm Is	Isaac Shoal	0	4	Total loss
1885	10	24	Skylark	Sch	Cb Is	N end Carter's Bar	0	7	Total loss

Year/Mo/Day			Vessel	Type	Station	Location	Lives lost	Lives saved	$ value of vessel and cargo lost
1885	10	29	*Annie*	Sl	Cb Is	Sand Shoal Inlet	0	1	All saved
1885	12	20	*James Boyce*	Sch	Wach/ Pa Bc	Dawson Shoal	0	8	All saved
1885	12	21	*Harriet E. Loundes*	Sl	As Bc	.75 mi SE	0	3	All saved
1885	12	25	*Davy Crockett*	Sl	Setk	1.25 mi N	0	2	Total
1885	12	27	*Lena Hunter*	Sch	Cp Hn	1.75 mi S	0	7	Total loss
1886	1	9	*Lillie Ernestine*	Sch	As Bc	1 mi SE	0	5	1,000
1886	1	17	*Serpho*	Ss	Lt Is	3 mi S	0	22	All saved
1886	2	5	*Emma Aery*	Sch	Cb Is	Carter's Bar	0	7	Total loss
1886	2	25	*Rebecca J.*	Sl	Wach	S end Cedar Island	0	2	Total loss
1886	3	2	*Mary Ann*	Sl	Cb Is	500 yds NE	0	3	All saved
1886	3	2	*Leona*	Sch	Hg Is	Outer bar Hog Island	0	6	Total loss
1886	3	3	*Two Brothers*	Sl	Pa Bc	1.75 mi NNW	0	2	All saved
1886	3	15	*John M. Price*	Sl	Hg Is	Tom's Inlet Bar	0	4	All saved
1886	3	24	*A. F. Kindberg*	Sch	Wach/ Pa Bc	Dawson Shoal Wachapreague Inlet	0	6	1,800
1886	4	2	*Julie A. Roe*	Sl	Wa Bc/ As Bc	Chincoteague Inlet Bar	0	4	Total loss
1886	4	7	*W. T. Sherman*	Sl	Wach	Wachapreague Bar	0	3	75
1886	4	8	*May Queen*	Bk	Lt Is	2 mi N	0	8	9,800
1886	4	16	*Bertha A. Watts*	Sch	Po Is	2 mi SW	0	6	Total loss
1886	6	2	*J. C. Wood*	Sl	As Bc	New Inlet Bar	0	4	All saved
1886	8	5	*Edwin J. Palmer*	Sch	As Bc	Williams Shoal	0	6	Total loss
1886	10	9	*James E. Kelsey*	Sch	Wa Bc	2 mi NE	0	5	All saved
1886	10	23	*Howard N. Johnson*	Sch	Cb Is	SE point Cobb Island	0	5	?
1886	10	24	*Howard N. Johnson*	Sch	Cb Is	SE point Cobb Island	0	11	Total loss
1886	10	30	*John Gibson*	Ss	Hg Is	Outer bar Hog Island	0	16	285
1886	10	31	*Fred*	Sl	Wach	N end Parra- more Beach	0	2	All saved
1886	11	19	*Clapeyron*	Ss	Fs Cp	Outer shoal False Cape	0	27	All saved
1886	12	3	*Bertram L. Townsend*	Sch	Hg Is	Outer bar Hog Island	0	9	600
1886	12	4	*Grace Leigh*	Sl	Sm Is	1.5 mi W	0	2	All saved
1886	12	5	*Pangussett*	Sch	Setk	.5 mi S	0	6	3,900
1886	12	5	*Emily A. Bartle*	Sch	Wa Bc	.5 mi S	0	6	Total loss
1886	12	6	*Annie F. Conlon*	Sch	Fs Cp	3 mi N	0	8	500

Year/Mo/Day	Vessel	Type	Station	Location	Lives lost	Lives saved	$ value of vessel and cargo lost
1886 12 12	Lizzie Jane	Sl	As Bc	2 mi SSE	0	2	All saved
1886 12 17	Nelson E. Newberry	Sch	Sm Is	Outer Middle Ground	0	8	35
1886 12 30	Pirate	Ss	Cp Hn	2 mi NW	0	16	All saved
1886 12 30	Lady Maud	Sl	Wach	Dawson Shoal	0	2	All saved
1887 1 8	Elizabeth	S	Lt Is	3 mi N	22	0	25,810
1887 2 18	Mary L. Vetra	Sch	Sm Is	Smith Island Inlet	0	2	All saved
1887 3 8	Rhein	Ss	Hg Is	Outer bar Hog Island	0	1,023	25,000
1887 3 20	R. F. Hastings	Sch	Hg Is	2.5 mi SW	0	7	All saved
1887 3 22	Samuel H. Walker	Sch	Hg Is	Outer bar Hog Island	0	9	All saved
1887 4 5	Nellie Potter	Sch	Cp Hn	6 mi NW	0	6	3,800
1887 4 6	Harry C. Shepard	Sch	Pa Bc	Little Machipongo Bar	0	9	All saved
1887 4 7	George L. Garlick	Sch	As Bc	Chincoteague Bar	0	2	All saved
1887 4 26	John H. Savage	Sl	As Bc	1 mi SE	0	2	All saved
1887 4 28	William C. Pruitt	Sl	As Bc	1 mi SE	0	3	All saved
1887 6 3	James E. Kelsey	Sch	Wa Bc	3.5 mi NNE	0	5	1,650
1887 7 15	Nellie Blanche	Sch	Wach	Wachapreague Bar	0	5	All saved
1887 7 21	A. H. Quimby	Sch	Cb Is	Carter's Bar	0	5	All saved
1887 9 18	Hygeia	Ss	Cb Is	.75 mi SE	0	0	All saved
1887 9 23	Ellen Holgate	Sch	Wach	Dawson Shoal	0	5	1,600
1887 10 17	Gertrude	Sch	Hg Is	Machipongo Inlet	0	0	All saved
1887 10 31	Manantico	Sch	Setk	1.25 mi N	2	3	?
1887 10 31	Mary D. Cranmer	Sch	DNM	1.75 mi S	0	6	Total loss
1887 10 31	Carrie Holmes	Sch	Cp Hn	1 mi N	0	7	Total loss
1887 10 31	Harriet Thomas	Sch	Setk	1 mi S	0	7	Total loss
1887 11 9	Macauley	S	Cp Hn	550 yds NE	0	19	All saved
1887 11 17	Bessie Morris	Sch	Fs Cp	2.5 mi SSE	0	7	Total loss
1887 11 20	Deutschland	S	Lt Is	2 mi SSE	0	19	?
1887 12 12	Lillie A. Warford	Sch	Wa Bc	3 mi NE	0	6	All saved
1887 12 21	Samuel Fillmore	Sch	Hg Is	1.5 mi W	0	3	All saved
1888 1 1	Ada Gray	Bk	Lt Is	2.75 mi SE	0	10	Total loss
1888 1 28	Florence Kellinger	Sch	Cb Is	Cobb Island Bar	0	3	All saved
1888 1 31	Levi Lewis	Sch	Sm Is	Smith Island Inlet	0	3	All saved
1888 2 12	Gray Eagle	Bk	Lt Is/ Fs Cp	2.75 mi S by Little Island	0	11	7,200
1888 2 13	Earnmoor	Ss	Wach	Metomkin Inlet	0	36	All saved

Year/Mo/Day			Vessel	Type	Station	Location	Lives lost	Lives saved	$ value of vessel and cargo lost
1888	3	8	John Young	Sch	Wach	Dawson Shoal	0	5	All saved
1888	3	12	Peerless	Sl	Sm Is	Isaac Shoal	0	2	25
1888	3	12	Florence Kellinger	Sch	Sm Is	2.5 mi SW by W	0	2	100
1888	3	29	Lizzie Jane	Sl	Wach	Dawson Shoal	0	2	All saved
1888	4	15	Anna Homan	Sl	Wach	3 mi ESE	0	3	All saved
1888	4	23	James Rothwell	Sch	As Bc/ Wa Bc	Williams Shoal	0	7	All saved
1888	5	15	Olustree	Bk	Sm Is	Isaac Shoal	0	8	Total loss
1888	7	13	Lady of the Lake	Sch	Wa Bc/ Pa Bc	Dawson Shoal	0	4	Total loss
1888	9	7	Esk	Sch	Pa Bc	2 mi S	0	7	Total loss
1888	11	25	Lizzie Jane	Sl	Cb Is	500 yds N	0	3	All saved
1888	12	11	Morning Light	Sch	As Bc	.5 mi E	0	3	All saved
1888	12	15	J. W. Luce	Sl	Cb Is	Carter's Bar	0	4	All saved
1888	12	15	Little Falkenburg	Sch	Sm Is	Isaac Shoal	0	6	All saved
1888	12	22	Tillie G. Cruse	Sch	Wach/ Pa Bc	Wachapreague Bar	0	5	100
1888	12	22	B. L. Burt	Sch	Wach	Wachapreague Bar	0	9	All saved
1888	12	22	Frank G. Dow	Sch	Hg Is	SE bar Hog Island Shoal	0	8	250
1888	12	22	Ida L. Hull	Sch	Wach/ Pa Bc	Wachapreague Bar	0	8	All saved
1888	12	22	Josie R. Burt	Sch	Wach	?	0	8	All saved
1889	1	13	Lady Ellen	Sch	Hg Is	SE bar Hog Island Shoal	0	6	2,500
1889	2	1	Mary and Emma	Sl	Hg Is	200 yds NW	0	6	All saved
1889	2	18	E. L. Pettingill	Bk	DNM/ Setk	2 mi N Dam Neck Mills	0	19	All saved
1889	3	3	William B. Wood	Sch	Wa Bc	?	0	8	Total loss
1889	3	10	Stony Brook	Sch	Wa Bc/ Pa Bc	Dawson Shoal	0	5	500
1889	3	14	Agnes Barton	Bg	DNM	.25 mi N	6	4	Total loss
1889	3	15	G. W. Bentley	Sch	Cp Hn	1.25 mi S	0	6	Total loss
1889	3	20	Benjamin C. Terry	Sch	Fs Cp	.75 mi N	0	7	Total loss
1889	4	6	Challenge	Sl	Pa Bc	6.5 mi NW	0	8	25
1889	4	7	Minnie Sylvia	Sl	Cb Is	4 mi SSW	0	1	All saved
1889	4	7	Northampton	Sch	Setk	2.25 mi S	3	1	Total loss
1889	4	7	Benjamin F. Poole	Sch	Setk	.25 mi N	0	9	20,000
1889	4	7	E. K. Rayfield	Sch	Sm Is	1.25 mi NNE	0	3	All saved
1889	4	7	Emma F. Hart	Sch	Setk	.75 mi N	0	7	8,130
1889	4	7	J. O. Fitzgerald	S	Cb Is	1 mi W by S	0	2	225
1889	4	7	Levi Lewis	Sch	Sm Is	3.5 mi WSW	0	3	125

Year/Mo/Day			Vessel	Type	Station	Location	Lives lost	Lives saved	$ value of vessel and cargo lost
1889	4	12	Emma McAdam	Sch	Cb Is	Carter's Bar	0	5	All saved
1889	4	21	Sunshine	Ss	Hg Is	3 mi W	0	4	30
1889	6	18	Constellation	S	Cp Hn	1.75 mi NE	0	317	15,000
1889	8	10	Harry Doremus	Sch	Me In	Metomkin Bar	0	3	All saved
1889	8	25	Prohibition	Sl	As Bc	1 mi W	0	0	All saved
1889	9	12	Godrevy	Ss	Cp Hn	.75 mi N by E	0	23	11,900
1889	10	05	Amy Dora	Ss	Wach	Dawson Shoal	0	21	230,000
1889	10	22	Baltimore	Ss	Cp Hn	90 yds NE	0	51	42,000
1889	10	23	Frank O. Dame	Sch	Lt Is	2 mi N	0	10	8,000
1889	10	23	General Harrison	Sl	Cp Hn	3.5 mi W	0	?	?
1889	10	23	Henry P. Simmons	Sch	Fs Cp/ WW	1.5 mi NE Wash Woods	7	1	Total loss
1889	10	26	Welaka	Sch	Cp Hn	800 yds NE	0	7	15,000
1889	11	15	Lizzie Jane	Sl	Me In	S Metomkin Inlet	0	4	All saved
1889	11	17	Ordovic	Bk	Cp Hn	2 mi NW	0	14	All saved
1889	12	1	Richard Rhodes	Sl	Cb Is	.5 mi SE	0	3	All saved
1889	12	11	Frank	Sl	Cb Is	.5 mi SE	0	2	All saved
1889	12	13	Medora Francis	Sch	Hg Is	2 mi S	0	3	All saved
1889	12	30	Annie E. Pierce	Sch	Wa Bc/ As Bc	3.5 mi NE Wachapreague Beach	0	7	All saved
1890	1	27	Caroline Miller	Ss	Sm Is	Isaac Shoal	0	18	All saved
1890	1	29	Pettiquamscott	Sch	Sm Is	Isaac Shoal	0	5	Total loss
1890	2	8	Wyandotte	Sl	Setk	2 mi N	0	4	235
1890	2	21	Eva I. Shenton	Sch	Cb Is	.5 mi NW	0	5	All saved
1890	3	15	J. W. Arthur	Sl	Sm Is	Isaac Shoal	0	4	100
1890	4	19	Frank C. Pettis	Sch	Sm Is	Isaac Shoal	0	4	Total loss
1890	7	18	Lizzie Jane	S	As Bc	Fox Shoal	0	2	All saved
1890	8	30	(Unnamed fishing boat)	?	Me In	1 mi ESE	0	2	Total loss
1890	9	27	John R. Walters	Sch	As Bc	2.75 mi SW	0	3	20
1890	9	27	John Young	Sch	Cb Is	Carter's Bar	0	6	Total loss
1890	9	29	Hattie Perry	Sch	Cp Hn	1 mi SSE	0	7	Total loss
1890	10	15	Marvin P. White	Sch	Cb Is	100 yds NW	0	3	All saved
1890	11	6	Josie Smith	Sl	Wa Bc	1.5 mi NE	0	4	10
1890	11	18	Lehman Blew	Sch	Po Is	2.5 mi S	0	6	Total loss
1890	11	20	Daniel Brown	Sch	Cb Is	Carter's Bar	0	7	200
1890	11	22	Undine	Sl	Wach	.75 mi SW	0	4	All saved
1890	12	3	Marion	Sch	Cb Is	4 mi SSE	0	4	All saved
1890	12	7	Union	Sch	Hg Is	.5 mi SW	0	3	10
1890	12	11	George C. Wainwright	Sch	Cb Is	1 mi S	0	4	All saved

Year/Mo/Day			Vessel	Type	Station	Location	Lives lost	Lives saved	$ value of vessel and cargo lost
1890	12	26	Phoebe Ann	Sch	Me In	.5 mi WSW	0	5	All saved
1891	1	9	Phoebe	Sch	Sm Is	4 mi SW	0	3	Total loss
1891	1	13	Sussex	Sch	Cb Is	1 mi S	0	4	All saved
1891	1	19	Acuba	Ss	Cp Hn	1.5 mi N	0	22	All saved
1891	3	14	Mary C. Carroll	Sch	Wach	Dawson Shoal	0	6	Total loss
1891	3	15	C. C. Cruser	Sch	Sm Is	Isaac Shoal	0	6	All saved
1891	3	22	L. B. Chandler	Sch	Cb Is	.5 mi NW	0	2	All saved
1891	3	27	Dictator	Bk	Setk	1 mi N	7	10	Total loss
1891	4	14	Strathome	Bk	Cp Hn	1 mi E by S	0	14	All saved
1891	4	29	William M. Bird	Sch	Po Is	3 mi SSW	0	9	All saved
1891	5	27	Libbie P. Hallock	Sch	Sm Is	7 mi NE	0	4	Total loss
1891	8	26	E. S. Newins	Sch	Pa Bc	3.5 mi NE	0	5	Total loss
1891	9	8	Ada	Sl	Sm Is	Fisherman's Island	0	1	All saved
1891	10	10	Despatch	Ss	As Bc	2.5 mi E by N	0	79	Total loss
1891	10	12	Challenge	S	Wach	.5 mi SW	0	0	All saved
1891	10	14	Harvey M. Anderson	Sch	Hg Is	2 mi E	0	7	?
1891	11	29	Harriet S. Brooks	Sch	Wach/ Pa Bc	.75 mi S Wacha- preague	0	5	All saved
1891	11	29	John Hooper	Sch	Sm Is	?	0	5	Total loss
1891	12	29	(Unnamed)	?	As Bc	2 mi N	0	4	100
1892	1	7	Ashburne	Ss	Wach/ Pa Bc	5.5 mi S Wacha- preague	0	26	All saved
1892	1	12	Miranda	Ss	Po Is	4 mi SSW	0	22	All saved
1892	1	19	William Armstrong	Ss	Hg Is/ Cb Is	12 mi S ½ mi E Hog Island	0	26	All saved
1892	1	20	H. W. Race	Sch	Setk	.2 mi NE	0	4	4,800
1892	1	26	James D. Dewell	Sch	Cp Hn	.35 mi E	0	8	?
1892	2	6	Polynesian	Ss	Cp Hn/ Setk	.875 mi NE Cape Henry	0	53	?
1892	2	21	Govino	Ss	Cb Is	Carter's Bar	0	28	All saved
1892	2	22	San Albano	Ss	Hg Is	6 mi NE by E	1	26	Total loss
1892	2	29	William Phillips	Sch	Cp Hn	?	0	12	Total loss
1892	3	31	E. K. Wilson	Sch	Me In	Cedar Island	0	5	Total loss
1892	4	18	M. Luella Wood	Sch	C Hn	.6 mi E by S	0	8	All saved
1892	8	1	Thomas W. Waters	Sch	Hg Is	Hog Island Bar	0	6	Total loss
1892	12	20	A. P. Newell	Sch	Hg Is	Hog Island Bar	0	6	Total loss
1892	8	18	Castlefield	Ss	Fs Cp	2 mi ENE	0	22	All saved
1892	12	20	A. P. Newell	Sch	Hg Is	Hog Island Bar	0	6	Total loss
1892	12	20	Magellan	Sch	Sm Is/ Cb Is	8 mi NE Smith Island	1	5	Total loss
1892	12	20	Robert H. Parker	Sch	Sm Is	1 mi SE	0	7	Total loss
1892	12	24	Mary E. H. G. Dow	Sch	Sm Is	Middle Ground	0	10	Total loss

Year/Mo/Day			Vessel	Type	Station	Location	Lives lost	Lives saved	$ value of vessel and cargo lost
1893	1	1	Edith Berwind	Sch	Sm Is	6 mi S	1	8	Total loss
1893	3	24	L. B. Chandler	Sch	Hg Is	Outer bar Hog Island	0	4	Total loss
1893	4	11	Charles E. Balch	Sch	Fs Cp	1 mi NE	0	9	All saved
1893	4	20	North Star	Sch	Lt Is	?	0	10	Total loss
1893	4	27	Helen	Ss	Fs Cp	2.25 mi SE by S	0	29	All saved
1893	10	4	C. C. Davidson	Sch	Setk	2.5 mi N	0	5	5,950
1893	10	4	Wm. Applegarth	Sch	Setk	200 yds E	0	6	Total loss
1893	10	8	Thomas Thomas	Sch	Wa Bc	Fox Shoal	0	3	225
1893	10	9	J. B. Denton	Sb	Hg Is	4 mi E	2	2	?
1893	10	23	Murciano	Ss	Wa Bc	1.25 mi S	0	33	All saved
1893	11	15	J. H. Elliott	Sch	As Bc	1 Mi SSE	0	4	?
1893	11	17	Major Pickands	Sch	Hg Is	Hog Island Shoal	0	10	2,000
1893	12	4	Prohibition	Sl	Me In	1.5 mi S	0	3	Total loss
1893	12	28	Fannie Brown	Sch	Cp Hn	.75 mi E by S	0	8	275
1894	1	7	Nettie	Bg	Lt Is	1.25 mi S	0	9	?
1894	1	22	Clythia	Bk	WW/ Fs Cp	3 mi S False Cape	0	17	Total loss
1894	1	22	Rappahannock	Ss	Cp Hn	.66 mi NE by E	0	52	12,000
1894	1	24	Josie Smith	Sl	Wa Bc	.25 mi S	0	3	Total loss
1894	3	8	Fanny Arthur	Sch	Cp Hn	.875 mi NNW	0	9	?
1894	4	9	Chester	Ss	Sm Is	7 mi NE	0	32	All saved
1894	9	1	Sarah C. Smith	Sch	As Bc/ Po Is	7 mi NE Assateague Beach	0	7	All saved
1894	9	16	John I. Brady	Ss	Cp Hn	1.25 mi NW	0	8	All saved
1894	10	17	W. L. Willis	Sb	Wa Bc	S end Williams Shoal	0	2	Total loss
1894	10	28	Nettie and Lena	Sch	Cb Is	.5 mi E	0	3	All saved
1894	10	31	(Unnamed)	Sb	Wach	3 mi SE	0	1	Total loss
1894	11	5	Benjamin M. Wallace	Sch	Cb Is	Carter's Bar	0	12	6,200
1894	11	11	Sachem	Sl	Wach	S end Cedar Island	0	4	All saved
1895	1	18	Govino	Ss	Cp Hn	.75 mi NNE	0	28	10,000
1895	1	18	Sophia Godfrey	Sch	As Bc	1 mi S	0	6	800
1895	1	19	Nathan Lawrence	Sch	Hg Is	6 mi SE	0	9	All saved
1895	2	8	Water Lily	Sch	As Bc	2.5 mi S	0	4	Total loss
1895	2	12	Elise Marie	Ss	Pa Bc	6.5 mi SW	0	35	All saved
1895	3	17	Zimri S. Wallingford	Sch	Me In	7 mi E	0	7	Total loss
1895	4	2	Oakdene	Ss	As Bc/ Po Is	3 mi NE Assateague Beach	0	20	Total loss
1895	4	29	Henry Parker	Sch	Sm Is	Isaac Shoal	0	6	Total loss

Year/Mo/Day			Vessel	Type	Station	Location	Lives lost	Lives saved	$ value of vessel and cargo lost
1895	5	5	Vandalia	Sch	Cp Hn	2.25 mi NW	0	11	All saved
1895	5	14	Midnight	Sl	Wach	.25 mi E	0	3	Total loss
1895	5	16	Josephine	Bktn	Lt Is/ DNM/ Fs Cp	1.5 mi SE Little Island	0	13	Total loss
1895	9	9	Benjamin A. Van Brunt	Sch	Sm Is	Isaac Shoal	0	9	All saved
1895	9	14	Centennial	Sch	Wach	1.75 mi ESE	0	5	Total loss
1895	9	29	Margaret	Ss	Cp Hn	4 mi NW	0	18	Total loss
1895	10	15	Cambay	Ss	Fs Cp	2.5 mi ESE	0	25	All saved
1895	10	23	H. J. Bradshaw	Sch	Cp Hn	4.25 mi NW	0	3	Total loss
1895	10	30	Carrie L. Godfrey	Sch	Pa Bc	Little Machipongo Inlet	0	8	Total loss
1895	11	2	Emily F. Northam	Sch	Cp Hn	.5 mi NW by N	0	7	2,500
1895	11	21	Lucy A. Davis	Sch	Wach/ Pa Bc	3 mi E Wachapreague	0	9	All saved
1896	2	5	Allie B. Cathrall	Sch	Fs Cp	.5 mi SSe	0	6	Total loss
1896	2	9	Caroline Hall	Sch	Sm Is	4 mi SW	0	7	Total loss
1896	3	15	R. F. Hastings	Sch	Wach	2.5 mi ESE	0	5	Total loss
1896	5	3	Samuel H. Sharp	Sch	Sm Is	6 mi SW by S	0	6	600
1896	5	6	John S. Beachman	Sch	As Bc	3 mi S	0	5	All saved
1896	9	1	L. A. Rose	Sch	As Bc	2.5 mi ESE	0	5	All saved
1896	10	2	Maggie E. Davis	Sch	As Bc	2.5 mi SSE	0	5	Total loss
1896	10	7	Hungry Negro	Sa	Pa Bc	1 mi E	?	?	?
1896	11	29	City of Philadelphia	Sch	Lt Is	25 mi NE	0	7	Total loss
1896	12	3	Walker Armington	Ss	Fs Cp	3 mi N	0	13	6,000
1896	12	17	Kildonan	Ss	Fs Cp	2 mi N	0	34	50,000
1896	12	31	Willehad	Ss	Cp Hn	1 mi N by E	0	65	All saved
1897	1	15	Haxby	Ss	DNM/ Setk	.2 mi NE Dam Neck Mills	0	24	600
1897	1	16	Staffa	Ss	Fs Cp	2.5 mi SE	0	22	Total loss
1897	1	30	Alliance	Ss	Cp Hn	2 mi NNW	0	197	All saved
1897	4	20	James Ponder	Sch	Cb Is	Carter's Bar	0	8	Total loss
1897	10	6	J. G. Conner	Sch	Wach	2 mi ESE	0	2	Total loss
1897	10	25	L. A. Rose	Sch	As Bc	1 mi SE	0	7	Total loss
1897	10	26	Polaria	Ss	Cp Hn / Setk	.875 mi NW Cape Henry	0	35	All saved
1897	11	23	Straits of Magellan	Ss	Lt Is	2 mi NW	0	27	All saved
1897	12	22	Annie E. Edwards	Sch	Cb Is	.5 mi NW	0	4	All saved
1897	12	22	R. B. Leeds	Sch	Cb Is	.5 mi NW	0	2	All saved
1897	12	23	Lizzie S. James	Sch	As Bc	2 mi S	0	6	All saved

Year/Mo/Day			Vessel	Type	Station	Location	Lives lost	Lives saved	$ value of vessel and cargo lost
1897	12	24	Katie J. Hoyt	Sch	Cb Is	5 mi SE	0	7	Total loss
1897	12	24	Mary J. Robbins	Sch	As Bc	1.5 mi S	0	3	250
1897	12	24	Samuel C. Holmes	Sch	As Bc	1.5 mi S	0	5	150
1897	12	25	Mascott	Sl	Hg Is	3 mi SE	0	2	All saved
1897	12	25	Virginia Rulon	Sch	As Bc	5 mi S	0	7	1,300
1898	1	9	Manson	Bg	As Bc	5 mi S	0	6	Total loss
1898	2	3	Stella B. Kaplan	Sch	Sm Is	5 mi SSW	0	8	All saved
1898	2	10	Annie M. Reynolds	Sch	Me In	1.5 mi ENE	0	4	Total loss
1898	2	16	Clipper	Sl	Setk	.5 mi S	0	2	?
1898	3	4	Gleadowe	Ss	Cp Hn/ Setk	2.25 mi SSE Cape Henry	0	23	10,000
1898	4	5	Sarah E. Palmer	Sch	Wach	1 mi ESE	0	9	All saved
1898	5	22	Eugene Hall	Sch	Hg Is	4 mi E	0	6	Total loss
1898	9	21	Hibernia	Ss	Fs Cp	2.25 mi SE	0	24	All saved
1898	11	17	Theresa Wolf	Sch	As Bc	5 mi SE	0	6	5,600
1898	11	27	William M. Wilson	Sch	Me In/ Wach	4 mi S Metomkin Inlet	0	6	Total loss
1898	12	5	Harp	Sl	Fs Cp/ WW	2 mi WSW Wash Woods	0	2	All saved
1898	12	7	Puritan	Sch	As Bc	1.5 mi S	0	4	All saved
1899	2	8	George E. Dudley	Sch	Cb Is	6 mi S	0	7	4,000
1899	2	9	Melvin R. Drew	Sch	Sm Is	4 mi SW	0	3	120
1899	2	10	C. R. Bennett	Ss	Sm Is	.5 mi SE	0	3	100
1899	2	12	Melvin R. Drew	Sch	Sm Is	1.3 mi NW	0	3	All saved
1899	3	5	Tamesi	Ss	Wa Bc	3 mi E	0	9	Total loss
1899	3	15	Brator	Ss	Cp Hn	1 mi E	0	26	All saved
1899	9	8	Annie	Sch	Sm Is	4 mi WSW	0	2	All saved
1899	9	19	Annie	Sch	Pa Bc	1.25 mi NW	0	2	All saved
1899	10	2	Hartfield	S	Fs Cp	2 mi E	0	23	All saved
1899	12	14	Rillie S. Derby	Sch	Hg Is	4.5 mi SE	0	7	Total loss
1900	1	11	Empress	Ss	Fs Cp	2.5 mi ENE	0	26	All saved
1900	2	13	C. A. White	Sch	Lt Is/ Fs Cp/ WW	2.5 mi N False Cape	0	9	1,000
1900	2	26	J. T. Ford	Sch	Wach	3 mi ESE	0	7	Total loss
1900	3	26	Vidar	Ss	DMN/ Lt Is	.75 mi SSW Dam Neck Mills	0	18	All saved
1900	4	22	Emily P. Wright	Sch	Cp Hn	1.5 mi NW	0	14	All saved
1900	4	25	Cordelia R. Price	Sch	Cb Is	1 mi W	0	3	Total loss
1900	5	1	Isle of Kent	Ss	Fs Cp	2.5 mi E	0	24	4,000
1900	9	10	Moonstone	Ss	Cp Hn	.67 mi NE	0	21	All saved

Year/Mo/Day			Vessel	Type	Station	Location	Lives lost	Lives saved	$ value of vessel and cargo lost
1900	12	1	S. B. Wheeler	Sch	Hg Is	4.5 mi SE	0	6	Total loss
1900	12	20	Volunteer	Sl	Pa Bc	Horseshoe Channel	0	4	Total loss
1900	12	21	Jennie Hall	Sch	DNM/ Setk	.25 mi NE Dam Neck Mills	3	5	Total loss
1900	12	24	Astoria	Sch	Sm Is/ Cb Is	Ship Shoal	0	4	Total loss
1900	12	24	Ocean King	Ss	Sm Is/ Cb Is	Ship Shoal	0	10	Total loss
1900	12	24	Rondout	Sch	Sm Is	8 mi NE	0	4	Total loss
1900	12	27	Kestrel	Sl	Hg Is	Hog Island Shoal	0	4	Total loss
1901	1	4	James Young	Sch	As Bc/ Wa Bc	Turner's Shoal	0	6	1,000
1901	2	5	John F. Kranz	Sch	Cp Hn	?	?	0	?
1901	3	11	Mary Standish	Sch	As Bc	1 mi W	0	6	Total loss
1901	4	29	Helga	Ss	Fs Cp	2.5 mi E	0	24	All saved
1901	5	25	Robinia	Ss	Cp Hn	1.5 mi NW	0	24	All saved
1901	7	14	Malden	Sch	Fs Cp	.25 mi SE	0	8	1,500
1901	7	26	Monhegan	Sch	As Bc	2 mi SSE	0	3	Total loss
1901	8	25	Cape Henry	Sch	Cp Hn	"Off" Cape Henry	0	0	100
1901	9	16	Jospeh J. Pharo	Sch	As Bc	1.5 mi SSE	0	8	All saved
1901	9	17	Edith G. Folwell	Sch	Cp Hn	1 mi N	0	17	All saved
1901	10	10	Maude and Ellis	Sl	Sm Is	3.5 mi N	0	6	All saved
1901	12	5	Virginia Rulon	Sch	Sm Is	Isaac Shoal	0	6	1,000
1902	2	25	Alice and Isabelle	Bk	As Bc	2.5 mi SE	0	15	2,000
1902	2	27	Emma M. Robin- son	Sch	As Bc	2.25 mi S	0	4	All saved
1902	2	28	Yeoman	Ss	Cp Hn	.66 mi E	0	45	All saved
1902	6	10	Thomas Wayman	Ss	Fs Cp	Pebble Shoal	0	22	All saved
1902	6	14	Falcon	Ss	Fs Cp	2 mi SE	0	23	5,000
1902	11	1	Express	Sch	Fs Cp	.5 mi NE	0	3	Total loss
1902	11	16	Onancock City	Sl	Sm Is	4.5 mi SW	0	3	Total loss
1902	12	16	Lillian Russell	Sch	Hg Is	4 mi ESE	2	0	Total loss
1902	12	21	Florence A.	Lch	Cp Hn	3 mi W	0	6	500
1903	1	10	Juno	Ss	Fs Cp/ Lt Is	2.5 mi ESE False Cape	0	24	All saved
1903	1	16	Noviembre	Ss	Fs Cp	2.5 mi ESE	0	26	All saved
1903	2	17	Rebecca	Sch	Hg Is	4 mi S	0	6	Total loss
1903	4	13	Daybreak	Ss	Fs Cp	2.25 mi E	0	23	?
1903	10	10	Alice Parks	Sch	Cb Is	30 yds E	0	3	All saved
1903	10	10	Georgia	Schbg	Va Bc/ Cp Hn	.37 mi N Virginia Beach	0	0	Total loss

Year/Mo/Day	Vessel	Type	Station	Location	Lives lost	Lives saved	$ value of vessel and cargo lost
1903 10 10	Hawk	Sl	Sm Is	1.25 mi N	0	4	All saved
1903 10 10	Mary Washington	Sl	Sm Is	1 mi N	0	0	All saved
1903 10 10	Missouri	Sl	Sm Is	3 mi NE	0	1	All saved
1903 10 10	Nellie W. Howlett	Sch	DNM/ Lt Is	3 mi S Dam Neck Mills	0	8	Total loss
1903 10 10	Ocean Belle	Schbg Va Bc		2.5 mi N	2	3	Total loss
1903 10 10	Oregon	Sl	Sm Is	4 mi NE	0	0	All saved
1903 10 11	Benjamin Russell	Sch	Hg Is	3 mi SSE	0	5	3,300
1904 1 3	Joseph J. Pharo	Sch	Cb Is/ Sm Is	8 mi S Cobb Island	0	6	Total loss
1904 1 11	Glencova	Bk	Fs Cb	2.5 mi E	0	27	All saved
1904 2 11	Henry B. Hyde	S	DNM/ Lt Is	2.5 mi S Dam Neck Mills	0	4	48,700
1904 4 8	Rosewood	Ss	Va Bc	1.25 mi N	0	22	All saved
1904 5 2	Frank Leaming	Sch	Cp Hn	1 mi SE	0	6	1,200
1904 6 10	Henry B. Hyde	S	DNM/ Va Bc	2.5 mi S Dam Neck Mills	0	4	0
1904 7 7	Robert J. Poulson	Sch	Sm Is	Isaac Shoal	0	2	800
1904 9 22	Henry B. Hyde	S	DNM/ Lt Is	2.75 mi S Dam Neck Mills	0	8	0
1904 11 11	Rebecca Palmer	Sch	Cb Is	Carter's Bar	0	13	All saved
1904 11 13	Robert J. Poulson	Sch	Hg Is	.5 mi SW	0	4	All saved
1905 2 3	D. M. Anthony	Sch	Fs Cp/ Lt Is	1.5 mi N	0	9	Total loss
1905 2 8	San Ignaciode Loyola	Bktn	Wach/ Pa Bc	2 mi S Wacha- preague	0	18	All saved
1905 2 24	Bangor	Ss	Lt Is/ DNM/ Fs Cp	.5 mi SE	0	28	All saved
1905 4 8	M. P. Howlett	Sch	As Bc	4 mi SE	0	4	Total loss
1905 5 5	Emmet Arthur	Sl	Wa Bc	6 mi SW	0	2	Total loss
1905 9 4	Aragon	Ss	Fs Cp	2.25 mi SSE	0	21	2,000
1905 9 4	Saxon	Bg	Fs Cp	2.25 mi SSE	0	4	Total loss
1905 10 11	Ada R. Terry	Sch	As Bc	1.75 mi SE	0	14	2,500
1905 12 15	Antigoon	Ss	Lt Is/ Fs Cp	2 mi SE	0	19	All saved
1905 12 15	Pendleton Sisters	Sch	Me In	5.5 mi NE	1	8	Total loss
1905 12 24	C. H. Moore	Sch	Lt Is	1 mi SSE	0	2	Total loss
1906 1 9	Fannie Palmer	Sch	Lt Is/ DNM	.75 mi N Little Island	0	12	20,000
1906 2 27	George M. Grant	Sch	Cp Hn / ? Va Bc		0	10	6,000
1906 3 22	Harry T. Hayward	Sch	Cp Hn	8 mi SE	0	11	24,000

Year/Mo/Day			Vessel	Type	Station	Location	Lives lost	Lives saved	$ value of vessel and cargo lost
1906	3	23	Asher J. Hudson	Tug	Lt Is/ DNM	250 yds NE	0	10	10,000
1906	3	31	Antonio	Bk	Cp Hn	.5 mi N	0	11	Total loss
1906	5	7	Alice	Sch	Wa Bc / As Bc	1.5 mi NE Wallops Beach	0	4	3,800
1906	9	25	Marion Grimes	Sch	As Bc	4.5 mi SW	0	15	Total loss
1906	10	20	George Farwell	Ss	Cp Hn	.75 mi SE	0	16	35,000
1906	12	7	Florence I. Lockwood	Sch	Wa Bc/ As Bc	2.5 mi E Wallops Beach	0	6	Total loss
1906	12	11	Ralph C. Hayward	Sch	Lt Is/ Fs Cp	.33 mi SE Little Island	0	9	All saved
1906	12	16	Edgar C. Ross	Sch	Cp Hn	?	0	6	450
1907	1	3	R. W. Hopkins	Sch	Cp Hn	1 mi N	0	9	All saved
1907	5	2	Glendy Stewart	Sch	Cp Hn	6 mi W	0	2	50
1907	5	4	Dora	Ss	Fs Cp/ WW	2.25 mi SSE	0	25	?
1907	8	12	Henry A. Littlefield	SchbgVa Bc		"Near" Virginia Beach	0	4	?
1907	8	16	Arleville H. Peary	Sch	As Bc	2.5 mi SW	0	7	500
1907	10	3	Foam	Yt	As Bc	1 mi W	0	6	1,000
1907	11	7	Wicomico	S	As Bc	1 mi SSE	0	28	Total loss
1907	11	26	Virginia	Sch	Hg Is	.5 mi WSW	0	4	All saved
1908	1	12	John E. Sevlin	Sch	Me In	5 mi NNE	0	9	Total loss
1908	4	16	Glenaen	Ss	Cb Is	?	0	25	10,000
1908	8	24	Margaret H. Vane	Sch	Cb Is	Carter's Bar	0	6	11,600
1908	10	31	Arleville H. Peary	Sch	Fs Cp/ WW	3.25 mi S	0	6	Total loss
1908	11	12	Florence Shay	SchbgLt Is/ Fs Cp		3.5 mi S Little Island	2	4	Total loss
1908	12	23	Avonmore	Ss	Cp Hn / Va Bc	8.5 mi W	0	26	5,500
1909	1	6	Anglo-African	Ss	Sm Is	4 mi S	0	38	Total loss
1909	1	18	Pendleton Satisfaction	?	Lt Is/ Fs Cp	600 yds S Little Island	0	8	All saved
1910	2	5	Jennie N. Huddell	Sch	Cb Is	2 mi SSE	0	5	Total loss
1910	2	6	Carrie A. Norton	Sch	Fs Cp/ Lt Is	2 mi N	0	8	9,500
1910	2	18	Norwood	S	Cb Is/ Sm Is	10 mi SSE Cb Is	0	18	Total loss
1910	3	7	Manchuria	Ss	Lt Is/ Fs Cp/ DNM/ WW	3.5 mi S Little Island	0	25	3,000
1910	4	1	Margherita	Ss	Fs Cp	2.25 mi E	0	28	20,000
1910	7	9	Nellie W. Craig	Sch	Cp Hn	3 mi NW	0	7	All saved

Year/Mo/Day	Vessel	Type	Station	Location	Lives lost	Lives saved	$ value of vessel and cargo lost
1911 12 3	*Sterling*	Ss	Cp Hn	3 mi W	0	37	2,900
1911 12 17	*Katherine D. Perry*	Sch	Sm Is	5 mi SW	0	9	Total loss
1912 3 25	*Gaston*	Sch	Cb Is	3 mi SE	0	4	Total loss
1912 3 25	*S. D. Carleton*	Sch	Cb Is	3 mi SE	0	5	Total loss
1912 11 2	*Reliance*	Ss	Cp Hn	7 mi W	0	3	1,900
1912 11 11	*Silverton*	Ss	Fs Cp/ WW	3 mi False Cape	0	23	All saved
1912 12 3	*Charmer*	Bk	Cp Hn	3.5 mi ENE	0	4	Total loss
1913 3 2	*Laura Tomkins*	Sch	Cb Is	2.5 mi SSW	1	1	Total loss
1913 4 24	*Harlseywood*	Ss	Cp Hn	1,400 yds E	0	30	500
1913 5 24	*Lucia*	Ss	Va Bc/ Cp Hn	7 mi NE Virginia Beach	0	45	?
1913 12 23	*Frieda*	Ss	Lt Is	1.5 mi S	0	32	All saved
1913 12 24	*Frieda*	Ss	Fs Cp	3.5 mi N	0	32	19,000
1914 1 22	*Levi S. Andrews*	Sch	Wach/ Pa Bc	2.5 mi SE	0	7	3,000
1914 2 3	*Trojan*	Ss	Cp Hn	.75 mi E	0	34	All saved
1914 2 20	*Riversdale*	Ss	Lt Is/ DNM/ Fs Cp	.5 mi N Little Island	0	23	13,000
1914 7 9	*Lizzie Godfrey*	Sch	Wa Bc/ As Bc	Williams Shoal	0	3	Total loss
1914 10 27	*USS Paulding*	Dest	Cp Hn / Va Bc	Lynnhaven Inlet	?	0	?
1914 11 15	*Massasoit*	Sch	Sm Is	"Off" Smith Island	0	10	Total loss

B. Alphabetical Listing of Shipwrecks on the Atlantic Coast of Virginia, 1875-1915

Vessel	Year/Mo/Day	Ton-nage	Master	Home port
?	1879 10 13	?	Sturges	?
?	1894 10 31	?	?	Wachapreague, Va.
?	1890 8 30	?	?	Accomack Courthouse, Virginia
*?	1891 12 29	?	none	*
A. D. Scull	1884 11 15	396	Kelly	Boston, Mass.
A. F. Kindberg	1886 3 24	226	Mount	New York City
A. H. Quimby	1887 7 21	68	Key	Millville, N. J.
A. M. Bailey	1885 3 22	66	Wescott	Somers Point, N. J.
A. M. Payne	1883 10 6	88	Abbott	Halifax, Nova Scotia
A. P. Newell	1892 12 20	241	Hunter	Philadelphia
A. S. Davis	1878 10 22	1,399	Ford	?
Acuba	1891 1 19	1,845	Steele	Sunderland, England
Ada	1891 9 8	6	Sullivan	Cape Charles City, Va.
Ada Gray	1888 1 1	566	Plummer	Portland, Me.
Ada M. Hallock	1880 1 11	?	?	New York City
Ada R. Terry	1905 10 11	69	Jorgenson	New York City
Adelia F. Cohen	1881 10 5	?	Somers	Philadelphia
Admiral	1879 3 2	?	?	Norway
Aeolus	1876 1 12	55	Boggs	Pungoteague Creek, Va.
Agnes Barton	1889 3 14	400	Knight	Baltimore
Agostino C.	1881 12 14	?	Langobarde	Castlemare, Italy
Albert C. Paige	1884 1 26	379	Haley	Morristown, N. J.
Albert Dailey	1883 1 7	238	Goldthwaite	Augusta, Me.
Alice	1906 5 7	61	Jones	Baltimore
Alice and Isabelle	1902 2 25	647	Leblais	Sables d'Orlonne, France
Alice Ida	1877 2 18	45	Price	Philadelphia
Alice Lea	1880 1 8	?	?	Wilmington, Del.
Alice Parks	1903 10 10	8	Widegon	Cape Charles, Va.
Alliance (USS)	1897 1 30	615	Manney	?
Allie B. Cathrall	1896 2 5	109	Collins	Wilmington, Del.
Alvira	1882 3 1	?	Saunders	Millville, N. J.

*Small boat of unknown type attached to the "Winter Quarter Light Ship"

Voyage from	to	Cargo	Dollar Value of Vessel	Cargo
?	?	?	?	?
Wachapreague	Parramore Beach	?	?	?
?	Folly Creek, Va.	?	30	?
?	?	none	150	0
Promised Land, N. Y.	Baltimore	fish & scrap	10,000	8,000
New York City	Richmond, Va.	phosphate	4,500	10,000
Washington, N. C.	Philadelphia	lumber	2,500	1,000
Great Egg Harbor, N. J.	Hatteras Inlet, N. C.	?	?	?
Breezy Point, West Indies	Baltimore	quano	3,500	1,000
Suffolk, Va.	New York City	lumber	8,500	2,000
Callao, Peru	Hampton Roads, Va.	guano	?	?
Philadelphia	Newport News, Va.	?	90,000	?
Cape Charles City	Smith Island, Va.	?	1,200	?
St. Thomas, Virgin Islands	Hampton Roads, Va.	iron ore	6,540	?
?	?	?	?	?
New York City	Assateague, Va.	?	6,000	?
Philadelphia	Richmond, Va.	coal	4,000	1,300
?	?	?	?	?
Pungoteague Creek	Machipongo, Va.	corn	5,000	200
Navassa, West Indies	Baltimore	fertilizer	?	?
Italy	Baltimore	sulphur	19,000	12,800
Charlestown, S. C.	New York City	phosphate rock	1,500	?
Baltimore	Bridgeport, Conn.	coal	10,000	1,500
Hampton, Va.	Maurice River, N. J.	oysters	2,800	1,650
Sables d'Orlonne	Philadelphia	?	100,000	?
Baltimore	New York City	gas pipes	2,000	8,000
?	?	lumber	?	?
?	?	?	200	?
St. Thomas, V. I.	Newport News, Va.	?	50,000	?
New Bern, N. C.	Bridgeport, Conn.	lumber	5,000	1,000
Pocomoke City, Md.	Millville	lumber	2,500	3,000

Vessel	Year/Mo/Day	Ton-nage	Master	Home port
Amaryllis	1883 8 19	1,109	Iliff	North Shields, England
Amy Dora	1889 10 5	1,708	Thompson	North Shields, England
Angie Predmore	1876 3 28	93	Parker	Barnegat, N. J.
Anglo-African	1909 1 6	4,186	?	London, England
Anna Homan	1888 4 15	22	Dunton	Chincoteague, Va.
Anne Dole	1884 4 4	186	Blackman	Somers Point, N. J.
Annie	1885 10 29	?	?	Cobb Island, Va.
Annie	1885 9 8	18	Lilliston	Newport News, Va.
Annie	1899 9 19	18	Lilliston	Newport News, Va.
Annie E. Edwards	1897 12 22	61	Brasure	Perth Amboy, N. J.
Annie E. Moore	1882 7 17	126	Carey	Seaford, Del.
Annie E. Pierce	1889 12 30	93	Still	Wilmington, Del.
Annie F. Conlon	1886 12 6	591	Seward	Portsmouth, N. H.
Annie M. Reynolds	1898 2 10	60	Pruitt	Chincoteague, Va.
Anthea Godfrey	1882 12 7	182	Price	Wilmington, Del.
Anthony Kelley	1875 12 18	59	Greenwood	Staten Island, N. Y.
Antigoon	1905 12 15	1,214	Calmelet	Antwerp, Belgium
Antonia	1878 5 22	?	Anderson	Liverpool, England
Antonio	1906 3 31	495	Longbardo	Castlemare, Italy
Aragon	1905 9 4	1,450	Blake	Boston, Mass.
Arleville H. Peary	1907 8 16	311	?	New York City
Arleville H. Peary	1908 10 31	311	?	New York City
Armenia Bartlett	1877 5 20	229	Smith	Philadelphia
Ashburne	1892 1 7	2,469	Brotherton	Sunderland, England
Asher J. Hudson	1906 3 23	136	Johnson	Philadelphia
Astoria	1900 12 24	1,281	Smith	New York City
Aurora Mills	1875 2 17	?	Brown	Philadelphia
Avonmore	1908 12 23	2,607	?	Liverpool, England
B. H. Jones	1882 8 7	216	Pearce	Perth Amboy, N. J.
B. L. Burt	1884 5 26	719	Johnson	Taunton, Mass.
B. L. Burt	1888 12 22	719	Johnson	Fall River, Mass.
Baltimore	1889 10 22	3,730	Simpson	Liverpool, England
Bangor	1905 2 24	3,372	Brown	Belfast, Ireland
Bateau Sharpley	1884 7 8	3	?	Chincoteague, Va.
Bedabedee	1884 12 15	95	Miller	Philadelphia
Benjamin A. Van Brunt	1895 9 9	1,192	Pearce	North Amboy, N. J.
Benjamin C. Terry	1889 3 20	260	Mathis	New York City
Benjamin F. Poole	1889 4 7	1,155	Charlton	Providence, R. I.
Benjamin M. Wallace	1894 11 5	61	Peterson	New York City

Voyage from	to	Cargo	Dollar Value of Vessel	Cargo
North Shields	Baltimore	general	125,000	200,000
Savannah, Ga.	Genoa, Italy	cotton	90,000	235,000
Barnegat	Norfolk, Va.	ballast	5,000	
South America	Baltimore	nitrate of soda	400,000	300,000
Cobb Island, Va.	Chincoteague, Va.	oysters	1,000	50
Philadelphia	Washington, D. C.	coal	6,000	1,450
Bone Island, Va.	Cobb Island	?	125	?
Norfolk, Va.	Chincoteague, Va.	lumber	500	400
Norfolk, Va.	Assateague, Va.	lumber	700	450
James River, Va.	Morris River, N. J.	oysters	6,000	500
Newberg, N. Y.	Washington, D. C.	plaster	8,000	1,000
New Bern, N. C.	New York City	lumber	6,000	1,500
Boston, Mass	Baltimore	?	25,000	?
Hampton Roads, Va.	Chincoteague	oysters	1,500	375
Wilmington	Petersburg, Va.	guano	6,000	11,000
York River, Va.	New York City	oysters	5,000	2,500
Mobile, Ala.	LaRochelle, France	lumber	90,000	?
Liverpool	Baltimore	?	?	?
Baltimore	Paysande, Uruguay	bones	20,000	?
Georgetown, S. C.	Philadelphia	lumber	178,000	?
Virginia	New York City	lumber	4,000	3,500
New York City	Norfolk, Va.	?	3,000	?
Philadelphia	Washington, D. C.	coal	10,000	1,600
Sunderland	Baltimore	?	100,000	?
Norfolk, Va.	?	?	35,000	?
New York City	Baltimore	?	10,000	?
Norfolk, Va.	?	sugar	33,000	?
Para, Brazil	Hampton Roads, Va.	?	75,000	?
Roundout, N. Y.	Baltimore	cement	6,000	2,500
Providence, R. I.	Baltimore	?	38,000	?
Brighton, Mass.	Baltimore	?	30,000	?
Liverpool	Baltimore	general	202,000	?
Pensacola, Fla.	Hamburg, Germany	turpentine resin	315,000	?
Chincoteague	?	?	75	?
Jamaica, West Indies	Philadelphia	coconuts	2,500	3,500
Fall River, Mass.	Baltimore	?	45,000	?
New York City	Norfolk, Va.	?	4,000	?
Providence	Baltimore	?	50,000	?
?	?	?	7,000	?

Vessel	Year/Mo/Day	Ton-nage	Master	Home port
Benjamin Russell	1903 10 11	154	Thomas	Bridgeton, N. J.
Bertha A. Watts	1886 4 16	146	Watt	Lunenberg, Nova Scotia
Bertram L. Townsend	1886 12 3	641	Tunnell	Philadelphia
Bessie Morris	1887 11 17	425	Wheaton	Philadelphia
Boston	1882 12 30	120	Jones	Philadelphia
Bradshaw	1884 7 23	?	?	Assawoman, Va.
Brator	1899 3 15	1,829	Hood	London, England
C. A. White	1900 2 13	232	Connor	Fall River, Mass.
C. C. Cruser	1891 3 15	13	Mister	Cape Charles City, Va.
C. C. Davidson	1893 10 4	116	Younger	Philadelphia
C. E. Scammell	1875 1 22	254	Smith	St. Johns, New Brunswick
C. H. Moore	1905 12 24	17	Hudgins	Newport News, Va.
C. R. Bennett	1899 2 10	32	Merritt	Chincoteague, Va.
Cambay	1895 10 15	1,694	Rowland	Newcastle, England
*Cape Henry	1901 8 25	?	None	Norfolk, Va.
Caroline Hall	1896 2 9	250	Mason	Wilmington, Del.
Caroline Miller	1890 1 27	622	Ryder	New York City
Carpione	1877 1 17	474	Ferari	Genoa, Italy
Carrie A. Norton	1910 2 6	559	?	New London, Conn.
Carrie Hall Lister	1881 12 22	142	Pierce	Seaford, Del.
Carrie Hall Lister	1883 2 3	142	Pierce	Wilmington, Del.
Carrie Holmes	1887 10 31	375	Holmes	Forked River, N. J.
Carrie L. Godfrey	1895 10 30	435	Cullen	Philadelphia
Castlefield	1892 8 18	1,485	Ching	Stockton, England
Celia	1884 3 30	29	Williams	New Bedford, Mass.
Centennial	1895 9 14	113	Thorington	Baltimore
†Challenge	1889 4 6	7	Delano	New York City
‡Challenge	1891 10 12	7	?	New York City
Charles E. Balch	1893 4 11	844	White	Bath, Me.
Charles H. Malleson	1880 4 13	?	?	Perth Amboy, N. J.
Charmer	1912 12 3	1,885	?	Perth Amboy, N. J.
Chester	1894 4 9	1,868	?	Rotterdam, Holland
Chiswick	1883 12 21	796	Watts	London, England

*"found adrift"
†on a "pleasure trip"
‡abandoned

Voyage from	to	Cargo	Dollar Value of Vessel	Cargo
Bogue Inlet, N. C.	Bridgeton	lumber	5,000	1,300
Cienfuegos, Cuba	Philadelphia	molasses	6,500	5,000
New York City	Baltimore	?	30,000	?
Elizabethport, N. J.	Savannah, Ga.	guano	21,000	?
New Bern, N. C.	Philadelphia	lumber	4,500	?
Franklin City, Va.	Assawoman, Va.	empty barrels	600	20
Daiquiri, Cuba	Baltimore	iron ore	134,000	?
Boston, Mass.	Baltimore	?	15,000	?
Smith Island, Va.	Cape Charles City	machinery	1,000	1,500
New Bern, N. C.	Atlantic City, N. J.	lumber	7,000	?
Bahia, South America	Baltimore	sugar	47,000	?
Norfolk, Va.	Ware River, Va.	shingles & tiling	500	75
Norfolk, Va.	Chincoteague	shingles	1,400	1,500
Bensaff, Africa	Baltimore	iron ore	105,590	?
?	?	none	1,500	0
Coles River, R. I.	Savannah, Ga.	fish scrap	12,000	3,000
New York City	West Point, Va.	general	60,000	25,000
Leith, Scotland	Baltimore	?	16,000	?
Jacksonville, Fla.	New York City	lumber	15,000	3,500
Rappahannock, Va.	New York City	wood	6,000	800
York River, Va.	New York City	wood	5,000	700
New Haven, Conn.	Norfolk, Va.	lumber	?	?
Charleston, S. C.	Wilmington, Del.	phosphate rock	8,000	3,000
Pensacola, Fla.	Norfolk, Va.	lumber	141,720	?
New Bedford, Mass.	Wilmington, N. C.	?	2,500	?
Philadelphia	New Bern, N. C.	coal	3,500	715
Wachapreague, Va.	?	?	1,000	?
?	?	none	800	0
New York City	Lamberts Point, Va.	?	40,000	?
Philadelphia	Norfolk, Va.	ballast	?	?
Newport News, Va.	Boston, Mass.	coal	50,000	?
Amsterdam, Holland	Baltimore	?	150,000	?
Ireland	Hampton Roads, Va.	?	200,000	?

Vessel	Year/Mo/Day	Tonnage	Master	Home Port
City of Philadelphia	1896 11 29	387	Dodd	Philadelphia
Clapeyron	1886 11 19	1,148	Ken	Marseilles, France
Clipper	1898 2 16	?	?	West Point, Va.
Clythia	1894 1 22	1,140	Heffermehl	Christiania, Norway
Constellation (USS)	1889 6 18	1,886	Harrington	Annapolis, Md.
Cordelia R. Price	1900 4 25	42	York	Somers Point, N. J.
D. Ellis	1881 1 28	70	Torry	Rockland, Me.
D. M. Anthony	1905 2 3	555	Hatfield	New York City
Daniel Brown	1890 11 20	204	Davis	New York City
Daniel S. Williams, Jr.	1884 3 30	629	Hyers	Perth Amboy, N. J.
Dauntless	1881 11 16	?	Leamon	Cherrystone, Va.
Dauntless	1882 2 21	?	Collins	Chincoteague, Va.
David F. Keeling	1881 5 23	209	Owens	Baltimore
Davy Crockett	1885 12 25	?	?	Norfolk, Va.
Daybreak	1903 4 13	2,922	Morris	West Hartlepool, England
Delphin	1877 1 20	69	Desroses	St. Pierre, West Indies
Despatch (USS)	1891 10 10	730	Coules	?
Deutschland	1887 11 20	1,251	Peters	Hamburg, Germany
Dictator	1881 4 21	578	Christensen	Tvedstrand, Norway
Dictator	1891 3 27	1,242	Jorgensen	Moss, Norway
Dolly Varden	1882 1 31	?	Hackney	Somers Point, N. J.
Dora	1907 5 4	2,290	Randall	Whitby, England
E. K. Rayfield	1889 4 7	8	Chandler	Onancock, Va.
E. K. Wilson	1892 3 31	71	Lupton	Beaufort, N. C.
E. L. Pettingill	1889 2 18	842	White	Portland, Me.
†*E. S. Newins*	1891 8 26	81	Gardner	Philadelphia
Earnmoor	1888 2 13	1,300	Grey	Newcastle, England
Edgar C. Ross	1906 12 16	399	Quillin	Seaford, Del.
Edith Berwind	1893 1 1	815	McBride	Philadelphia
Edith Fowle	1882 4 30	23	Pater	Chincoteague, Va.
Edith G. Folwell	1901 9 17	1,263	Kelsey	Hartford, Conn.
Edwin J. Palmer	1886 8 5	197	Gardner	Providence, R. I.
Elise Marie	1895 2 12	3,568	Reiners	Hamburg, Germany

*on a navel cadet cruise

†on a fishing trip

Voyage from	to	Cargo	Dollar Value of	
			Vessel	Cargo
Charleston, S. C.	Philadelphia	phosphate rock	12,500	?
Cartagena, Spain	Baltimore	iron ore	144,000	?
?	?	?	150	?
Genoa, Italy	Baltimore	statue marble	45,000	29,000
Annapolis, Md.	?	equipment & stores	380,000	?
James River, Va.	New Jersey	oysters	1,600	350
Norfolk, Va.	New York City	corn	2,000	2,100
New York City	Norfolk, Va.	?	10,000	?
James River, Va.	New York City	wood	7,000	1,000
New York City	Baltimore	?	25,000	?
Cobb Island, Va.	Cherrystone	oysters	1,000	65
Hog Island, Va.	Chincoteague	oysters	400	50
Charleston, S. C.	Baltimore	lumber	8,000	?
St. Georges Is., Md.	Norfolk	none	2,000	0
Santiago, Cuba	Baltimore	iron ore	150,000	?
Martinique, West Indies	Baltimore	sugar	6,000	6,800
Washington, D. C.	New York City	?	135,000	?
Hamburg	Baltimore	?	19,000	?
Boston, England	Baltimore	?	25,000	?
Pensacola, Fla.	Hartlepool, England	timber	?	?
New Inlet, Va.	Great Egg Harbor, N. J.	oysters	1,000	?
Trinidad, West Indies	Baltimore	asphalt	109,000	?
Onancock, Va.	Magothy Bay, Va.	?	600	?
New Bern, N. C.	Philadelphia	lumber	3,000	1,000
Pisagua, Chili	Hampton Roads, Va.	nitrate of soda	3,000	1,000
Philadelphia	?	?	9,000	?
Santiago, Cuba	Baltimore	iron ore	100,000	30,000
Georgetown, S. C.	Baltimore	lumber	21,000	?
Port Tampa, Fla.	Baltimore	phosphate rock	35,000	11,000
James River, Va.	Chincoteague	oysters	1,000	200
Washington, D. C.	Portsmouth, N. H.	coal	54,000	?
Providence	Philadelphia	scrap iron & barrels	3,000	1,200
Hamburg	Baltimore	?	60,000	?

Vessel	Year/Mo/Day	Ton-nage	Master	Home Port
Elizabeth	1887 1 8	1,239	Halberstadt	Bremen, Germany
Elizabeth A. Baizley	1882 1 29	?	Townsend	Camden, N. J.
Elizabeth White	1880 12 29	126	Lear	New York City
Ella T. Little	1883 11 1	449	Crawford	Philadelphia
Ellen Holgate	1887 9 23	168	Betto	Philadelphia
Ellie	1879 11 24	?	?	Chincoteague, Va.
Ellie Bodine	1879 10 20	?	?	Tuckerton, N. J.
Ellie Bodine	1879 12 25	?	?	Tuckerton, N. J.
Elysia A.	1880 12 29	88	Holmes	St. Johns, New Brunswick
Emily A. Bartle	1886 12 5	214	Lawrence	Philadelphia
Emily F. Northam	1895 11 2	332	Johnson	Philadelphia
Emily P. Wright	1900 4 22	97	Leathen	Stonington, Conn.
Emma Aery	1886 2 5	330	Hall	New York City
Emma D. Endicott	1885 7 1	336	Bowen	Philadelphia
Emma F. Hart	1889 4 7	400	Keene	Camden, Me.
Emma G. Edwards	1878 12 23	?	?	Camden, N. J.
Emma M. Robinson	1902 2 27	63	Stuart	Chincoteague, Va.
Emma McAdam	1889 4 12	167	Brown	Calais, Me.
Emmet Arthur	1905 5 5	22	Hill	Chincoteague, Va.
Empress	1900 1 11	?	Stewart	West Hartlepool, England
Esk	1888 9 7	148	Watt	Lunenburg, Nova Scotia
Eugene Hall	1898 5 22	320	Sawyer	New York City
Eva I. Shenton	1890 2 21	92	James	Baltimore
Express	1902 11 1	22	Billops	Newport News, Va.
Falcon	1902 6 14	3,049	Ross	Newcastle, England
Fannie Brown	1893 12 28	508	Hardcester	Richmond, Va.
Fannie K. Shaw	1876 12 9	295	Balano	Thomaston, Me.
Fannie Palmer	1906 1 9	2,258	Nash	Boston, Mass.
Fanny Arthur	1894 3 8	614	Douglas	?
Figogna	1883 2 28	843	Nicolini	Genoa, Italy
Flora Curtis	1878 12 2	?	?	Manasquan, N. J.
*Florence A.	1902 12 21	?	?	Lynnhaven, Va.
Florence I. Lockwood	1906 12 7	299	Taylor	Norfolk, Va.
Florence Kellinger	1888 1 28	18	Long	Onancock, Va.
Florence Kellinger	1888 3 12	18	Long	Onancock, Va.
Florence Shay	1908 11 12	405	?	New York City
Flying Scud	1884 8 23	10	Fletcher	Onancock, Va.

*on a pleasure trip

Voyage from	to	Cargo	Dollar Value of Vessel	Cargo
Hamburg, Germany	Baltimore	kainite & barrels	26,810	?
Baltimore	Providence, R. I.	coal	15,000	3,600
York River, Va.	Philadelphia	railroad ties	3,000	1,155
Philadelphia	Richmond, Va.	pig iron	8,000	1,000
New Haven, Conn.	Norfolk, Va.	?	2,000	?
Chincoteague	Indian River, Del.	?	?	?
New York City	York River, Va.	ballast	?	
?	?	?	?	?
St. Thomas, Virgin Islands	New York City	salt	3,000	1,200
New York City	Virginia	?	3,000	?
New York City	Norfolk, Va.	?	15,000	?
Old Point, Va.	Hatteras, N. C.	?	10,000	?
Norfolk, Va.	New Haven, Conn.	coal	12,000	1,280
New York City	Baltimore	cement	5,000	3,000
Nassau, Bahamas	Boston, Mass.	lumber	11,000	?
?	?	lumber	?	?
James River, Va.	New York City	wood	2,000	350
New York City	Baltimore	copper	2,000	2,000
James River, Va.	Chincoteague	oysters	1,000	300
Galveston, Tex.	Newport News, Va.	general	194,400	?
Maracaibo, Venezuela	Providence, R. I.	dyewood	7,500	3,500
Red Beach, Me.	Norfolk, Va.	plaster	18,000	2,500
Chester, Pa.	Smith Island, Va.	stone	4,000	1,000
Mathews County, Va.	Hampton, Va.	wood	525	?
Mobile, Ala.	Norfolk, Va.	lumber	196,040	?
Charleston, S. C.	Richmond	phosphate rock	16,500	?
St. Mary's, Ga.	Baltimore	lumber	10,000	5,000
Boston	Baltimore	?	100,000	?
Baltimore	Cardenas, Cuba	coal	30,750	?
Parma, Italy	Baltimore	iron ore	45,000	?
?	?	?	?	?
?	?	?	1,500	?
Norfolk, Va.	New York City	lumber	2,500	4,000
Cobb Island, Va.	Norfolk, Va.	oysters	900	250
Norfolk, Va.	Cobb Island, Va.	?	700	?
Norfolk, Va.	New York City	paving blocks	9,800	?
Wachapreague, Va.	Metomkin, Va.	fish & scrap	300	400

Vessel	Year/Mo/Day	Ton-nage	Master	Home Port
Foam	1907 10 3	64	?	New York City
Francisco Bella Gamba	1878 1 4	430	Brigwont	Genoa, Italy
Frank	1883 12 23	16	Clayville	Onancock, Va.
Frank	1889 12 11	16	Lilliston	Cape Charles City, Va.
Frank C. Pettis	1890 4 19	25	Doane	Norfolk, Va.
Frank G. Dow	1888 12 22	411	Kelley	Providence, R. I.
Frank Jameson	1877 11 25	181	Jameson	Rockport, Me.
Frank Leaming	1904 5 2	257	Cramer	Norfolk, Va.
Frank O. Dame	1889 10 23	688	Shailer	Boston, Mass.
Franklin	1878 11 17	?	?	?
*Fred	1884 4 27	15	Penn	Guilford, Conn.
Fred	1886 10 31	16	Littiston	Guilford, Conn.
Frieda	1913 12 23	1,633	?	Boston, Mass.
Frieda	1913 12 24	1,633	?	Boston, Mass.
G. B. Claxom	1881 10 22	?	Claxom	Locustville, Va.
G. W. Bentley	1889 3 15	113	Doane	Provincetown, Mass.
Galathea	1877 3 26	475	Steansen	Tvedstrand, Norway
Gaston	1912 3 25	1,442	?	Baltimore
General Harrison	1889 10 23	?	?	?
George C. Wainwright	1890 12 11	52	Chapman	Newport News, Va.
George E. Dudley	1899 2 8	407	Wilson	New Haven, Conn.
George F. Wright	1876 6 30	?	Summers	Onancock, Va.
George Farwell	1906 10 20	977	Chisholm	New York City
George L. Garlick	1887 4 7	22	Chamberlin	Somers Pt., N. J.
George L. Treadwell	1877 1 27	113	Taylor	Portsmouth, N. H.
George M. Grant	1906 2 27	1,254	Pelton	New Haven, Conn.
George White	1882 11 20	42	Parker	Tuckerton, N. J.
Georgia	1903 10 10	1,609	?	New York City
*Gertrude	1887 10 17	10	?	Baltimore
Gertrude T. Browning	1882 12 17	134	Showell	Somers Pt., N. J.
Giambattista Primo	1880 10 22	516	Dagnino	Genoa, Italy
Gleadowe	1898 3 4	2,138	Harris	London, England
Glenaen	1908 4 16	3,227	?	Whitby, England
Glencova	1904 1 11	2,369	Bowles	Dundee, Scotland
Glendy Stewart	1907 5 2	9	Bradshaw	Norfolk, Va.

*abandoned

Voyage from	to	Cargo	Dollar Value of Vessel	Dollar Value of Cargo
Tarpon Springs, Fla.	New York City	general	3,000	7,000
Genoa	Baltimore	?	30,000	?
New Inlet, Va.	Chincoteague, Va.	?	800	?
Cobb Island, Va.	Norfolk, Va.	oysters	700	150
Rappahannock River, Va.	New Haven, Conn.	oysters	2,000	230
Providence, R. I.	Baltimore, Md.	fish	12,000	5,000
Rockport, Me.	Richmond, Va.	ice	8,000	500
New York City	Norfolk, Va.	?	6,000	?
Providence, R. I.	Norfolk, Va.	?	35,000	?
?	?	?	?	?
Guilford	Parramore Beach, Va.	?	600	?
Folly Creek, Va.	Norfolk, Va.	potatoes	600	150
Sabine, Tex.	Baltimore	sulphur	473,750	?
Sabine, Tex.	Baltimore	sulphur	473,750	?
Locustville	fishing trip	fish	?	?
Provincetown	Fishing Bay, Va.	?	?	?
Cadiz, Spain	Hampton Roads, Va.	?	11,000	?
Providence, R. I.	Hampton Roads, Va.	?	20,000	?
?	?	?	?	?
Cobb Island, Va.	Norfolk, Va.	oysters	2,500	320
New Haven	Norfolk, Va.	?	15,000	?
Messongo, Va.	New York City	ballast	6,800	0
Jacksonville, Fla.	New Haven, Conn.	lumber	45,000	?
Chincoteague, Va.	Atlantic City, N. J.	clams	400	50
Norfolk, Va.	New York City	corn	12,000	3,000
Brunswick, Ga.	Perth Amboy, N. J.	railroad ties	25,000	?
Jersey City, N. J.	Wachapreague, Va.	?	2,000	?
Newport News, Va.	Beverly, Mass.	?	60,200	?
?	?	?	600	?
James River, Va.	Philadelphia	lumber	6,000	1,100
Ipswich, England	Baltimore	?	34,000	?
Delaware break-water	Norfolk, Va.	?	75,000	?
Port Tampa, Fla.	Norfolk, Va.	phosphate	280,000	50,000
?	Baltimore	nitrate	125,000	?
Hampton Roads, Va.	Lynnhaven River, Va.	oysters	1,500	?

Vessel	Year/Mo/Day	Ton-nage	Master	Home Port
Godrevy	1889 9 12	1,106	Jamieson	London, England
Govino	1892 2 21	2,220	Gilalty	Sunderland, England
Govino	1895 1 18	2,279	Alderson	Sunderland, England
Grace Leigh	1886 12 4	14	Bolton	Petersburg, Va.
Gray Eagle	1888 3 12	442	Powell	Baltimore
Guiseppe Messone	1878 2 9	495	Merble	Genoa, Italy
H. J. Bishop	1883 3 13	21	Larkins	Brookhaven, N. Y.
H. J. Bradshaw	1895 10 23	22	Linman	Newport News, Va.
H. M. Somers	1884 4 4	31	Ingersoll	Somers Pt., N. J.
H. Prescott	1877 1 24	101	Meriman	Portland, Me.
H. W. Race	1892 1 20	?	Jackson	New York City
Hannah Morris	1880 4 16	?	?	Windsor, N. J.
Hansa	1879 11 2	?	?	Germany
Harlseywood	1913 4 24	2,701	?	Middlesboro, Nova Scotia
Harp	1898 12 5	5	O'Neal	Norfolk, Va.
Harriet E. Loundes	1885 12 21	13	Whealton	Chincoteague, Va.
Harriet S. Brooks	1891 11 29	231	Smith	Philadelphia
Harriet Thomas	1887 10 31	475	Edgell	Baltimore
Harry C. Shepard	1887 4 6	214	Booye	Somers Pt., N. J.
Harry Doremus	1889 8 10	48	Benjamin	New York City
Harry T. Hayward	1906 3 22	1,203	Calcord	Thomaston, Me.
Hartfield	1899 10 2	1,867	Christie	Liverpool, England
Harvey M. Anderson	1891 10 14	?	?	?
Hattie Mary	1879 3 11	?	?	Chincoteague, Va.
Hattie Perry	1890 9 29	174	Chase	New Bedford, Mass.
Hawk	1903 10 10	6	Mister	Cape Charles, Va.
Haxby	1897 1 15	3,445	Brown	West Hartlepool, England
Helen	1893 4 27	2,031	Bugby	Belfast, Ireland
Helen Hasbrouck	1884 5 26	309	Bennett	New York City
Helga	1901 4 29	1,900	Braastead	Grimstead, Norway
Henrietta	1881 3 3	33	Larkin	Norfolk, Va.
Henry A. Littlefield (USS)	1907 8 12	?	?	?
Henry B. Hyde	1904 2 11	2,583	Pearson	San Francisco, Cal.
Henry B. Hyde	1904 6 10	2,583	none	San Francisco, Cal.
Henry B. Hyde	1904 9 22	2,583	Demalo	San Francisco, Cal.
Henry Doremus	1883 10 18	48	Lamberson	New York City
Henry P. Simmons	1889 10 23	648	Grace	Philadelphia

Voyage from	to	Cargo	Dollar Value of Vessel	Cargo
Santiago, Cuba	Baltimore	mineral	70,015	?
Sunderland	Baltimore	?	150,000	?
Serpho, Greece	Baltimore	iron ore	114,035	?
Magothy Bay, Va.	Petersburg	oysters	500	75
Rio de Janeiro, Brazil	Baltimore	iron	8,000	?
Belfast, Ireland	Baltimore	?	?	?
Baltimore	Hog Island, Va.	?	2,000	?
Hampton, Va.	?	?	500	?
Chuckatuck, Va.	Great Egg Harbor, N. J.	oysters	1,000	350
Chesapeake Bay	Portland, Me.	oysters	3,500	630
Hampton, Va.	New York City	lumber	5,500	?
Bremerhaven, Germany	Baltimore	barrels & salt	?	?
Bremen, Germany	Baltimore	ballast	?	?
Mobile, Ala.	Holland	lumber	175,000	?
Edenton, N. C.	False Cape, Va.	fish	550	?
Hog Island, Va.	Tom's Cove, Va.	oysters	1,500	200
Wachapreague, Va.	Petersburg, Va.	guano	3,000	5,000
New Haven, Conn.	Baltimore	?	?	?
Newark, N. J.	Port Deposit, Va.	phosphate	9,000	11,000
Norfolk, Va.	Fire Island, N. Y.	lumber	2,000	600
Punta Gorda, Fla.	Baltimore	phosphate rock	67,500	?
South America	Philadelphia	iron ore	66,000	?
?	?	?	?	?
?	Chincoteague, Va.	lumber	?	?
Philadelphia	New Bedford	coal	5,000	650
?	?	?	?	?
Liverpool, England	Hampton Roads, Va.	?	75,000	?
Belfast	Baltimore	iron ore	192,000	?
New York City	Baltimore	?	7,000	?
Daiquiri, Cuba	Baltimore	?	79,500	?
Norfolk	Isaac Shoals, Va.	?	1,000	?
?	?	?	?	?
New York City	Baltimore	coal	52,000	?
New York City	Baltimore	none	?	0
New York City	Baltimore	none	?	0
Folly Creek, Va.	New York City	potatoes	5,000	2,800
Charleston, S. C.	Baltimore	phosphate rock	31,500	?

Vessel	Year/Mo/Day			Tonnage	Master	Home Port
Henry Parker	1895	4	29	226	Crammer	New York City
Hibernia	1898	9	21	2,371	Cameron	Whitby, England
Howard N. Johnson	1886	10	23	96	Granger	Baltimore
Howard N. Johnson	1886	10	24	96	Granger	Baltimore
Hungry Negro	1896	10	7	?	?	?
Hygeia	1887	9	18	24	Spady	Norfolk, Va.
Ida C. Schodcraft	1884	8	18	320	Booye	Somers Pt., N. J.
Ida L. Hull	1888	12	22	498	Gibson	Barnstable, Mass.
Isle of Kent	1900	5	1	1,961	Sutherland	Newcastle, England
Ivanhoe	1885	1	9	95	Tingle	Philadelphia
*J. B. Denton	1893	10	9	?	?	Red Bank, Va.
J. C. Wood	1886	6	2	5	Shorpley	Chincoteague, Va.
†J. F. Knapp	1880	2	1	?	?	Smith's Landing, N. J.
J. G. Connor	1897	10	6	26	Tull	Chincoteague, Va.
J. H. Chapman	1881	12	9	?	Leamon	Keyport, N. J.
J. H. Crittenden	1884	9	17	12	Brown	Norfolk, Va.
J. H. Elliott	1893	11	15	71	Aydelott	Philadelphia
J. J. Spencer	1878	1	6	210	Haskell	Boston, Mass.
J. O. Fitzgerald	1889	4	7	9	Mason	Chincoteague, Va.
J. Ricardo Jova	1881	1	2	?	Dale	Philadelphia
J. T. Ford	1900	2	26	17	Edwards	Crisfield, Md.
J. W. Arthur	1890	3	15	11	Clark	Norfolk, Va.
J. W. Luce	1888	12	15	22	Stiles	Onancock, Va.
Jacob T. Alburgher	1877	12	1	256	Newell	Philadelphia
James Anderson	1877	11	18	39	Derrickson	Wilmington, Del.
James Boyce	1885	12	20	454	Crossley	?
James D. Dewell	1892	1	26	603	Chatfield	New Haven, Conn.
James E. Kelsey	1886	10	9	102	Longstreet	Manasquan, N. J.
James E. Kelsey	1887	6	3	102	Longstreet	Manasquan, N. J.
James Ford	1879	11	13	?	?	Fall River, Mass.
James M. Vance	1879	3	31	?	?	Philadelphia
James Ponder	1897	4	20	272	Maxwell	Tuckerton, N. J.
James Rothwell	1888	4	23	498	Lambert	Boston, Mass.
James W. Brown	1881	11	23	161	Elwell	Belfast, Me.
James Young	1901	1	4	261	Bulger	Thomaston, Me.
Jane Emson	1883	3	11	329	Greene	Taunton, Mass.
Jas. B. Johnson	1884	6	17	148	Rose	Somers Pt., N. J.
Jason	1879	11	26	?	?	?

*on a "fishing trip"
†abandoned

Voyage from	to	Cargo	Dollar Value of Vessel	Dollar Value of Cargo
New York City	Norfolk, Va.	?	6,000	?
Galveston, Tex.	Norfolk, Va.	general	161,565	?
Richmond, Va.	Smith Island, Va.	stone	3,000	150
Richmond, Va.	Smith Island, Va.	stone	3,000	150
?	?	?	?	?
?	?	?	3,000	?
Richmond, Va.	Philadelphia	railroad ties	6,000	2,000
Taunton, Mass.	Baltimore	?	35,000	?
New Orleans, La.	Newport News, Va.	general	240,000	?
Philadelphia	Chincoteague, Va.	?	35,000	?
Red Bank	?	fish & scrap	75	?
Hog Island, Va.	Chincoteague	oysters	500	100
?	?	?	?	?
James River, Va.	Chincoteague	oysters	1,000	80
Norfolk, Va.	Rappahannock, Va.	?	600	?
Smith Island, Va.	York River, Va.	oysters	600	200
Hampton, Va.	New York City	wood	3,000	350
Boston	Washington, D. C.	pitch & lumber	6,000	3,000
Chincoteague	?	clams	700	25
New York City	Richmond, Va.	railroad iron	7,000	12,750
Crisfield	Long Branch, N. J.	?	500	?
Smith Island, Va.	Norfolk	oysters	500	70
Norfolk, Va.	Wachapreague, Va.	lumber	2,000	250
Philadelphia	Richmond, Va.	pig iron	12,000	5,000
Philadelphia	Norfolk, Va.	coal	1,500	300
New Haven, Conn.	Norfolk, Va.	?	8,000	?
Brunswick, Ga.	Elizabethport, N. J.	railroad ties	17,000	2,000
Wishart's Pt., Va.	New York City	wood	5,000	500
Wishart's Pt., Va.	New York City	wood	3,000	450
Baltimore	Hoboken, N. J.	coal	?	?
?	?	?	?	?
Bermuda Hundreds, Va.	New York City	railroad ties	3,000	1,000
Boston	Philadelphia	?	24,000	?
Baltimore	Jacksonville, Fla.	general	10,000	10,000
Bermuda Hundreds, Va.	New York City	lumber	3,000	3,000
Norfolk, Va.	New York City	railroad ties	8,000	3,000
Mattapony River, Va.	Philadelphia	railroad ties	2,500	2,000
?	?	railroad iron	?	?

Vessel	Year/Mo/Day	Ton-nage	Master	Home Port
Jennie Hall	1900 12 21	412	Lamson	Machias, Me.
Jennie N. Huddell	1910 2 5	279	?	New York City
Jennie Sweeny	1878 2 4	643	Hudson	Philadelphia
Joanna H. Cann	1881 2 10	1,169	Tooker	Yarmouth, Nova Scotia
John E. Sevlin	1908 1 12	1,107	?	Thomaston, Me.
John Eills	1881 1 26	762	Simpson	St. John, New Brunswick
John F. Kranz	1901 2 5	?	?	?
John Gibson	1886 10 30	445	Young	Georgetown, S. C.
John H. Savage	1887 4 26	?	Savage	Chincoteague, Va.
John Hooper	1891 11 29	92	Thomas	Somers Pt., N. J.
John I. Brady	1894 9 16	?	Freeburger	Baltimore
John M. Price	1886 3 15	26	Birch	Chincoteague, Va.
John M. Rogers	1884 11 6	19	Booth	Chincoteague, Va.
John McDonnell	1881 11 4	?	Coulborn	Philadelphia
John R. Walters	1890 9 27	9	Booth	Chincoteague, Va.
John S. Beachman	1896 5 6	234	Strout	Richmond, Va.
John S. Higgins	1880 11 14	47	Cook	Provincetown, Mass.
John Young	1888 3 8	87	Burden	Perth Amboy, N. J.
John Young	1890 9 27	87	Burden	New York City
Joseph J. Comstock	1884 12 9	21	Bolton	Norfolk, Va.
Joseph J. Pharo	1901 9 16	261	Thornblom	New York City
Joseph J. Pharo	1904 1 3	261	Berry	New York City
Josephine	1895 5 16	940	McLean	Baltimore
Josie R. Burt	1888 12 22	722	Burt	Fall River, Mass.
Josie Smith	1890 11 6	12	Mumford	Chincoteague, Va.
Josie Smith	1894 1 24	12	Daisey	Chincoteague, Va.
Julie A. Roe	1886 4 2	32	Marshall	Baltimore
Julius Webb	1878 3 25	134	Loveland	New York City
Juno	1903 1 10	2,430	Hummel	Fredericksvaern, Norway
Katherine D. Perry	1911 12 17	1,125	?	New York City
Katie Collins	1881 10 30	?	Mathis	Philadelphia
Katie J. Hoyt	1897 12 24	220	Adams	Dennis, Mass.

Voyage from	to	Cargo	Dollar Value of Vessel	Cargo
Port of Spain, Trinidad	Baltimore	asphalt	15,000	1,000
Norfolk, Va.	New York City	lumber	4,000	4,000
Galveston, Tex.	Philadelphia	cotton	30,000	130,000
Antwerp, Belgium	Baltimore	?	65,000	?
Salem, Mass.	Newport News, Va.	?	40,000	?
Waterford, Ireland	Hampton Roads, Va.	?	20,000	?
?	?	?	?	?
Alexandria, Va.	New York City	general	50,000	75,000
Fiske's Cove, Va.	Chincoteague	oysters	800	50
Cape Hatteras, N. C.	Atlantic City, N. J.	lumber	6,500	1,200
Baltimore	?	?	20,000	?
Hog Island, Va.	Tom's Cove, Va.	oysters	1,500	200
?	?	?	1,500	?
Nansemond River, Va.	Philadelphia	railroad ties	8,000	2,250
Hog Island, Va.	Chincoteague	oysters	500	100
Richmond	New Haven, Conn.	pig iron	4,000	2,000
Boston, Mass.	Norfolk, Va.	fish & apples	1,000	800
New York City	York River, Va.	?	2,000	?
Nansemond River, Va.	New York City	wood	4,000	550
Ship Shoal Inlet, Va.	Norfolk	oysters	2,000	270
New York City	Bermuda Hundreds, Va.	?	3,000	?
New York City	Richmond, Va.	?	6,000	?
Rio de Janeiro, Brazil	Baltimore	coffee	166,140	50,000
New Bedford, Mass.	Baltimore	?	10,000	?
?	?	?	500	?
Metomkin Inlet, Va.	Assateague, Va.	oysters	600	30
Deal's Island, Md.	Maurice River, N. J.	oysters	2,500	240
New York City	Virginia	?	2,000	?
Santiago, Cuba	Baltimore	iron ore	28,500	?
Portland, Me.	Norfolk, Va.	?	20,000	?
Jacksonville, Fla.	Perth Amboy, N. J.	lumber	15,000	8,940
Norfolk, Va.	Derby, Conn.	lumber	3,000	2,000

Vessel	Year/Mo/Day	Ton-nage	Master	Home Port
Kestrel	1900 12 27	10	Wright	New Haven, Conn.
Kildonan	1896 12 17	2,337	Renwick	Dundee, Scotland
Kwasind	1881 1 20	984	Sprague	Sackville, New Brunswick
L. A. Rose	1896 9 1	145	Rose	Somers Pt., N. J.
L. A. Rose	1897 10 25	145	Rose	Somers Pt., N. J.
L. B. Chandler	1891 3 22	39	Hudson	New Castle, Del.
L. B. Chandler	1893 3 24	39	Swift	Chincoteague, Va.
L. S. Levering	1881 3 2	299	Corson	Wilmington, Del.
Lady Ellen	1889 1 13	203	Clark	New York City
Lady Maud	1886 12 30	10	Warren	Onancock, Va.
Lady of the Lake	1888 7 13	48	Chatham	Crisfield, Md.
Laura Tomkins	1913 3 2	16	?	Chincoteague, Va.
Lehman Blew	1890 11 18	275	Sharp	Camden, N. J.
Lena	1884 12 27	450	Mortensen	Norway
Lena Hunter	1883 12 16	285	Fisher	Philadelphia
Lena Hunter	1885 12 27	285	Fisher	Philadelphia
Leona	1886 3 2	202	Lippincott	New York City
Levi Lewis	1888 1 31	14	Reid	Newport News, Va.
Levi Lewis	1889 4 7	14	Bell	Norfolk, Va.
Levi S. Andrews	1914 1 22	669	?	Philadelphia
Lewis A. Rommell	1884 1 15	334	Jeffries	Philadelphia
Libbie P. Hallock	1891 5 27	79	Shaw	Somers Pt., N. J.
Lilla	1877 1 20	544	Pecasso	Genoa, Italy
Lillian Russell	1902 12 16	18	Parson	Cape Charles, Va.
Lillie A. Warfield	1884 10 24	171	Mount	Philadelphia
Lillie A. Warford	1883 12 23	171	Mount	Perth Amboy, N. J.
Lillie A. Warford	1887 12 12	171	Pierce	Manasquan, N. J.
Lillie Ernestine	1886 1 9	54	Terry	Patchogue, N. Y.
Little Falkenburg	1888 12 15	217	Cranmer	Tuckerton, N. J.
Lizzie	1884 10 10	86	Cramer	Somers Pt., N. J.
Lizzie Godfrey	1914 7 9	73	?	?
Lizzie Jane	1884 1 10	11	?	Chincoteague, Va.
Lizzie Jane	1886 12 12	11	Whealton	Chincoteague, Va.
Lizzie Jane	1888 3 29	11	Whealton	Chincoteague, Va.
Lizzie Jane	1888 11 25	11	Whealton	Chincoteague, Va.
Lizzie Jane	1889 11 15	11	Whealton	Chincoteague, Va.

Voyage from	to	Cargo	Dollar Value of Vessel	Cargo
New Haven	Jacksonville, Fla.	?	5,000	?
Glasgow, Scotland	Newport News, Va.	?	125,000	?
Hamburg, Germany	Baltimore	general	30,000	7,000
Claremont, Va.	New York City	wood	2,000	1,000
James River, Va.	New York City	wood	1,000	300
Norfolk, Va.	Cobb Island, Va.	?	1,800	?
James River, Va.	New Haven, Conn.	oysters	2,000	600
Philadelphia	Alexandria, Va.	coal	10,000	?
New York City	Norfolk, Va.	fertilizer	3,000	12,000
Chincoteague, Va.	Wachapreague, Va.	?	1,000	?
New York City	Baltimore	salt	3,000	250
Chincoteague	Norfolk, Va.	?	800	?
Virginia	Philadelphia	wood	3,000	900
Natal, Brazil	Philadelphia	sugar	15,000	28,000
New York City	Richmond, Va.	?	10,000	?
Roundout, N. Y.	Washington, D. C.	stone	?	?
New York City	West Point, Va.	phosphate	10,000	10,000
Ship Shoal Inlet, Va.	Norfolk, Va.	oysters	700	100
Magothy Bay, Va.	Chuckatuck, Va.	oysters	650	100
Philadelphia	Savannah, Ga.	coal	7,000	2,500
Charleston, S. C.	Baltimore	phosphate rock	33,000	?
Morris Canal, N. J.	Jersey City, N. J.	sand	2,000	300
Genoa	Baltimore	?	15,000	?
Norfolk, Va.	Hog Island, Va.	?	2,000	?
Nansemond River, Va.	New York City	wood	7,000	700
Nansemond River, Va.	New York City	wood	3,000	800
Wishart's Pt., Va.	New York City	wood	3,600	800
New York City	York River, Va.	?	4,000	?
New York City	James River, Va.	?	8,000	?
Camden, N. J.	Parramore Island, Va.	lumber	1,500	1,500
?	?	oysters	?	?
New Inlet, Va.	Chincoteague	?	800	?
Cobb Island, Va.	Chincoteague	oysters	1,200	40
Wachapreague, Va.	Chincoteague	?	1,000	?
Chincoteague	?	?	600	?
Chincoteague	Metomkin Inlet, Va.	?	1,000	?

Vessel	Year/Mo/Day	Ton-nage	Master	Home Port
Lizzie Jane	1890 7 18	11	Whealton	Chincoteague, Va.
Lizzie S. James	1897 12 23	182	Howard	Philadelphia
Lucia	1913 5 24	4,286	?	Trieste, Austria
Lucy A. Davis	1895 11 21	621	Loring	Portland, Me.
M. Luella Wood	1892 4 18	557	Spaulding	Rockland, Me.
M. P. Howlett	1905 4 8	46	Mullen	Philadelphia
Mabel Thomas	1881 3 28	35	McKenzie	New Haven, Conn.
Macauley	1887 11 9	1,038	Bennett	Baltimore
Maddalena Seconda	1882 12 4	473	Schiafino	Genoa, Italy
Madora Francis	1880 12 19	24	Hudson	Chincoteague, Va.
Madora Francis	1883 10 18	24	Thornton	Chincoteague, Va.
Magellan	1892 12 20	226	Dixon	New Brunswick, Nova Scotia
Maggie Bell	1882 5 5	?	Lynch	Chincoteague, Va.
Maggie E. Davis	1896 10 2	44	Whealton	Chincoteague, Va.
Maggie E. Gray	1880 11 22	406	Crockett	Baltimore
Major Pickands	1893 11 17	984	Laithwait	Portland, Me.
Malden	1901 7 14	538	McKown	Boston, Mass.
Manantico	1887 10 31	177	Emmons	Middletown, Conn.
Manchuria	1910 3 7	2,997	?	West Hartlepool, England
Manson	1898 1 9	264	Crapo	New Bedford, Mass.
Margaret	1895 9 29	299	Fitzgerald	New Haven, Conn.
Margaret H. Vane	1908 8 24	246	?	Baltimore
Margherita	1910 4 1	3,269	?	Trieste, Austria
Marion	1890 12 3	1,009	Wade	New London, Conn.
Marion Grimes	1906 9 25	72	Osborn	New York City
Marvin P. White	1890 10 15	28	Bloxom	Norfolk, Va.
Mary A. Harmon	1878 2 27	320	Scaife	Philadelphia
Mary and Emma	1889 2 1	?	?	Machipongo Creek, Va.
Mary Ann	1881 10 9	?	Cobb	Cobb Island, Va.
Mary Ann	1886 3 2	?	?	Cobb Island, Va.
Mary C.	1882 4 27	?	Williams	New Castle, Del.
Mary C. Carroll	1891 3 14	174	Campbell	Somers Pt., N. J.
Mary D. Cranmer	1887 10 31	214	Parker	Tuckerton, N. J.
Mary E. H. G. Dow	1892 12 24	1,139	Philpot	Bath, Me.
Mary J. Robbins	1897 12 24	24	Gaskell	Port Norris, N. J.

Voyage from	to	Cargo	Dollar Value of Vessel	Cargo
Norfolk, Va.	Chincoteague	shingles/laths	1,200	300
New Bern, N. C.	New York City	lumber	7,000	1,500
Newport News, Va.	Cadiz, Spain	general	?	?
Brunswick, Ga.	New York City	lumber	15,000	20,000
Port Royal, S. C.	Baltimore	phosphate rock	20,000	?
James River, Va.	Philadelphia	oysters	5,000	700
Baltimore, Md.	Boston, Mass.	coal	20,000	2,200
Hamburg, Germany	Baltimore	kainite & barrels	10,000	?
Montevideo, Uruguay	Baltimore	bones	20,000	8,000
Philadelphia	Chincoteague	general	1,500	1,000
Newport News, Va.	Hog Island, Va.	coal	1,200	50
Newport News, Va.	Halifax, Nova Scotia	coal	6,000	2,620
Hog Island, Va.	Chincoteague	oysters	200	50
New York City	Chincoteague	coal	2,000	200
Portsmouth, N. H.	Baltimore	?	12,000	?
Philadelphia	Norfolk, Va.	?	40,000	?
Boston	Savannah, Ga.	?	16,000	?
Albany, N. Y.	Richmond, Va.	lumber	?	?
Newport News, Va.	Tampico, Mexico	coal	16,500	?
Bermuda Hundreds, Va.	Philadelphia	railroad ties	2,500	1,700
New London, Conn.	Tampa, Fla.	?	40,000	?
Beaufort, N. C.	Bridgeport, Conn.	lumber	10,000	3,200
New Orleans, La.	Norfolk, Va.	general	100,000	100,000
New London	Norfolk, Va.	?	15,000	?
?	?	fish	3,600	250
Norfolk	Cobb Island, Va.	?	2,000	?
Philadelphia	Baltimore	?	?	?
Machipongo Creek	Hog Island, Va.	?	200	?
Cobb Island	Seaside, Va.	?	200	?
Cobb Island	?	oysters	200	?
James River, Va.	Sinepuxent Bay, Del.	oysters	2,500	300
Carteret, N. J.	Richmond, Va.	phosphate	3,000	8,000
James River, Va.	New York City	?	?	?
Baltimore	Portsmouth, N. H.	coal	60,000	6,100
James River, Va.	Port Norris	oysters	2,000	150

Vessel	Year/Mo/Day	Tonnage	Master	Home Port
Mary L. Vetra	1887 2 18	21	Travis	Eastville, Va.
Mary Standish	1901 3 11	272	Gillchrist	Boston, Mass.
Mary Washington	1903 10 10	8	Rowley	Newport News, Va.
Mary Wood	1877 5 24	35	Arthur	New York City
Mascott	1897 12 25	14	Parker	Somers Pt., N. J.
Massasoit	1914 11 15	1,212	?	?
Maude and Ellis	1901 10 10	?	?	?
May Queen	1886 4 8	184	Asquini	Baltimore
Medora Francis	1889 12 13	24	Babbit	Chincoteague, Va.
Melvin R. Drew	1899 2 9	48	Amory	Norfolk, Va.
Melvin R. Drew	1899 2 12	48	Amory	Norfolk, Va.
Memento	1882 3 1	?	Means	Onancock, Va.
Midnight	1895 5 14	6	Johnson	New York City
Minnie Sylvia	1889 4 7	?	?	Cobb Island, Va.
Miranda	1892 1 12	1,668	Wallace	West Hartlepool, England
Missouri	1903 10 10	8	Rowley	Newport News, Va.
Monhegan	1901 7 26	23	Yarrow	New York City
Montevue	1878 1 4	185	Leek	New York City
Moonstone	1900 9 10	2,076	Williams	London, England
Morning Light	1888 12 11	?	?	Chincoteague, Va.
Murciano	1893 10 23	2,410	Avalucca	Bilbao, Spain
N. C. Price	1875 12 7	38	Williams	Cape May, N. J.
Nathan Lawrence	1895 1 19	771	Haskell	Fall River, Mass.
Nederland	1882 1 17	1,738	Sluendrecht	Rotterdam, Holland
Nellie Blanche	1887 7 15	140	Johnson	Key West, Fla.
Nellie Potter	1887 4 5	104	Wahab	Washington, D. C.
Nellie W. Craig	1910 7 9	492	?	New York City
Nellie W. Howlett	1903 10 10	568	Gheen	Philadelphia
Nelson E. Newberry	1886 12 17	659	Warren	New York City
Nettie	1894 1 7	503	Lowry	New York City
Nettie and Lena	1894 10 28	32	?	Camden, N. J.
Nettie Murphy	1881 1 11	1,373	Raymond	Yarmouth, Nova Scotia
Nipote	1878 3 28	428	Dumwick	Fiume, Austria
North Carolina	1880 8 18	?	?	Liverpool, England

Voyage from	to	Cargo	Dollar Value of Vessel	Cargo
Norfolk, Va.	Smith Island, Va.	stone	1,500	75
New York City	City Point, Va.	?	5,000	?
?	?	?	?	?
Chuckatuck, Va.	New York City	oysters	5,000	200
Chincoteague	James River, Va.	?	1,000	?
?	?	?	?	?
?	?	?	?	?
San Andres, Colombia	Baltimore	coconuts	11,700	?
Norfolk, Va.	Machipongo, Va.	?	1,200	?
Cobb Island, Va.	Norfolk	oysters	1,000	120
?	?	oysters	1,000	100
Onancock	Norfolk, Va.	corn & potatoes	700	600
Norfolk, Va.	New York City	?	500	?
Cobb Island	?	none	125	
West Hartlepool	Delaware break-water	?	6,000	?
?	?	?	?	?
New York City	Annapolis, Md.	?	3,750	?
Hampton Roads, Va.	New York City	pine wood	3,000	600
Sabine Pass, Tex.	Rotterdam, Holland	lumber	85,300	?
Chincoteague	Fiske's Cove, Va.	oysters	500	50
New Orleans, La.	Lambert's Point, Va.	cotton & grain	60,000	178,180
Cape May	Norfolk, Va.	ballast	4,500	?
Boston, Mass.	Newport News, Va.	?	30,000	?
Rotterdam	Baltimore	general	130,950	?
New York City	Baltimore	general	3,000	3,500
New York City	Washington, D. C.	general	5,000	?
Norfolk, Va.	Charleston, S. C.	coal	13,200	?
Jacksonville, Fla.	New York City	?	30,000	?
Baltimore	New York City	coal	30,000	3,000
Turk's Island, West Indies	Norfolk, Va.	salt	?	?
James River, Va.	Maurice River, N. J.	oysters	2,500	300
Tusket, Nova Scotia	Norfolk, Va.	ballast	75,000	?
Fleetwood, England	Baltimore	?	?	?
Smithville, N. C.	Baltimore	ballast	?	?

Vessel	Year/Mo/Day	Ton-nage	Master	Home Port
North Point	1878 3 7	455	Jones	Kingston, Jamaica
North Star	1893 4 20	47	Haje	Stonington, Conn.
Northampton	1889 4 7	36	Lawson	Eastville, Va.
Norwood	1910 2 18	1,718	?	Mailland, Nova Scotia
Noviembre	1903 1 16	3,655	Ybarraran	Bilbao, Spain
Oakdene	1895 4 2	1,594	Sandale	Sunderland, England
Ocean Belle	1903 10 10	1,593	Adams	New York City
Ocean King	1900 12 24	201	Chase	New York City
Ocean Star	1881 12 15	?	Rider	Somers Pt., N. J.
Ocean Star	1884 4 10	113	Adams	Somers Pt., N. J.
Olga	1883 12 21	547	Nicoli	Genoa, Italy
Olustree	1888 5 15	470	Nicholson	Boston, Mass
Onancock City	1902 11 16	13	?	Chincoteague, Va.
Ordovic	1889 11 17	825	Austin	Caernarvon, Wales
Oregon	1903 10 10	8	Winder	Cape Charles, Va.
Osborn Curtis	1878 1 4	48	Mount	Perth Amboy, N. J.
Osborn Curtis	1880 3 11	?	?	?
Ossipee	1877 11 25	365	?	New York City
Pangussett	1886 12 5	196	Anderson	Norfolk, Va.
Pantser	1877 3 26	350	Johnson	Liverpool, England
Paulding (USS)	1914 10 27	742	?	?
Pearl Nelson	1882 2 24	?	?	Provincetown, Mass.
Pecora	1882 12 7	75	Branin	Bridgeton, N. J.
Peerless	1878 12 1	?	?	Baltimore
Peerless	1888 3 12	14	Bell	Onancock, Va.
Pendleton Satisfacton	1909 1 18	524	?	Belfast, Me.
Pendleton Sisters	1905 12 15	798	Davies	New York City
Peter J. Hart	1884 12 15	40	Sharpley	Chincoteague, Va.
Pettinquamscott	1890 1 29	22	West	Norfolk, Va.
Phoebe	1891 1 9	26	West	Norfolk, Va.
Phoebe Ann	1890 12 26	32	Pearsall	Patchogue, N. Y.
Pirate	1886 12 30	218	Hughes	Glasgow, Scotland

Voyage from	to	Cargo	Dollar Value of Vessel	Cargo
Kingston	Philadelphia	fruit, rags, & wood	17,000	5,000
New York City	Hatteras, N. C.	?	3,000	?
Cherrystone, Va.	Cape Charles, Va.	?	?	?
Bonair, West Indies	Boston, Mass.	salt	15,000	5,500
Galveston, Tex	Rotterdam, Holland	general	120,000	?
Hamburg, Germany	Baltimore	salt & cement	30,000	16,000
Newport News, Va.	Providence, R. I.	coal	38,725	?
New York City	Baltimore	?	25,000	?
New York City	Ship Shoal, Va.	?	1,500	?
Somers Pt.	Chincoteague, Va.	?	3,000	?
Westport, England	Baltimore	?	12,000	?
New York City	Baltimore	?	18,000	?
Chincoteague	Norfolk, Va.	oysters	900	300
Lobos de Afuera, Peru	Hampton Roads, Va.	guano	40,000	?
?	?	?	?	?
Assawoman, Va.	New York City	pine wood	4,000	300
?	?	?	?	?
Denia, Spain	New York City	almonds & raisins	14,000	30,000
New York City	Norfolk, Va.	railroad iron & firebrick	7,000	?
Liverpool	Hampton Roads, Va.	?	15,000	?
?	?	?	?	?
Wilmington, N. C.	Plymouth, Mass.	tar	?	?
South Creek, N. C.	Philadelphia	lumber	2,000	1,300
Baltimore	?	?	?	?
Norfolk, Va.	Machipongo, Va.	general	700	300
Brunswick, Ga.	Perth Amboy, N. J.	lumber	30,000	?
Port Arthur, Tex.	Noank, Conn.	lumber	40,000	13,000
New York City	Franklin City, Va.	coal	2,500	500
Ship Shoal Inlet, Va.	Norfolk	oysters	300	250
Cobb Island, Va.	Norfolk	oysters	450	250
New York City	Norfolk, Va.	?	1,500	?
Baltimore	Kingston, Jamaica	lumber	77,000	?

Vessel	Year/Mo/Day	Ton-nage	Master	Home Port
Polaria	1897 10 26	2,724	Strange	Hamburg, Germany
Polynesian	1892 2 6	2,023	Dougall	Glasgow, Scotland
Prohibition	1889 8 25	6	Terlington	Chincoteague, Va.
Prohibition	1893 12 4	6	Mumford	Chincoteague, Va.
Puritan	1898 12 7	116	Sargent	Belfast, Me.
R. B. Leeds	1885 4 12	35	Hammond	Somers Pt., N. J.
R. B. Leeds	1897 12 22	35	Hilton	Philadelphia
R. F. Hastings	1887 3 20	31	Bool	Eastville, Va.
R. F. Hastings	1896 3 15	31	Collins	Chincoteague, Va.
R. W. Hopkins	1907 1 3	935	Clark	Thomaston, Me.
Ralph C. Hayward	1906 12 11	604	Lawry	Fall River, Mass.
Ralph Howes	1876 2 20	143	Burgess	Belfast, Me.
Rappahannock	1894 1 22	3,883	Penwell	Liverpool, England
Rebecca	1903 2 17	141	Thomas	Norfolk, Va.
Rebecca J.	1886 2 25	14	Jeffers	Chincoteague, Va.
Rebecca Palmer	1904 11 11	2,556	Clark	Boston, Mass.
Reliance	1912 11 2	25	?	Norfolk, Va.
Rescue	1885 5 21	68	Key	Bridgeton, N. J.
Rhein	1887 3 8	3,075	Reman	Bremen, Germany
Richard Rhodes	1889 12 1	19	Williams	Newport News, Va.
Rillie S. Derby	1899 12 14	419	Naylor	Philadelphia
Riversdale	1914 2 20	1,785	?	Sunderland, England
Robert H. Parker	1892 12 20	380	Smith	Somers Pt., N. J.
Robert J. Poulson	1904 7 7	29	Madkins	Cape Charles, Va.
Robert J. Poulson	1904 11 13	29	Madkins	Cape Charles, Va.
Robert W. Brown	1880 12 7	177	Miller	Key West, Fla.
Robinia	1901 5 25	2,038	Lash	North Shields, England
Rondout	1900 12 24	815	Buhr	New York City
Rosalie Starita	1881 2 8	422	Maresca	Naples, Italy
Rosewood	1904 4 8	1,757	McGregor	South Shields, England
S. B. Wheeler	1900 12 1	280	Fedderman	Baltimore
S. D. Carleton	1912 3 25	1,874	?	New York City
S. E. Barnes	1876 3 28	42	LaForge	Staten Island, N. Y.
Sachem	1894 11 11	9	Figs	Chincoteague, Va.
Sagitta	1882 1 9	980	Taylor	Windsor, Nova Scotia
Sallie Coursey	1880 11 7	179	Pardee	Wilmington, Del.

Voyage from	to	Cargo	Dollar Value of Vessel	Dollar Value of Cargo
Galveston, Tex.	Norfolk, Va.	cotton & coffee	140,000	?
Liverpool	Baltimore	general	?	?
Chincoteague	?	furniture	250	400
Franklin City, Va.	Cobb Island, Va.	?	220	?
Charleston, S. C.	New York City	lumber	3,000	2,000
Parker's Bay, Md.	Absecom, N. J.	oysters	4,000	50
James River, Va.	Maurice, N. J.	oysters	2,000	300
Wachapreague, Va.	Chincoteague, Va.	oysters	1,000	200
Chincoteague	Norfolk, Va.	oysters	600	375
Gulfport, Miss.	Baltimore	lumber	51,720	?
Mystic, Conn.	Norfolk, Va.	?	12,000	?
Belfast	Baltimore	plaster, hay, & corn	7,000	1,200
Newport News, Va.	Liverpool	general	563,000	?
New York City	Norfolk	?	2,500	?
Hog Island, Va.	Chincoteague	oysters	500	130
Boston	Hampton Roads, Va.	?	100,000	?
James River, Va.	Lynnhaven River, Va.	oysters	4,400	?
Washington, N. C.	Millville, N. J.	lumber	2,600	2,000
Bremen	Baltimore	general	80,000	30,000
Cobb Island, Va.	Norfolk, Va.	oysters	1,500	200
Jacksonville, Fla.	Philadelphia	lumber	40,000	9,000
Port Arthur, Tex.	Rotterdam, Holland	lumber	150,000	?
Richmond, Va.	New Haven, Conn.	lumber	12,000	3,780
Hog Island, Va.	Norfolk, Va.	?	1,500	?
?	Norfolk, Va.	oysters	2,500	600
Philadelphia	Fort Monroe, Va.	coal	4,000	750
Charleston, S. C.	Baltimore	?	100,000	?
New York City	Baltimore	?	7,000	?
Catania, Italy	Baltimore	brimstone	42,000	?
Gulfport, Miss.	Rotterdam, Holland	lumber	152,000	?
Philadelphia	Claremont, Va.	?	2,000	?
Providence, R. I.	Hampton Roads, Va.	?	40,000	?
Staten Island	Nansemond, Va.	ballast	3,000	0
Cobb Island, Va.	Franklin City, Va.	clams	500	100
Spain	Baltimore	iron ore	12,000	8,000
Georgetown, S. C.	Roundout, N. Y.	lumber	8,000	3,400

Vessel	Year/Mo/Day			Ton-nage	Master	Home Port
Sallie Solomon	1885	9	20	32	Jones	Baltimore
Samuel C. Holmes	1897	12	24	79	Evans	Wilmington, Del.
Samuel Fillmore	1887	12	21	6	Johnson	Chincoteague, Va.
Samuel Fish	1884	2	28	214	Teel	Thomaston, Me.
Samuel H. Sharp	1896	5	3	249	Crowley	New York City
Samuel H. Walker	1887	3	22	594	Kelly	Taunton, Mass.
San Albano	1892	2	22	1,291	Lajasuaga	Bilbao, Spain
San Ignaciode Loyola	1905	2	8	3,228	De La Torre	San Sebastian, Spain
San Marcos	1875	1	8	2,238	Burrage	Liverpool, England
Sandringham	1880	11	5	737	McKay	Glasgow, Scotland
Sarah C. Smith	1894	9	1	297	Corson	Philadelphia
Sarah E. Palmer	1898	4	5	1,226	Whittier	Bath, Me.
Sarah Shubert	1884	10	14	157	Ewan	Philadelphia
Saxon	1905	9	4	?	?	?
Scindia	1881	9	4	1,000	Roberts	Hull, England
Serpho	1886	1	17	1,059	Hastia	Sunderland, England
Shekinah	1883	1	12	84	Shaw	Bridgeton, N. J.
Silverton	1912	11	11	6,682	?	Leith, Scotland
Skylark	1885	10	24	388	Evans	Boston, Mass.
Sophia Godfrey	1895	1	18	257	McCarty	Bridgeton, N. J.
Southern Belle	1878	1	23	582	Robbins	Yarmouth, Nova Scotia
Staffa	1897	1	16	2,146	Ostergard	West Hartlepool, England
Stella B. Kaplan	1898	2	3	1,079	Potter	Greenport, N. Y.
Sterling (USS)	1911	12	3	5,663	?	?
Stony Brook	1889	3	10	101	Wells	Port Jefferson, N. Y.
Straits of Magellan	1897	11	23	1,657	Hackland	Glasgow, Scotland
Strathome	1891	4	14	1,038	Urquart	Maitland, Nova Scotia
Sunshine	1889	4	21	31	?	Cape Charles City, Va.
Sussex	1891	1	13	63	Whealton	Wilmington, Del.
*Swiftsure	1880	5	9	?	?	England
T. W. Wiltbank	1883	12	20	7	Mason	Chincoteague, Va.
Tamesi	1899	3	5	178	McHenry	Norfolk, Va.
Theresa Wolf	1898	11	17	307	Bowen	Somers Pt., N. J.

*abandoned

Voyage from	to	Cargo	Dollar Value of Vessel	Cargo
Norfolk, Va.	Wicomico River, Va.	?	900	?
York River, Va.	New York City	wood	4,000	250
Potomac River	Chincoteague	?	400	?
New London, Conn.	Hampton, Va.	hay	10,000	435
Norfolk, Va.	New York City	wood	3,700	600
Baltimore	Bridgeport, Conn.	coal	35,000	3,000
New Orleans, La.	Hamburg, Germany	cotton, grain, & oil	75,000	120,000
Passages, Spain	Philadelphia	?	50,000	?
Galveston, Tex.	Liverpool	general	350,000	?
Galveston, Tex.	Liverpool	cotton	235,000	?
Georgetown, S. C.	Boston, Mass.	lumber	3,000	3,500
Portsmouth, N. H.	Norfolk, Va.	?	40,000	?
Philadelphia	Petersburg, Va.	coal	7,500	1,275
Georgetown, S. C.	Philadelphia	lumber	?	?
South America	Norfolk, Va.	?	95,000	?
Gibraltar, Spain	Baltimore	iron ore	62,000	?
New York City	Elizabeth City, N. C.	?	2,500	?
Leith	Charleston, S. C.	fertilizer	150,000	?
Philadelphia	Norfolk, Va.	coal	3,000	2,000
New York City	Suffolk, Va.	salt	2,000	1,600
Genoa, Italy	Baltimore	marble	?	?
New Orleans, La.	Newport News, Va.	grain	125,400	?
Boston, Mass.	Newport News, Va.	?	30,000	?
Annapolis, Md.	Hampton Roads, Va.	?	200,000	?
New York City	Baltimore	salt	3,000	1,000
Cork, Ireland	Baltimore	?	20,000	?
Lobos de Afuera, Peru	Hampton Roads, Va.	guano	100,000	?
Hog Island, Va.	Machipongo, Va.	?	4,000	?
Norfolk, Va.	Cobb Island, Va.	?	500	?
?	?	?	?	?
Myrtle Is., Va.	Metomkin, Va.	oysters	300	35
Norfolk	Westerly, R. I.	?	6,000	?
Bermuda Hundreds, Va.	Philadelphia	wood	5,000	1,000

Vessel	Year/Mo/Day	Ton-nage	Master	Home Port
Thomas and William Dickerson	1884 11 26	41	Dickerson	Onancock, Va.
Thomas Thomas	1893 10 8	44	Harris	Norfolk, Va.
Thomas W. Waters	1892 8 1	92	Eason	Baltimore
Thomas Wayman	1902 6 10	2,210	Williams	Newcastle, England
Tillie G. Cruse	1888 12 22	97	Bailey	Somers Pt., N. J.
Trojan	1914 2 3	4,017	?	Liverpool, England
Tunis	1878 12 28	?	?	London, England
Two Brothers	1886 3 3	7	Somers	Yorktown, Va.
Two Sisters	1883 11 11	26	Yates	Somers Pt., N. J.
Undine	1883 12 1	10	?	Chincoteague, Va.
Undine	1890 11 22	10	Booth	Wachapreague, Va.
Union	1890 12 7	19	Bowen	Philadelphia
Vandalia	1895 5 5	53	Baetrez	New London, Conn.
Vidar	1900 3 26	1,543	Sorensen	Frederickshall, Norway
Vienna	1883 3 21	21	Steelman	Onancock, Va.
Virginia	1907 11 26	44	?	Norfolk, Va.
Virginia Rulon	1897 12 25	280	Leek	New York City
Virginia Rulon	1901 12 5	280	Cramer	Philadelphia
Volunteer	1900 12 20	6	Bowden	Chincoteague, Va.
W. E. Heard	1879 11 3	?	?	Yarmouth, Nova Scotia
W. L. Willis	1894 10 17	?	?	Chincoteague, Va.
W. T. Sherman	1886 4 7	23	Bunting	Chincoteague, Va.
Walker Armington	1896 12 3	914	Drinkwater	Rockland, Me.
Water Lily	1895 2 8	37	Peterson	New York City
Water Witch	1879 1 28	?	?	Baltimore
Welaka	1889 10 26	433	Mahoney	Belfast, Me.
West Wind	1878 1 24	332	Rider	Sligo, Ireland
Wicomico	1907 11 7	141	?	Tappahannock, Va.
Willehad	1896 12 31	4,998	Kuhman	Bremen, Germany
William Allen	1881 3 10	316	Steelman	Perth Amboy, N. J.
William Allen	1881 8 7	?	Steelman	Perth Amboy, N. J.
William Armstrong	1892 1 19	2,255	McKenzie	New Castle, England
William B. Wood	1889 3 3	599	Davidson	Bridgeton, N. J.
William C. Pruitt	1887 4 28	9	Hill	Chincoteague, Va.
William H. VanName	1876 2 18	97	Holmes	New York City
William M. Bird	1891 4 29	808	Barrett	Somers Pt., N. J.
William M. Wilson	1898 11 27	252	Bragg	Tuckerton, N. J.

Voyage from	to	Cargo	Dollar Value of Vessel	Dollar Value of Cargo
Baltimore	Metomkin, Va.	guano	2,000	1,500
Chincoteague, Va.	Philadelphia	fish	1,000	400
New York City	Norfolk, Va.	stone	5,000	2,000
Coosa, S. C.	Norfolk, Va.	phosphate rock	90,000	?
James River, Va.	Philadelphia	lumber	4,000	850
New Orleans, La.	Hamburg, Germany	general	240,000	?
?	?	?	?	?
Yorktown	Wilmington, Del.	oysters	250	50
Chincoteague, Va.	James River, Va.	?	1,600	?
Chincoteague	Wachapreague, Va.	?	800	?
Chincoteague	Wachapreague	?	800	?
Hog Island, Va.	Norfolk, Va.	oysters	600	300
?	?	line	3,000	?
New York City	Norfolk, Va.	?	80,000	?
Machipongo, Va.	Tuckerton. N. J.	oysters	1,000	300
Norfolk	Hog Island, Va.	?	2,500	?
Bermuda Hun-dreds, Va.	Elizabeth, N. J.	railroad ties	7,000	2,000
New Haven, Conn.	Suffolk, Va.	?	5,000	?
Hog Island, Va.	Chincoteague	oysters	400	30
Newry, Ireland	Baltimore	ballast	?	?
?	?	fish	?	?
Wachapreague, Va.	Chincoteague	oysters	800	140
Providence, R. I.	Newport News, Va.	?	25,000	?
Norfolk, Va.	New York City	?	13,000	?
?	?	?	?	?
Union Island, Ga.	Providence, R.I.	lumber	18,000	?
Georgia	Dublin, Ireland	pine timber	13,000	15,000
?	?	coal	20,000	250
Baltimore	Bremen	general	365,000	?
Baltimore	Hoboken, N. J.	coal	10,000	1,900
Halifax, Nova Scotia	Norfolk, Va.	coal	3,000	1,500
New Orleans, La.	Le Havre, France	cotton	150,000	200,000
Sagua, West Indies	Philadelphia	sugar	16,000	60,000
Hog Island, Va.	Chincoteague	oysters	800	50
New York City	York River, Va.	none	12,000	0
Kennebeck River, Me.	Philadelphia	ice	35,000	2,500
Philadelphia	Norfolk, Va.	coal	3,000	1,000

Vessel	Year/Mo/Day	Ton- nage	Master	Home Port
William Phillips	1892 2 29	592	Potter	New Bedford, Mass.
William T. Elmer	1884 1 5	185	Emmons	Hartford, Conn.
Winchester	1877 3 22	16	McDonald	Liverpool, England
Winged Racer	1877 12 3	80	Hawes	Wellfleet, Mass.
Wm. Applegarth	1893 10 4	101	Younger	Baltimore
Wolverton	1883 3 7	620	Dyer	Portland, Me.
Woodruff Sims	1880 9 25	?	?	New York City
Wyandotte	1890 2 8	8	Elliot	Norfolk, Va.
Yeoman	1902 2 28	4,378	Lang	Liverpool, England
Zimri S. Wallingford	1895 3 17	296	Higbee	Portsmouth, N. H.
Zulu Chief	1881 10 19	?	Jerome	Atlantic City, N. J.

Voyage from	to	Cargo	Dollar Value of Vessel	Cargo
Pisagua, Chile	Hampton Roads, Va.	saltpeter	47,890	?
New York City	West Point, Va.	phosphate	8,000	6,000
?	?	?	?	?
Philadelphia	Baltimore	coal	2,400	400
Scranton Mills, N. C.	Newark, N. J.	lumber	6,000	?
Cardenas, Cuba	New York City	sugar	37,700	57,000
Chickahominy, Va.	New York City	lumber	?	?
Fisherman's Inlet, Va.	Norfolk	oysters	385	?
Galveston, Tex.	Liverpool	cotton	500,000	860,000
Georgetown, S. C.	Boston, Mass.	lumber	6,000	5,000
Atlantic City	Yorktown, Va.	?	300	?

Notes

Chapter 1
The Development of the United States Life-Saving Service

1. *The New York Times,* 22 June 1923, p. 17.

2. United States Life-Saving Service (USLSS), *Annual Report of the United States Life-Saving Service for the Fiscal Year Ending 30 June 1876* (Washington, D.C.: Government Printing Office, 1876), p. 69.

3. *The Norfolk Virginian,* 24 May 1874, p.1.

4. Sumner I. Kimball, *Regulations for the Government of the Life-Saving Service of the United States, January 1873* (Washington, D.C.: Government Printing Office, 1873), p. 11.

5. Ibid., p. 7.

Chapter 2
Early Casualties

1. Statistics were compiled from information taken from the USLSS Annual Reports in the years 1876 to 1915.

2. Ibid.

3. USLSS, *Annual Report,* 1879, p.20.

4. Ibid.

5. Ibid., p. 22.

6. *The Norfolk Virginian,* 29 October 1878, p.1.

7. A wreck in as bad a condition as the Davis was in would not have been searched—it would have been too dangerous. Only if a wreck were stranded and not in imminent danger of breaking up would the life-savers go out and try to salvage as much of the cargo as possible, *after* they had rescued the crew.

There are many instances of the surfmen risking their lives to save a sailor hanging from the rigging of a ship or perched precariously on a mast. And they would indeed "search" a ship to look for other crew members, if told by one of the crew that several were below decks. But most often, all crew members would be above the water, having scrambled to the masts and crosstrees to be away from the churning waters, minus those who had drowned. In those days, it seems that there was a much more callous regard for life than today. Some sailors didn't even know the names of those they sailed with.

8. USLSS, *Annual Report,* 1881, p. 164.

9. Ibid.

Chapter 3
The Sea Takes Its Toll

1. USLSS, *Annual Report,* 1881, p. 180.

2. When there was a loss of life in a shipwreck or a question of wrongdoing on the part of the life-savers, an investigation was conducted by those inspectors having jurisdiction in a particular area. It helped to clear up any question of impropriety on the part of the life-savers (i.e., if a captain of a ship felt that the life-savers had not done all they could to save his crew or cargo, he might have lodged a complaint with the district superintendent, and it would have to be investigated). The significance of the investigation was that it provided a decision which both parties, the captain of the ship and the life-savers, could abide by.

3. USLSS, *Annual Report,* 1882, p. 179.

Chapter 4
Ever Watchful

1. USLSS, *Annual Report,* 1883, p. 204.

2. USLSS, *Annual Report,* 1884, p. 26.

3. Special Meeting of the Council of the Town of Virginia Beach, Virginia, 9 November 1950, transcript, Virginia Beach Maritime Historical Museum Archives.

4. USLSS, *Annual Report,* 1886, pp. 244-45.

5. USLSS, *Annual Report,* 1887, p. 33.

Chapter 5
The Toll Mounts

1. USLSS, *Annual Report,* 1888, p. 25.

2. Ibid., p. 159.

3. USLSS, *Annual Report*, 1889, pp. 296-98.

4. USLSS, *Annual Report*, 1890, p. 39.

5. Ibid., p. 40.

6. Ibid., p. 40.

7. USLSS, *Annual Report*, 1889, p. 224.

8. Ibid., p. 226.

9. Ibid., p. 225.

Chapter 6

Surfmen's Peril

1. "A War Ship Ashore," *The Norfolk Virginian*, 19 June 1889, p.1.

2. "Five Days Without Food," *The Norfolk Virginian*, 1 November 1889, p.1.

3. Ibid.

4. USLSS, *Annual Report*, 1890, p. 28.

5. "Five Days Without Food,", p. 1.

6. "The International Marine Conference," *The Norfolk Virginian*, 1 November 1889, p.1.

7. USLSS, *Annual Report*, 1891, pp. 51-52.

8. "The Wreck of the Dictator," *The Norfolk Virginian*, 29 March 1891, p. 1.

9. USLSS, *Annual Report*, 1891, p. 54.

10. Ibid., p. 59.

11. "Drinkwater Case," *The Norfolk Virginian*, 16 April 1891, p.1.

12. "Life-Saving Signals," *The New York Times*, 9 October 1891, p. 9.

Chapter 7

A Light in the Fog

1. USLSS, *Annual Report*, 1892, p. 37.

2. Ibid., p. 38.

3. USLSS, *Annual Report*, 1893, p. 32.

4. Ibid., p. 34.

5. USLSS, *Annual Report*, 1894, pp. 32-33.

6. Ibid., p. 202.

7. Ibid., p. 101.

8. Ibid., p. 201.

9. Ibid., pp. 137-38.

Chapter 8

Tragedy on the Coast

1. USLSS, "Investigation of the Loss of Three Lives by the Wreck of the Schooner *Jennie Hall* near the Dam Neck Mills Life-Saving Station, 22 December 1900," National Archives, p.2.

2. Ibid., p.2.

3. Ibid., p. 25

4. Ibid., pp. 7-8.

5. Ibid., p. 8.

6. USLSS, "Report of the Assistant Inspector Investigating the Loss of Three Lives at the Wreck of the Schooner *Jennie Hall* near the Dam Neck Mills Station, 22 December 1900," National Archives, p.9.

7. Ibid., p.9.

8. Ibid., p. 30.

9. "Investigation, Jennie Hall," p. 8.

10. Ibid., p. 31.

11. USLSS, "Investigation of the Wreck of the Schooner *Lillian Russell*, Testimony of John H. DeWald, Surfman Number Two, Hog Island Life-Saving Station, 16 December 1902," National Archives, p. 2.

12. Ibid.

13. USLSS, "Report of Investigation over Loss of Life and Wreck of the Schooner *Lillian Russell*, Hog Island Bar, Virginia, 4 January 1903," National Archives, p.3.

14. USLSS, "Report of the Investigation over Loss of Life and Wreck of the Schooner *Lillian Russell*, Hog Island Bar, Virginia," attached letter from Frank Parson, Jr. to Keeper J. E. Johnson, 20 December 1902, National Archives, p.1.

15. USLSS, *Annual Report*, 1904, p. 216.

16. Ibid., p. 20.

17. USLSS, "Wreck Report, *Ocean Belle*, 10 October 1903, Virginia Beach Station, Seventh District, J. W. Partridge, Keeper," National Archives, p. 4.

18. Ibid., pp. 4-5.

19. Ibid., p. 5.

20. USLSS, *Annual Report*, 1904, p. 217.

Chapter 9

Farewell to Sail

1. *The Virginian Pilot*, 12 February 1904, p. 2.

2. Ibid., p. 1.

3. USLSS, "Wreck Report, *Henry B. Hyde,* 11 February 1904, Dam Neck Mills Station, Seventh District, James E. Woodhouse, Keeper," National Archives, p. 4.

4. *The Virginian Pilot,* 12 February 1904, p. 1.

5. USLSS, "Wreck Report, *Arleville H. Peary,* False Cape Station, Seventh District, William H. O'Neal, Keeper," National Archives, p. 5.

6. "Vessel's Tow Line Cut Loose by Barge's Crew, Is Charge," *The Virginian Pilot,* 14 November 1908, p. 1.

7. USLSS, "Wreck Report, *Florence Shay,* 12 November 1908, Little Island Station, Seventh District, J. W. Partridge, Keeper," National Archives, p. 2.

8. USLSS, *Annual Report,* 1911, p. 77.

9. USLSS, "Investigation of the Circumstances Attending the Wreck of the Schooner *Laura Tompkins* of Chincoteague, Virginia, on 2 March 1913, in the Vicinity of Cobb Island Life-Saving Station on Which Occasion Loss of Life Was Sustained," National Archives, p. 5.

10. Ibid., p. 6.

11. USLSS, "Wreck Report, *Frieda,* 23 December 1913, Little Island Station, Seventh District, John W. Partridge, Keeper," National Archives, attached typewritten letter from Sumner I. Kimball to Keeper John W. Partridge.

Bibliography

Government Documents

Kimball, Sumner I. *Organization and Methods of the United States Life-Saving Service.* Washington, D. C.: Government Printing Office, 1890.

───── . *Regulations for the Goverment of the Life-Saving Service of the United States,* January 1873. Washington, D. C.: Government Printing Office, 1873.

United States Coast Guard. *The Annual Report of the United States Coast Guard 1916.* Washington, D. C.: Government Printing Office, 1917.

United States Life-Saving Service. *Annual Report of the United States Life-Saving Service for the Fiscal Year Ending 30 June 1874 - 30 June 1915.* Washington, D.C.: Government Printing Office, 1874-1915.

───── . Register of Wreck Reports Received from Life-Saving Stations 1884-1895. U. S. Coast Guard Record Group 26, National Archives. Washington, D.C.

───── . "Wreck Report. *Antonio.* 31 March 1906. Cape Henry Station. Seventh District. Nelson Holmes, Keeper." U. S. Coast Guard Record Group 26, National Archives. Washington, D. C.

───── . "Wreck Report. *Arleville H. Peary.* 31 October 1908. False Cape Station. Seventh District. William H. O'Neal, Keeper." U. S. Coast Guard Record Group 26, National Archives. Washington, D. C.

───── . "Wreck Report. *Charmer.* 3 December 1912. Cape Henry Station. Seventh District. Nelson Holmes, Keeper." U.S. Coast Guard Record Group 26, National Archives. Washington, D. C.

───── . "Wreck Report. *D. M. Anthony.* 3 February 1905. False Cape Station. Seventh District. William H. O'Neal, Keeper." U. S. Coast Guard Record Group 26, National Archives. Washington, D. C.

———."Wreck Report. *Florence Shay.* 12 November 1908. Little Island Station. Seventh District. J. W. Partridge, Keeper." U. S. Coast Guard Record Group 26, National Archives. Washington, D.C.

———."Wreck Report. *Frieda.* 23 December 1913. Little Island Station. Seventh District. J. W. Partridge, Keeper." U. S. Coast Guard Record Group 26, National Archives. Washington, D. C.

———."Wreck Report. *Frieda.* 24 December 1913. False Cape Station. Seventh District. Thomas H. Delon, Keeper." U. S. Coast Guard Record Group 26, National Archives. Washington, D. C.

———."Wreck Report. *George Farwell.* 20 October 1906. Cape Henry Station. Seventh District. Nelson Holmes, Keeper." U. S. Coast Guard Record Group 26, National Archives. Washington, D. C.

———."Wreck Report. *Harry T. Hayward.* 22 March 1906. Cape Henry Station. Seventh District. Nelson Holmes, Keeper." U. S. Coast Guard Record Group 26, National Archives. Washington, D. C.

———."Wreck Report. *Henry B. Hyde.* 11 February 1904. Dam Neck Mills Station. Seventh District. James E. Woodhouse, Keeper." U. S. Coast Guard Record Group 26, National Archives. Washington, D. C.

———."Wreck Report. *Henry B. Hyde.* 11 February 1904. Little Island Station. Seventh District. Otto V. Halstead, Keeper." U. S. Coast Guard Record Group 26, National Archives. Washington, D. C.

———."Wreck Report. *Henry B. Hyde.* 10 June 1904. Dam Neck Mills Station. Seventh District. William H. Partridge, Keeper." U. S. Coast Guard Record Group 26, National Archives. Washington, D. C.

———."Wreck Report. *Henry B. Hyde.* 10 June 1904. Virginia Beach Station. Seventh District. J. S. Partridge, Keeper." U. S. Coast Guard Record Group 26, National Archives. Washington, D. C.

———."Wreck Report. *Henry B. Hyde.* 22 September 1904. Dam Neck Mills Station. Seventh District. James W. Woodhouse, Keeper." U. S. Coast Guard Record Group 26. National Archives. Washington, D. C.

———."Wreck Report. *Henry B. Hyde.* 22 September 1904. Little Island Station. Seventh District. Otto V. Halstead, Keeper." U. S. Coast Guard Record Group 26, National Archives. Washington, D. C.

———."Wreck Report. *Jennie Hall.* 21 December 1900. Dam Neck Mills Station. Seventh District. Bailey T. Barco, Keeper." U. S. Coast Guard Record Group 26, National Archives. Washington, D. C.

————.Investigation of the Loss of Three Lives by the Wreck of the Schooner *Jennie Hall* near the Dam Neck Mills Life-Saving Station, 22 December 1900." U.S. Coast Guard Record Group 26, National Archives. Washington, D. C.

————."Report of the Assistant Inspector Investigating the Loss of Three Lives at the Wreck of the Schooner *Jennie Hall* near the Dam Neck Mills Life-Saving Station, 22 December 1900." U. S. Coast Guard Record Group 26, National Archives. Washington, D. C.

————."Investigation of the Circumstances Attending the Wreck of the Schooner *Laura Tompkins* of Chincoteague, Virginia, on 2 March 1913, in the Vicinity of Cobb Island Life- Saving Station on Which Occassion Loss of Life Was Sustained." U. S. Coast Guard Record Group 26, National Archives. Washington, D. C.

————."Investigation of the Wreck of the Schooner *Lillian Russell*. Testimony of John H. DeWald, Surfman Number Two, Hog Island Life-Saving Station, 16 December 1902." U. S. Coast Guard Record Group 26, National Archives. Washington, D. C.

————."Report of Investigation Over Loss of Life and Wreck of the Schooner *Lillian Russell*, Hog Island Bar, Virginia, 4 January 1903." U. S. Coast Guard Record Group 26, National Archives. Washington, D. C.

————."Wreck Report. *Ocean Belle*. 10 October 1903. Virginia Beach Station. Seventh District. J. W. Partridge, Keeper." U. S. Coast Guard Record Group 26, National Archives. Washington, D. C.

Newspapers

The New York Times, 8, 30, 31 December 1875; 7 March 1876; 24 October 1878; 8 January, 30 April, 28 November 1882; 28 November 1884; 2 April 1885; 9 January 1887; 28, 29, 30 March, 14 October 1891; 9 July 1895; 26 July 1896; 22 October 1897; 29 November 1889; 30 November 1899; 11 October 1903; 2, 31 January, 6 February 1915.

The Norfolk Virginian, 24 May, 28 August 1874; 3, 4, 7, 8 January 1875; 24, 27, 29 October 1878; 1, 3, November 1887, 18, 19 June, 25, 26, 27 October, 1 November 1889; 29, 30 September 1890; 27, 29, 30 March, 16 April 1891; 21 January, 1 March 19 April 1892; 3, 4, 5, 6, 7, October 1893.

The Public Ledger, Norfolk, Virginia, 14, 15, 16 December 1876; 22, 26, 27 March 1877; 20, 21 April 1881; 1 January 1883; 31 October, 1, 2, 3, November 1887; 24, 25, 26, 28 October 1889; 28, 29, 30 March 1891; 19 September, 12, 16 October 1903; 14 January, 23, 24 March 1906.

The Virginian Pilot, Norfolk, Virginia, 1 August, 9, 10, 11, 12 October 1903; 12 February, 12 June, 4, 23, September 1904; 1, 2, 3, 4, 5, 6, 7 April 1906; 12, 13, 14 November 1908; 8 March 1911.

Books and Periodicals

"The American Life-Saving Service." *Harper's New Monthly Magazine* (December 1881-May 1882): 357-73.

Baughman, James P. *Charles Morgan and the Development of Southern Transportation.* Nashville, Tennessee: Vanderbilt University Press, 1968.

Bennett, Robert F. *Surfboats, Rockets, and Carronades.* Washington, D. C.: Government Printing Office, 1976.

Billias, George A. "Nathanial T. Palmer's Fleet of Great Schooners." *American Neptune* 20(1960): 236-42. Bloomfield, Howard V. L. *The Compact History of the United States Coast Guard.* New York: Hawthorne Books, 1966.

Burgess, Robert H., Ed. *Coasting Captain: Journals of Captain Leonard S. Tawes, Relating His Career in Atlantic Coastwise Sailing Craft from 1868-1922.* Newport News, Virginia: Mariner's Museum, 1967.

Capron, Walter C. *The U. S. Coast Guard.* New York: Franklin Watts, 1965.

Chapelle, Howard I. *The American Fishing Schooners 1825-1935.* New York: W. W. Norton, 1973.

————. *The History of American Sailing Ships.* New York: W. W. Norton, 1935.

Engle, Eloise, and Lott, Arnold S. *America's Maritime Heritage.* Annapolis, Maryland: Naval Institute Press, 1975.

Evans, Stephen H. *The United States Coast Guard 1790-1915.* Annapolis, Maryland: The United States Naval Institute, 1968.

Gurney, Gene. *The United States Coast Guard: A Pictorial History.* New York: Crown Publishers, 1973.

Hutchins, John G. B. *The American Maritime Industries and Public Policy 1789-1914*. Cambridge, Massachusetts: Harvard University Press, 1941.

Kaplan, H. R., and Hunt, J. F. *This is the Coast Guard*. Cambridge, Maryland: Cornell Maritime Press, 1972.

Kilmarx, Robert A., Ed. *America's Maritime Legacy: A History of the U. S. Merchant Marine and Shipbuilding Industry Since Colonial Times*. Boulder, Colorado: Westview Press, 1979.

Laurence, Frederick Sturgis. *Coasting Passage*. Concord, Massachusetts: Charles S. Morgan Publisher, 1968.

Lawrence, Samuel A. *United States Merchant Shipping Policies and Politics*. Washington, D. C.: The Brookings Institution, 1966.

"The Life-Saving Service." *The Nation*. 69: 182-83.

Lonsdale, Adrian L., and Kaplan, H. R. *A Guide to Sunken Ships in American Waters*. Arlington, Virginia: Compass Publications, 1964.

Morgan, Charles S. *Coastal Shipping Under Sail 1880-1920*. Everett, Massachusetts: Fidelity Press, 1979.

Morris, Paul C. *American Sailing Coasters of the North Atlantic*. Chardon, Ohio: Bloch and Osborn Publishing Company, 1973.

———. *Four-Masted Schooners of the East Coast*. Orleans, Massachusetts: Lower Cape Publishing, 1975.

Parker, William James. *The Great Coal Schooners of New England 1870-1909*. Mystic, Connecticut: (n.p.), 1948.

Shepard, Birse. *Lore of the Wreckers*. Boston: Beacon Press, 1961.

Stick, David. *Graveyard of the Atlantic*. Chapel Hill, North Carolina: University of North Carolina Press, 1952.

Walker, Carroll. *Norfolk: A Pictorial History*. Virginia Beach, Virginia: The Donning Company, 1975.

Index